D0728032

KIDNAPPED BY NUNS

AND OTHER STORIES FROM

A LIFE ON THE RADIO

By Bob Fuss

Retired CBS News Correspondent

kidnappedbynuns.com
bobfuss@kidnappedbynuns.com

Cover Photo by Larry Downing

First Edition 2015
Printed in the United States

ISBN-13: 978-1508488132
ISBN-10: 1508488134

Table of Contents

FOREWORD

This book contains a lot of journalism and some history; dispatches from all corners of the globe, a collection of contemporaneously written travelogues, and hopefully some humor.

But it is at its core a memoir, which means the stories are how I remember them. Memories can change over time and if there are any errors, they are inadvertent.

As a network news correspondent I lived under strict rules about expressing political opinions. I couldn't say anything publicly, have a bumper sticker on my car, or even write a letter to my Congressman. I followed those rules and strived the best I could to make sure no personal bias crept into my reporting. But now that I am retired I am free to express how I really feel about the presidents and other politicians I covered. These opinions are mine and certainly don't reflect those of any of my employers.

This book is dedicated to my father, who always wanted me to dedicate a book to him

IN THE BEGINNING

The offer was serious.

As I looked out to the pristine white sand beach from the thatched meeting house with no walls, the chief of this small village in Fiji told me I could choose any of the local girls and marry her and stay with my own hut in this little slice of paradise.

I must admit there have been times I've looked back at that moment in my twenties and questioned my choice, but there were so many adventures I would have missed in forty years as a radio correspondent: Visiting Cuba with the Pope, huddling with rebels during an uprising in the Philippines, covering half a dozen presidential campaigns, 15 Academy Awards shows and welcoming in the new millennium with the King of Tonga.

As a boy I always planned to be a lawyer. A Supreme Court Justice actually, but first things first. I was born on New York's Long Island and spent my first five years there before my family moved to Los Angeles.

The move was actually because of me. Born with a whole range of birth defects similar to spina bifida, my parents were told I was unlikely to live past childhood. The lesson of never fully trusting doctors took hold early.

Pretty much everything below the waist was deformed in some way: my feet pointed the wrong direction, my knees didn't bend, internal organs were messed up, and lower vertebra were missing. Years later as I reported on abortion rights battles it would sometimes occur to me that if ultrasound tests had been used in the early 1950s there was no doubt a well-meaning doctor would have recommended terminating me.

Though I learned quickly to get around by pushing a chair or a wagon or anything else that was handy before learning to walk on crutches, my parents worried living in snow and ice in the winters would be too difficult for me. While it wasn't the only reason they decided to move to California, it was the main one.

They loaded up their rambler station wagon with three kids and a dog and headed west. My father had interviews lined up and joined an accounting firm soon after arriving in Los Angeles, where he would become a partner and stay the rest of his working life. Years later when I lived in New York and Washington and took up skiing there was some irony, but my parents loved California and hated the cold weather and were always happy they had moved.

They grew up in Brooklyn and met as teenagers. My father Milton was a natural athlete and my mother Carrie first noticed him on the basketball court. Though both were Jewish, neither would end up practicing the religion.

My mother's Uncle Mickey Marcus was a hero in the creation of Israel. A West Point graduate and Army colonel, he helped organize and lead the new Israeli Army in 1948. His exploits were dramatized in the movie "Cast a Giant Shadow," starring Kirk Douglas as Mickey, and while my mother tells me he was indeed larger than life, she complains the portrayal of her aunt by Angie Dickinson was completely wrong.

My mother was 18 when she married my father, who was 20 and already in the Army. Neither family was particularly thrilled with the idea and my mother traveled on her own to Alabama, where my dad was stationed at the time. Married by a Southern judge, my mother swore she could hear my father's knees buckle when the judge, who took a liking to her, tried to give them something special and called his sister over to play some music and then declared them married "in Jesus's name."

My dad saw action in France as a medic in the infantry and like so many men of his generation never talked much about it later. He went to college on the GI bill and earned both a law degree and an accounting degree. He liked accounting more than law and spent his life as a CPA. He helped people run their businesses and file their taxes but never let them cheat, even a little.

My mother started college but it would be decades later when she would go back and finish; she then continued earning more degrees, ending up working as a marriage and family counselor. During the war she worked as a lab technician for the Army, drawing blood from prisoners of war at one point.

My older brother Michael was born when my dad was still overseas.

My memories of my first five years in New York are pretty foggy, glimpses really. I remember a fig tree in front of our house, I remember my mother was upset when I got the measles, and that I got a present that was hidden in the closet when my sister Lorri was born when I was three. I remember my first day at kindergarten.

Later in life when I spent time with my nephews and nieces I remember feeling a little sad to think that the wonderful experiences we had together when they were one and two and three years old might contribute to their lives in important ways, but like me when they got older they probably wouldn't remember any of it.

I was always a busy and active kid and never let anything slow me down. Every parent wants to protect his or her child, not only from getting hurt but also from failure, disappointment, and frustration. My parents were no different. I know now how hard it must have been for them to watch me leap into tasks I shouldn't have been able to do and figure it out as all kids do, by trial and error. For me that meant a lot of falling down and I am so grateful they let me.

My mother was chided at times by other parents for not rushing to pick up her handicapped child when I fell, not understanding the extraordinary gift she was giving me, the confidence to try new things and the knowledge that if I fell down it was up to me to figure out a way to get back up.

And so I ran and jumped and climbed and played baseball and football and wrestled and never let anyone else's view of what I "should" be able to do hold me back. I loved the Slip'N Slide (a backyard toy that consists of a long "carpet" of plastic, made slippery from a stream of water from a garden hose) but I was dangerous because I'd run up to it and throw my crutches wildly to the side when I leaped on it. Soccer was scary too, since I hit the ball with the crutches and never played gently. I broke one crutch when I hit a basketball at full speed and lost one when a wave knocked me down at the beach.

But I'm sure my mom was dying inside when I started to skateboard. I would stand facing sideways and use both crutches on the same side to build up speed—and I was very fast. I remember people scattered when I would fly through Disneyland on my skateboard. I'm sure it was against their rules even then, but who was going to tell a little kid on crutches he had to walk?

Oddly one thing I never tried to do as a kid was go on an escalator. For some reason I was always hesitant about it and there was always an elevator or the stairs. So I never used one until I was 18 and in Moscow. I was on a tour with friends and we took a ride on Moscow's subway. We went down an elevator but at the station we were exiting there was no elevator or stairs, only the longest escalator I've ever seen going up to the street. I could barely make out where it ended. I studied it for a minute or two, and then got on because there was no choice. It turned out to be easy. Now I always take the escalator because elevators are too slow.

It is not easy to know how much of what we are comes from our parents, but I always considered myself a good mix. From my mother came exuberance for life, a sense of adventure and joy, and a sense of optimism that rarely wavered. From my father came an important balance of caution and reserve, and an understanding of the importance of perseverance and hard work. Also from him I gained what every son most wants from his father: the knowledge that from the time we wore wacky headdresses in Indian Guides to the times I sent him tapes of my stories traveling with the president, he was always proud of me.

My first brush with journalism was not encouraging.

Several times as a small boy my picture or name would get into the paper in a story about one of the Christmas parties or other big events sponsored by what was then called the Crippled Children's Society. (I never quite understood why "crippled" became a dirty word. It is descriptive and accurate. Then "handicapped," another perfectly good word, fell into disrepute replaced by "disabled." I sometimes hear "differently abled" or "physically challenged," which make no sense since they describe everyone to one degree or another.)

At any rate, every time I was in the paper they got the story wrong: my name or age or what the event was. My first introduction to journalists certainly didn't lead me to want to become one.

Plus, I couldn't spell. I was awful. Before every spelling test in school I'd memorize all the words and get 100 percent, then forget them all the next day. Later, in essay tests I'd use my atrocious handwriting to hide my horrible spelling by blurring the letters I wasn't sure of. Since I was an "A" student the teacher just assumed I spelled it right. At least until computers came along with spell check, writing was clearly not the profession for me.

I used to be smart when I was a kid, but other factors played in to my graduating from Stanford at 19.

When I started first grade in California there was no such thing as mainstreaming. Kids with disabilities, whether physical or developmental, were segregated in special schools. The schools I went to were small and they often combined two grades in a single classroom. They were prepared for kids with seizures or who needed help getting to the bathroom but didn't know quite what to do with a kid who learned all the material for both grades.

So they started skipping me ahead, one grade at a time.

Eventually they brought in a special teacher for the two "gifted students" they had. He would take Donald LeStrange and me for an hour or two a day. We would open the encyclopedia, and starting with "A," just find things that interested us and we would learn about them. It was great fun.

There were also field trips. I remember one where we milked a goat, but the one where I played with a lion was much more exciting. I think I was eight.

The field trip was to a veterinary hospital out in the country. The rooms were organized in a circle around a central courtyard and our class was in one watching a cat get spayed. One whiff of the ether and I had to get out. Never the type to bother the teacher with such trivialities such as permission, I opened the sliding glass door to the courtyard outside and went exploring.

I found a lion cub.

He was tied with a chain and playing with a beach towel. I had a dog at home and I knew that game. So I picked up one end of the towel and started playing tug of war. We were having a great time when someone finally noticed I was missing and came looking for me. I didn't understand why they were all so upset; the baby lion and I were just playing.

It's amazing to think back now, but there was no scandal; no one got fired or went to jail or sued anyone. But I have a feeling the next class took a different field trip.

I liked school and was good at it, though looking back at some old report cards my mother saved, I discovered a pattern. I always had top grades in academic subjects but on the "citizenship" side there was always a lower mark for "obedience." I never did get good at that. Being slightly disrespectful of authority is a common trait among journalists and helps us do our job.

I was also a bit of a ham and liked the spotlight. Even at four and five I would organize my friends and put on shows. Acting was fun and I was often in school plays. So when a casting agent came to the summer day camp I attended looking for some handicapped kids for a TV show I got on the list.

Rancho del Valle was the Crippled Children's Society's center in the San Fernando Valley where I grew up. I loved the place; it was where I learned to swim. There was also a sheltered workshop there where disabled adults were brought every day to "work." As I look back at the wonderful times I had at the day camp, as well as at Camp Paivika, the summer sleepover camp in the mountains and all the terrific people who worked and volunteered there, I am struck by the fact that I never remember at any of those places meeting a successful handicapped adult. One who had a real job and lived an independent life. When I began volunteering to teach disabled children to swim in Northern Virginia decades later, I like to think I was also doing some teaching by example.

The casting agent was from the "Lassie" TV show. Three other kids and I were chosen for an episode about handicapped kids taken out to the woods to plant trees with Lassie and the Ranger. (He was on for a few seasons after Timmy.)

I would be out of school a week making a TV show, get to meet Lassie, and they were going to pay me $300! I was a ten year old on top of the world.

My first shock was that there was more than one Lassie. There were lots of them, including one just for fight scenes. And there were a few "Laddie" puppies on the set, training to be future Lassies. Lassie didn't like to play; she was all business. And she was a he! But they did have golf carts and sometimes let me drive one around the back lot.

Our teacher in the show was played by Bonita Granville, who had been a movie star before marrying Jack Wrather, who owned the production company that made "Lassie." She didn't do much acting at that point in her life but wanted to do this role. Years later we met when I was covering a Reagan fundraiser and reminisced about the show.

The episode was built around my character, a sad and angry little boy who always felt sorry for himself because he needed crutches to walk. Talk about playing against type. My big scene was after the little trees we planted burned in a fire and I had to cry as Lassie came over to console me. They told me to think of something sad and I thought about my own dog dying and the tears flowed.

Then of course came the happy ending when Lassie pulled me over to see new growth on my burnt tree and I finally got to smile. Hamlet it was not, but it almost changed the course of my life. The director and others were sure I had a real future as a child actor and I went to see an agent and had professional pictures taken (and have never looked that good since).

But my parents and I were in agreement that academic pursuits were a better future course. I got to hold the money in cash at the bank before putting it in my first savings account. There were lots of residual payments for reruns, the last when the show was sold to Japan. By the time I left for college at 16 I had $1,000, which was put to good use when I spent six months studying abroad.

The schools for disabled children were good but limited. I wouldn't be able to take the kind of advanced courses I would need to get into a good college. My mother fought long and hard with the Los Angeles School District trying to convince them to let me into a regular school. Their greatest fear seemed to be that I would get hurt and they would get sued, but she finally succeeded and convinced the principal of Charles Evans Hughes Junior High School to take a chance and let me in.

And so in seventh grade at the age of 10 I entered a regular school for the first time. I then attended Taft High School and joined the debating team. I loved to argue and did well in debate, though I lost one debate in which my partner and I demolished the opposition. The judge said I was too sarcastic and I'm sure I was.

My classmates voted me "most serious" and I was terribly insulted. I thought I was hysterically funny but other people rarely see us as we see ourselves. Maybe I got funnier later.

In my senior year in high school I was called one day into the counselor's office. There, I met a man from the California Department of Rehabilitation who told me the state would like to help me to be "rehabilitated," so I could work someday and be independent. That seemed cool. He said they could pay for my tuition and books at any of the state colleges or universities. When I told him I had already gotten into Stanford, he said they could pay the equivalent of a state school's tuition, and for my books. I said sure, since any little bit my parents could save would be welcome. I checked in once or twice at school and after I graduated met with a state counselor and explained what I was doing and what my plans were. He said they couldn't do much to assist in getting me a job as a radio reporter but felt I was in good shape. The file was closed and I was declared officially rehabilitated.

A KIDNAPPING LAUNCHES MY CAREER

When I got to Stanford I had every intention of becoming a lawyer. I majored in political science, joined the debate team and had no doubts about my future. I wasn't particularly close to my freshman roommate Peter, the most classic math and science nerd you can imagine. He was brilliant when it came to computers and equations and yet halfway through our first year burst into a room full of people to excitedly announce he had discovered a medicine cabinet behind the mirror above our dressers.

The first friend I made lived across the hall— a tall, lanky fellow from Wyoming who had never seen a bagel and liked to smoke a pipe. He started briefly as an engineering major, but his love was radio and television. It was serendipity writ large and if Pete Williams, who later went on to be a much acclaimed NBC News correspondent hadn't lived across the hall, I never would have gone into journalism.

Like me, Pete wasn't a big drinker and was part of a small minority at Stanford in 1970 that didn't smoke marijuana. (Each freshman dorm voted how to use a small allotment of student activity funds and ours, like most of the others, used it to buy marijuana for parties.) Pete did have an edge over me, though, when it came to swearing. I couldn't bring myself to say the four-letter words that everyone in college used in every other sentence. Already desperately out of place socially at the age of 16 and at just under five feet, not tall enough to see the mirror in my dorm room, much less open the medicine cabinet behind it, I needed to do something about the swearing.

So I invented my own language and started swearing in it. My favorite curse word was "scararamosh" and when people asked what that was I told them it was Southern Tibetan. They were all very smart kids but many spent years thinking there really was a Southern Tibetan language and I swore in it. By the time I left Stanford I could swear with the best of them but still use my Southern Tibetan phrases from time to time.

Pete kept trying to convince me to come join him at the campus radio station KZSU and I resisted since I was pretty busy with classes and the debate team, which involved traveling to other schools for tournaments. But one day I gave in and went to check out the radio station, located in the basement of the building that held the drama department. That day changed my life.

I soon was spending most of my spare time (and not a small amount of time when I should have been in class) at the radio station. It was 1970 and the campus was roiling with anti-war protests. There were sit-ins and teach-ins and rallies and occasionally riots and we covered every one of them at KZSU and covered them all live.

I would drive my golf cart to wherever the action was, hook up to one of the phone lines KZSU had in key locations all over the campus and start broadcasting. There couldn't have been better training for live radio; we would sometimes go for hours without stopping.

Most of the other close friends I would make at Stanford were connected to the radio station and I began spending most of my time there. Once they made the mistake of letting me do a shift as a music DJ. In an era of the Grateful Dead and Rolling Stones, I played Carole King and the Carpenters. After that I stuck to news.

I actually had two golf carts while at Stanford, which is a very spread-out campus. The first lasted until I crashed it into a brick wall. I was driving through White Plaza, the center open area of the campus, and took a turn at full speed, my usual style, and the three-wheeled cart tipped on its side. I fell out, but somehow the cart righted itself and continued at full speed across the Plaza without me. It was straight out of a movie as I screamed at people to get out of the way of the driverless golf cart. The only casualty was the cart when it reached the wall.

My parents bought the next golf cart, which lasted a lot longer, though not due to my driving. There were a number of pathways for pedestrians and bicycles with white posts to ensure that cars couldn't get in. I could clear them with about two inches on each side and took them at full speed. I never crashed the second golf cart, though in my senior year it was stolen by some fraternity guys who drove it into Lake Lagunita. After that, my parents (very generous and forgiving souls) bought me a car.

By the end of my freshman year I was totally smitten with radio. It was fun and exciting and people knew who I was. I could interview professors and the president of the university and it was all very cool.

Instead of going home that first summer I stayed on as a paid (sort-of) staff person who would help keep the radio station running during the summer months when there weren't many student volunteers. I lived in a room rented out at an absurdly cheap rate, including wonderful home-cooked meals by a lovely faculty couple who lived in one of the big stately homes Stanford provides for top teachers.

In the spring of my sophomore year I left for six months to attend an overseas campus. I chose Vienna because in high school I had switched from Spanish to German and that was the foreign language I was most comfortable in (though far from fluent).

It was a great time in Vienna. All the students lived together in a big building down the street from the Opera House right in the center of town. The next street over was one of two where street prostitution was legal. The prostitutes wore bizarre costumes with metal frames that made their breasts into pointed lethal weapons and we would practice our German with them, annoying them greatly since we never actually bought their services. We also shared a little restaurant. They and their customers would meet in the front room and we'd hang out in the back eating Wiener Schnitzel.

The school building was organized around a courtyard that you had to walk through to get to the dining hall, which made a perfect place to drop water balloons, which was one of our favorite pastimes. We also learned every word of Crosby, Stills & Nash's first album, since it was the only thing we had for the record player other than German opera and classical music.

We would have classes four days a week and then jump on a train and go visit someplace. I traveled all through Austria and beyond with my Eurail pass and a small group of friends, some of whom would stay friends forever.

We went once to Florence to visit the Stanford campus there, which was at an incredible villa. But there wasn't enough room for all of us with the one friend we had there, so I slept outside in the parking lot in the back of a VW Bus. It was a great trip and I fell in love with Florence, especially the ice cream.

My parents and sister Lorri came to visit. I planned to meet them in Split, on the coast of what is now Croatia. I was on a group field trip to Sarajevo and then a few of us traveled together down to the coast. We somehow missed a connection on our train and ended up in a bizarre little Potemkin town in one of my strangest travel adventures.

There were five of us and we got off the train in a town having no idea where we were or how we would get out. We were told there were no more trains that night and we would have to stay over and try to leave in the morning. The Communist government of what was then Yugoslavia had decided this was going to be a tourist destination and built a big fancy hotel that no one ever visited. They were pretty shocked when we showed up.

Then things started going wrong. First, one of my friends tried to fix a broken toilet in his room; the tank was up above and the seat he was standing on to reach it gave way and he ended up with a severe cut on his leg. We managed to find a doctor and got him fixed up. Then the next morning we split up. The others went to the train station to head back to Vienna because they had had enough adventure while I decided on the bus station to try to find my way to Split, where I was supposed to meet my parents.

My suitcase had broken during this wild excursion. The others kindly took most of my things and I piled the essentials into a shopping bag and the next morning headed to the bus station, which was right out of a Charlie Chaplin movie. It was mobbed with people and as soon as a bus pulled up, everyone would rush it and fill all the seats. By the time there was an announcement of where the bus was going (and often there wasn't) it was too late to get a seat.

It had been a pretty crazy 24 hours so I decided on a new tactic, which turns out to be a pretty good philosophy of life. If you can't find a bus that is going where you want to go, then you need to want to go wherever the bus is going.

So I just got on the next bus that pulled in and sure enough it took me to Split, where my parents were greeted by their bedraggled son carrying his possessions in a torn shopping bag.

I covered my first U.S. president on that trip to Vienna, when Richard Nixon came to visit and there were massive protests in the streets. I covered them and then mailed the cassettes back to KZSU for them to put on the radio with their very own foreign correspondent.

Vienna is also where I made a decision I had been moving towards since that first day Pete convinced me to try the radio station. I was going to give up my plan to become a lawyer and go into broadcasting.

When I got back to the Stanford campus I changed my major from political science to communications and told my parents. My father was worried for me. He knew more about prejudice than I did and thought the law was a much better choice since I could work for myself and not rely on other people to hire me.

I didn't believe for a minute that people would discriminate against me because I walked on crutches but I was naive and he was right. Happily it all worked out in the end and he was always my biggest fan.

I moved into a trailer for my junior and senior years with Pete Williams, Lloyd Snook, and Francis Dickerson. We had a red phone with a direct line to KZSU where we spent most of our time. The trailers had been built years before as temporary student housing but were a great place to live and were still "temporary" ten years later when I went back for a reunion.

I owe my career to Patty Hearst, the newspaper heiress kidnapped in 1974 by a ragtag radical group called the Symbionese Liberation Army. Much to the chagrin of her parents, she was living with her older boyfriend Steven Weed in Berkeley at the time and the SLA radicals broke into their apartment, beat Weed up and took Patty Hearst screaming in the night.

She was nineteen and so was I. I had just finished my last quarter at Stanford in January but my graduation was in May, so I was staying in campus housing while looking for a job. I wasn't finding one. I had applied to every radio station in San Francisco and Oakland and a few in Los Angeles and no one wanted to hire me.

I was especially upset I couldn't get an open entry-level position at KCBS, the all-news station in San Francisco. I knew quite a few people there and I had sold them stories while still in school. I had an interview with the news director, who then turned me over to the assistant news director who oversaw the desk assistants. She told me she couldn't hire me because sometimes desk assistants needed to run across the newsroom to quickly get a cart (the way recorded audio was played then) to the studio. This was long before the Americans with Disabilities Act prohibited such blatant discrimination. I was flabbergasted and asked her to give me a cart and I would show her how fast I could run it to the studio.

She refused.

She later went on to become a network news executive in New York who I always did my best to avoid.

I was very angry at the blatant bias I had faced that day but it was the best thing that could have happened to me. I never could have risen so quickly to become a network correspondent if she had hired me. And there is some satisfaction knowing that I was heard almost daily on KCBS for most of my 40 years on the radio.

It all turned out for the best because Patty Hearst got kidnapped.

Unable to find a job, I was selling freelance stories. My main client was UPI Radio (a network with more than a thousand stations at the time but sadly now defunct). We used their service at KZSU and I would sell them stories from time to time while still in school. I got $5 a cut for sound from a news story and $10 for a story I wrote and voiced.

When I heard about the kidnapping, I jumped in the car and rushed to the Hearst family mansion in nearby Hillsboro, carefully noting the closest pay phone at a gas station along the route. A tape had arrived in which the SLA, about half a dozen white radicals led by an African American ex-con who named himself Cinque, claimed credit for the kidnapping.

The plaintive voice of Patty Hearst asking, "Mom, Dad, help!" could be heard along with the sign-off used on all the taped messages that followed: "Death to the fascist insect that preys upon the life of the people."

I knew this story would be huge (though I couldn't imagine where it would lead me) and also knew at least one other freelancer was there who did work for UPI Radio. So as soon as I had what I needed I ran to my car and drove like a madman to the gas station and called UPI Radio in New York and told them I was ready to give them the story. As I was feeding it in, the other freelancer called and was told, "Thanks anyway, we already have it."

For the next few months I was UPI Radio's reporter for the Hearst kidnapping, one of the biggest stories of 1974. My position was locked in when I got a phone right at the Hearst house so I could file more quickly. Like all the other phones for news organizations it was installed on the large trees outside the house where a major news encampment soon developed.

The SLA had delusions of grandeur and just plain delusions. The intent of the kidnapping and the increasingly bizarre ransom demands for free food for the poor was to spur a race war in which Cinque could emerge as the general. But it was less bizarre when you consider the times. The San Francisco Bay area in 1974 was a hotbed of radical politics of all stripes and the SLA, as crazy as they were, found allies and sympathizers. It was a story that captivated the nation and was filled with wild twists and turns, none stranger then when Patty Hearst announced in the most memorable of the tapes that she had joined her captors. She denounced her parents and declared she would now battle with the SLA against the "fascist insects."

The scene at the Hearst house was often surreal. With a huge media contingent outside, Randolph Hearst, conservative publisher of the San Francisco Examiner and the son of famed publisher William Randolph Hearst, was trying to figure out how to satisfy his daughter's kidnappers while his wife Catherine kept calling in all manner of psychics and assorted lunatics.

The low point came when an effort to satisfy the SLA with a giant food give-away in Oakland ended in a riot. Or maybe for the Hearsts it was when the heiress turned radical was photographed by a security camera holding a gun as she joined her former captors in a bank robbery.

I turned twenty just three weeks after Patty Hearst did and was now being heard every day on a thousand radio stations around the country. I was still learning how to be a reporter but was on a national network and frequently, instead of $5 a piece, I would be paid what seemed at the time a princely flat rate of $50 a day.

I also was learning from some of the best, especially Richard Threlkeld, who was covering the story for CBS News. My admiration and desire to write as well as he did sometimes went too far and more than once I'd listen to a story I recorded and realize I was imitating Threlkeld and repeating lines I heard him use.

I also saw the future I imagined some day as I watched him give his runner a lunch order that included a split of Champagne and sternly tell the young man to make sure it was French and not domestic. Sadly, by the time I became a CBS News correspondent those halcyon days of lavish spending were over.

The end of the SLA came in a fiery shootout in Los Angeles. They were found in a house there and a barrage of tear gas and bullets ended with the house burning up with most of the SLA inside. It was a terrible wait at the Hearst mansion as the daughter who had been kidnapped and tortured, and then joined her captors, condemned her parents, and robbed a bank was presumed burned to death on live television.

But Patty Hearst wasn't in the house and was eventually found, arrested, convicted of bank robbery, and sent to prison. I never thought that was a just outcome and her sentence was commuted by President Jimmy Carter after two years. She later got a full pardon from President Bill Clinton and went on to live a normal life.

It's hard to know how much of the kind of prejudice I faced at KCBS would have held me back elsewhere, but by the time most executives at UPI Radio first saw me or learned I was four foot eleven and on crutches I was already a well-established presence on their network. While it took a few months more of freelancing before they hired me, the die was pretty well cast that they would. Though I learned many years later there was substantial panic and debate when they first found out I was disabled.

My first out-of-town assignment came from UPI in the fall when former President Richard Nixon, who had just resigned, was very sick with phlebitis. They wanted to send me to Long Beach, near Los Angeles, to cover him. The offer was $50 a day plus all my expenses. I was thrilled but did have a little problem.

They would fly me down and pay for my hotel, food, and rental car. But I couldn't rent a car because I wasn't 21 yet. This didn't seem like good information to share with UPI Radio, which now considered me their main reporter in California. So my father rented the car and I drove his Cadillac (with portable hand controls) for the two weeks or so that Nixon was hospitalized and at one point close to death.

We all knew roughly when Nixon would be arriving at the hospital but his people were determined not to let any of us see him come in. I decided to look around. I took off my press credential and just wandered. I found Secret Service agents hanging around a bank of elevators and just rode up and down for a while.

I guess with my crutches I didn't look out of place in a hospital. I never lied about who I was but just let them think I belonged. I was the only reporter to see Nixon come in and was able to describe to the others what he looked like and that he was wearing pancake make-up in case a photographer had found him.

I was still by any account a novice reporter and not old enough to rent a car but I was definitely getting noticed.

I worked for a year as a freelance radio reporter, with youthful confidence after the Hearst story that UPI Radio would hire me when they had an opening. I didn't even try to find another job.

I made about $4,000 that year and I had a good life. I shared a three-bedroom apartment in Mountain View, where rent was cheap long before it became Silicon Valley. The complex had a swimming pool and a sauna and my roommates from college, Lloyd Snook and Francis Dickerson, were with me. Once a week we'd go out to dinner, often with Francis's girlfriend and future wife Lynne. We'd alternate between McDonald's and our favorite Chinese restaurant, Mister Chows.

Each day I would look for stories in the area and often would end up in San Francisco. I sometimes would pop into the UPI bureau and if I went to lunch in Chinatown and got a parking ticket (which was pretty unavoidable covering news in the city) I could generally come out even and call it a good day.

I remember one day heading out to Travis Air Force Base near Sacramento for the arrival of a plane filled with orphans from Vietnam being brought to America. It was there I started to learn the critical skill of being able to describe action as it was happening, capturing the drama and the emotion and getting it all into a thirty-second package.

When the call finally came from UPI it wasn't quite what I expected. They wanted me to go to Dallas and write the broadcast wire, the written news product for radio and television stations. They said I would learn a lot and then later would come to New York to work at the radio network. They wanted me there right away, so of course I said yes.

My green Chevrolet Vega hatchback couldn't hold all my stuff, so I rented a small U-Haul trailer and convinced my roommate Lloyd to drive with me to Texas (I'm happy to say we've remained close friends ever since).

My parents were visiting Palm Springs so we stopped there for the first night, and then barreled ahead on a two-day drive to Dallas. We unhooked the trailer at the Holiday Inn, I drove Lloyd to the airport for a flight home and I was on my own in a very strange land.

Texas is just different. On one of my first nights, there I was, listening to talk radio and callers were complaining about the problem of "imported beef" and it took me a while to figure out they were talking about beef from Oklahoma.

I had a nice apartment in North Dallas and would eat great barbecue at a nearby place with a big pit in the back where the smoke never stopped rising. The culture took some getting used to. I returned home one day to find my neighbors in the parking lot roasting a goat over a spit.

I also found out about chiles. There was a place near me with an all-you-can-eat pizza lunch, which was perfect both for my taste and my budget. One day I had a few slices and thought I'd try one more, though I didn't recognize the topping. I took one bite and thought I was going to die on the spot. The pizza was covered in jalapeño peppers. I suffered the rest of the day and everyone at work that night thought it was hysterically funny.

The bureau manager in Dallas was Max Vanzi, a terrific guy who used to host marathon poker games at his house where players would come and go depending on their shifts at work. My shift was 3 pm to 11 pm, which suited me well since I like to sleep in.

I would take the stories written for newspapers and re-write them into packages of short conversational news summaries that a DJ at a radio station could rip off the wire and read cold on the air. I was writing stories from Albuquerque and Oklahoma City and Cheyenne and scores of other places I had never been.

If I had a question I could contact the reporter who wrote the story on the message wire. There was no e-mail or instant messaging yet, but the new UPI computer system would let you send a message on a wire that was read by everyone in Dallas's region. A different wire was used for messages outside the region that could be read by every bureau in the country.

At night after managers had gone home and things slowed down we would use our regional message wire for entertainment. Someone would start, often with a line from the movie "Casablanca" and then someone in the next city would message the next line. It could go on for hours.

But things were never slow on Friday nights in the fall. If Texas has a state religion it is football, and on Friday nights it is high school football.

The bureau would be fully staffed because every score from every game across the state had to be reported. There were hundreds of them and if the scores from the high schools in Lubbock or Waco weren't on the wire there would be hell to pay on Monday morning. A network of stringers was set up and at every school there was someone who was supposed to call UPI after the game, but a few always slipped through the cracks. We then had to hit the phones calling bars and fire stations and anyone else we could find to learn the score of the high school football game in their town.

Most of my fellow broadcast writers didn't want to be writing for the radio wires. They wanted to be writing newspaper stories, which had more prestige; their bylines would be in the papers. I was enthused and energetic and learned fast and was soon put in charge of the night shift.

I tried to put out the best product I could and was unaware of how much the others resented taking orders from me until they invited me out one night after our shift and told me. It was a bad night and a hard lesson. Though things got better I realized supervising others was not for me. I would later enjoy teaching and mentoring others, but not running an office. I would later turn down management jobs in favor of staying a reporter, even when Bill Ferguson many years later wanted me to run the UPI Radio Network.

I would keep looking for stories to do in Dallas so I'd be on the radio and the people in New York wouldn't forget about me. I was working one Saturday on a story on the upcoming opening of the new Dallas-Fort Worth airport, which would be the biggest and most modern in the nation and was of course over budget and behind schedule. I learned its opening would be delayed again and besides filing a radio story I wrote one for the national wires.

Not long after that, the phone rang and Dan Rather was calling for me. Walter Cronkite was still the CBS Evening News anchor, but Rather was a star and anchoring the Saturday night news. He called because our competitor AP didn't have the story of another delay in the opening of the new airport and he wanted to talk to me personally before putting it on the air to make sure I had my facts straight. He asked about my sources and he was satisfied.

Years later, I would have plenty of opportunity working at CBS News to see the occasionally eccentric side of Dan Rather, but was always impressed he would call a rookie wire reporter on a Saturday to make sure my story was accurate before putting it on his broadcast.

I continued to call Frank Sciortino, the UPI Radio manager, once a month to say "hi" and ask if there were any openings in New York yet. After nine months, the answer was "yes.

WILD RIVERS

I've always been drawn to water. I love rivers, lakes, and oceans and have spent a lot of time snorkeling, kayaking, sailing, and running rivers in rubber rafts.

My first river trip was on the Rogue in Oregon, a perfect Disney river with deer along the bank, cliff swallows around each corner, river otters frolicking, and rapids that felt scary but were pretty safe.

It was a wonderful way to travel. We were camping in pristine wilderness, which would only be otherwise accessible by backpacking. I loved the thrill of the rapids, the beauty and stillness of the canyon, and going to sleep in a tent to the sounds of the nearby river. Plus, it is pretty lazy camping with the gear carried on the boats and a professional crew cooking all the meals and doing the dishes. Some outfitters excelled at food (cakes baked to perfection in a Dutch oven placed in hot coals) and there was pride in setting up the portable outdoor toilet with the grandest river views. A flag system assured privacy except on those rare occasions when another raft trip floated by, when the proper river etiquette was to stay seated and wave.

My big concern was always my crutches. If I fell out (as happened from time to time) I would float with my life jacket and could swim to safety, but my metal crutches would sink to the bottom of the river so I always made sure they were tied in tight, especially when I was taking rapids in a small inflatable kayak and they were on a raft.

I did a new river each year: the Middle Fork and Main Salmon, Snake and Selway in Idaho, the Kern, Stanislaus and Klamath in California, the Green in Utah and the granddaddy of them all, the Colorado through the Grand Canyon.

COLORADO RIVER 1980

I walked through the terminal at the Las Vegas airport, past the ticket counters and slot machines in a place I had been many times before. But it wasn't the same. People were rushing every which way, the sound was deafening, and I felt like I needed someplace to hide.

I had just returned from 18 days floating down the Colorado River through the Grand Canyon and getting used to civilization again wasn't easy.

It had been almost three weeks since sitting at the hotel pool in St. George, Utah, trying to figure out which of the other people was as crazy as I was, getting ready to float through 280 miles of the roughest whitewater in the country in small wooden boats.

From the upper edge of Marble Canyon looking down on our starting point on the river, the water was a deep forest green and slow moving. As we posed for pictures and spoke of the lazy looking river below us, our guides smiled knowingly.

The brightly painted dories are made of wood and hold four passengers and a boatman, who maneuvers it with two heavy oars.

They are graceful craft, less forgiving than rubber rafts when they hit rocks but more nimble negotiating the currents and far better looking.

As the boats are loaded we are given life jackets and shown how to put them on. "They will be your best friend," we are told and only later would we realize how true that was. Everything we would need for 18 days, including all our food, was loaded on the five wooden dories and a supply raft. It didn't look like enough but it would have to be. There are no supermarkets at the bottom of the Grand Canyon.

Less than half a mile downriver we went through our first little riffle, the lowest level of whitewater and not enough to even get wet. But it was an important milestone because you can't row up a whitewater river and so from this point on, the only way out was either a grueling hike on one of the handful of trails to the rim or 280 miles downstream to Lake Mead.

At our lunch stop we received our first lecture and the subject was toilet training. Going to the bathroom in the Grand Canyon is a whole new experience. The river environment is fragile and with the number of people floating down the Colorado, human waste is a problem. Our group leader, who like so many boatmen goes only by his nickname Fleet, is clearly uncomfortable explaining what comes next but goes bravely on. There are two problems and number two is the more complex one, since solid waste must be transported downstream and out of the canyon to be disposed of properly. A portable unit (called the P-U) will be set up at each camp to use for that purpose (basically a toilet seat on a base with a big black garbage bag underneath). As for number one, we have to avoid dry sand or rocks, since chemicals can leach out in the sun, so must use wet sand by the river or the river itself.

That doesn't afford much privacy, so the rule is that men head downriver along the beach and women upriver. Those who needed to put the new lessons to immediate use took a lengthy hike over boulders to an isolated spot in the appropriate direction. After a few days we would simply walk to the end of the beach.

That afternoon we floated down fairly quiet water until camp, the first of 17 patches of shoreline we would call home. We find a spot on the beach and lay out our sleeping bags. It is far too warm for tents. We slept all over the beach that first night but as the days went by we realized that lugging sleeping gear and clothes wasn't worth it. So except for one privacy-minded couple we ended up most nights close together. There are no secrets on the river.

The trip was put together by the Stanford Alumni Association and came with lectures from a full-time naturalist, John Olson. The first was on the geology of the canyon. It was a far cry from anything in a classroom as John pointed across the river to a wall showing several million years of geologic history in its layers. Rocks, never of great interest to me, came alive, and in time all among us knew our Toroweap Limestone from our Vishnu Schist.

Sometimes there would be unscheduled lessons in nature. One came when my fellow traveler Kevin was doing what men do downstream at the river's edge, when a rattlesnake began moving next to him in the wet sand. His exact words aren't as important as the volume with which they were screamed, and within moments we were all upon this poor snake (not to mention poor Kevin), receiving our first lesson on the pink rattlesnake, a variety found only in the Grand Canyon.

Our most frequent animal companions were lizards and birds, including eagles and bats, which would swoop over us every night at dusk.

On day two we hit our first big rapid, called House Rock. Water levels change dramatically on the Colorado depending how much water is released at Glen Canyon Dam to make electricity for Southern California and this day the water was low, too low to safely run House Rock.

The guides took the boats through the narrow chute alone and we had our first taste of canyon hiking. Temperatures were near 100 and the rocks were hot to the touch and sharp enough to cut through your hands. We were at the top of a ridge and there didn't appear to be any way down. But our boatmen had told us this was the route, so inch by inch we worked our way down to the beach on the other side of House Rock Rapid.

As we watched our dories go though without a scratch were was some grumbling, why did we have to make that awful hike while our guides had all the fun? We soon had our answer.

A small private raft group came though House Rock while we watched from the beach. The first raft to enter spun around, taking on water, but the second, smaller raft got sucked into a swirling whirlpool (called a "hole") and surfaced far downriver, upside down. The occupants were washed through the rapid in their life jackets. No one was seriously hurt but the point had been made.

Though the rapids were thrilling, especially when we came close to flipping, my favorite times on the river were the quiet stretches. The soundlessness of the canyon is total, an awesome quiet that took some getting used to. Our hearing became more acute; we could hear lizards walking and rapids half a mile before we reached them.

Time also changed. The first day everyone looked at their wrists for watches that were stored safely back in St. George and guessed at the time of day, still caring out of habit. By the third day we were on river time: up at first light, breakfast, loading the boats, floating downriver. Lunch came when we were hungry, camp was when the guides decided, dinner was when it was ready and bedtime was when the stars came out. We could compute the day of the week by counting back to the day we started but by day four that was getting harder, and after that I had no idea what day it was.

Our group, ranging in age from 16 to 70, was pulling closer in a way you only can when cut off from the outside world, an intense closeness we all knew would be temporary. We were free to be ourselves and just deal with the basics of eating, sleeping, and surviving. We were becoming a community cut off, alone and happy.

As we moved down the canyon the rocks got older and we floated deeper into the earth's history. At the lowest point we were surrounded by sheer walls of two-billion-year-old shiny black schist, polished to a sparkling finish and sculpted by the power of the water. The canyon walls were the limits of our universe, an occasional plane passing far overhead the only reminder there was life outside.

At mile 31.7 we reached Vesey's Paradise, one of several spots along the river that didn't seem to belong in the Grand Canyon. It is a grotto filled with waterfalls, ferns, and flowers just a short walk away from our world of hot rocks and sand. You can't see the rim of the Grand Canyon floating along the Colorado except from a few places, just as it is only from a few spots along the rim you can catch a glimpse of the river below. As we dropped in elevation, floating deeper into the canyon, we left behind the outer canyon walls and could only see the walls closest to us. The canyon was casting its spell as we began to understand how this place dwarfed us.

All of human history is but a moment in the life of this canyon and the experience of surveying the millennia in the canyon walls floating down the river that carved them was, more than anything else, humbling.

The water in the river is icy cold, since it comes from the bottom of a dam, but it is the only place to take a bath. Willpower was the key, along with encouragement from those plunging around you, as you jumped in the water screaming, soaped up quickly with biodegradable soap, and rinsed before changing your mind. I found by the time my hair was rinsed I could no longer feel my legs but getting clean felt good and the sun warmed me up way too quickly.

When we weren't wet, the problem was finding shade, as the sun shows no mercy. When the afternoon winds come up it feels like being inside a hair dryer. Without the river this would be an unbearable place.

The water will slowly, imperceptibly warm up as we head down river to Lake Mead, 280 miles from our starting point, where it will feel like a warm bath. But there is a lot of cold water to get through first.

All big rapids have names. Some are Native American like Kwagnut, others from events like President Harding Rapid, named after news of his death reached a river party there, and some you would rather not know about, like Dubendorff Rapid, named for an adventurer who drowned there in 1909.

As we approached the midpoint of our journey, heading through some wet and bumpy rapids named Hance and Sockdolager, the guides began speaking in hushed tones about a "golden trip," in which neither boats nor passengers are damaged. Superstition prevented too much talk but halfway through we were "golden," and if we could finish that way it would be a rare trip.

We stopped briefly at the junction of the Little Colorado, a warm side river turned aquamarine from dissolved salts. The warm water felt nice and we floated through a small rapid with just our life jackets. It is an experience in which you come to feel the power of the river against your body and realize that if you ever had to fight this river you would lose. If this were a skirmish with the forces of flowing water, a few of us later would feel the full impact of battle.

My first task at any camping site was to look for two sturdy trees between which to tie my small backpacking hammock, the envy of all my new friends. If successful, I would then place my sleeping bag in the hammock and begin the often-comical exercise of trying to get into it without being tossed on the ground. Most nights, though, the canyon had no trees to offer. Sometimes there wasn't even sand and we made our beds on slabs of rock.

The first of the monster rapids came at mile 98.3. Crystal is rated 9.5 on a scale of ten (with ten being unrunnable) and the water level was bad for running Crystal. On the left, rocks jutted out by the canyon wall and on the right was a huge hole, a whirlpool that could swallow one of our boats with ease. Just beyond the narrow chute was an area of sharp rocks and tricky currents making rescue difficult if someone got washed overboard.

Because hiking over rocks does have its special challenges with crutches, I was offered the chance to ride through Crystal as the others walked around it and I didn't hesitate. I had come to the river to ride the rapids and this was one of the biggest.

I sat in the front of the boat in the middle, the worst spot for getting hit by waves but being the only passenger it was critical that the weight be balanced and I be able to move quickly right or left if the boat started to flip over. I tightened my life jacket and Wren at the oars rubbed his hands dry on the back of my shirt. He was more nervous than I was. He knew what was coming.

As we began our approach, the critical phase where the proper angle to the rapid must be achieved, the roar of the water blocked all other sound and it suddenly struck me that we were in the current and there was no way out except through the rapid, a thought that I found oddly calming.

I was holding on all with all my strength as the waves hit and we slipped by the hole with a perfect maneuver as the rest of the group took pictures from the cliff above.

The rapids were getting bigger and closer together: Sapphire, Waltenberg, Bedrock. This was the canyon's roughest stretch, but also the site of a magical place called Matkatamiba, which was not easy to reach, but not to be missed.

Climbing up a slippery shallow river in a side canyon so narrow you could touch both walls at once, I gained new respect for salmon. With some help in a few bad spots and after a fall into a well-placed pool, I finally made it to the top and a mystical place.

Matcat, as it's called, resembles a lost Incan city more than a part of the Grand Canyon. It has large, flat surfaces as smooth as marble with courtyards and balconies, all created by naturally flowing water. We played ball in a huge natural amphitheater and soaked in a "jacuzzi," all part of the sculpted rock that had been molded by water over the centuries. Going down the steep water chutes of Matcat Canyon was far easier than climbing up.

Then came Lava Falls, a name that sends shivers down the spines of river runners. It is the toughest rapid on the toughest river, a place where people have died and boats have been smashed to bits. Back at the company boathouse in Hurricane, Utah, there is a picture on the wall showing a giant motorized raft, the kind that breezes through the rapids our wooden dories have to fight through, being flipped in Lava. The look of sheer terror on the faces of passengers and guides told the story.

Water level is critical to a successful run through Lava and we'll wait as long as we need to, to get the proper flow. Only volunteers are taken through and then only if they climb the hill to look at it. "Study it," says our head boatman, Fleet. "I don't want you on the boats unless you have taken a good look at what you might have to swim through."

The sight takes my breath away: waves 20 feet high in a narrow chute, where all the energy the river musters is focused on whatever small craft ventures there. A big black rock where boats are smashed is the most obvious obstacle but you have to get close to it. Those who study the river know the other side is worse.

The decisions are made. Twelve of us will ride and 19 will walk around.

After much discussion and debate the boatmen decide on a strategy for today's run, a route that Grand Canyon Dories first ran commercially, and one that requires split-second timing of the oar strokes.

As we head back to the boats, our guides aren't the hellbent folks of the days before. They are deadly serious and carrying a terrible responsibility. Some of us joked about cracking up in Lava, but each of them has seen it happen.

Life jackets are tightened, hats and glasses locked safely away, and grips strengthened. If we flip, we are told, we shouldn't try to get back in the boat. That was the rule for all the other rapids, but Lava has its own rules. A swimmer alone has a better chance of making it than an out-of-control flipped boat, which would likely smash against the rocks.

One at a time our wooden boats head into Lava Falls, we flash "thumbs up" signs, and remember we are a "golden trip" with no accidents and this is the big one. It seems to take forever as we paddle into the current. The river is eerily calm above Lava, only the roaring sound tells what lies ahead. We passed the point of no return where the river takes control. One way or another we will go through Lava Falls.

The waves are huge, the sound like thunder, the ride like being on a bucking bull while firehoses were being shot from all directions. Holding on with my eyes closed to the constant splash I couldn't tell where in the rapid we were. The boatman was being tossed and sprayed as much but couldn't afford to lose his place. One wrong turn would send the boat into the black rock.

I lost count of the waves, one after another, we crashed over and through them, the time between them seeming like an eternity. I wasn't so much afraid of the boat hitting something as being thrown out of it, ending up in that water all alone. I would have that experience a few years later, but this time we got past the last big wave and could look back and see the churning whirlpool and the back of the black rock and knew we had made it. Some of the boats had a rougher time taking on more water but we all made it through.

Lava was the last big rapid. We had conquered the Colorado and had done it as a "golden trip," with no damage to the boats or anything more serious than cuts and sprains to the passengers. From the bottom of the boats that night came hidden and very well padded bottles and the Lava Falls party lasted well into the night.

As we approached the end of our trip there was one more adventure ahead. Those of us who secretly wanted to fall into a rapid at least once were given the chance at Mile 217 rapid. It wasn't a huge rapid, but it wasn't small, either. What distinguished it was a lack of dangerous rocks or other obstacles, and plenty of room to rescue a swimmer in calm water downstream.

Four of us swam the rapid. Mark, Michael, and Robert were teenage brothers and I was feeling very old at 28. But the daredevil in me is never far from the surface and those three were just the ones to bring it out.

As we approached, we were told to stay with the main current, swim left as we approached the rock wall, and most important, stay together.

We dropped into the water and were immediately separated, racing down the Colorado, totally in its control. I lost sight of the others and saw only white as water splashed and surged around me. I heard screaming and made out my name being called. "Ferry left," I was being told. I remembered the rock wall and began swimming left as hard as I could. It's hard to tell in a rapid if your swimming is actually moving you since the force of the water is so strong. But I managed to get back into the main current and away from the rock wall in time to see Robert stuck in an eddy (a spot where the current is reversed that can hold you in place).

There was absolutely nothing I could do to reach him as I struggled to keep my head above water long enough to keep breathing. As I was beginning to think this might have been a mistake and started yelling out some very nasty things, a second set of waves slammed into me, driving water up my nose and holding me under. "Your life jacket will always bring you back up," I remember being told. They forgot to say that sometimes it can take a while.

Robert managed to swim out of the eddy and we were all together to watch our rescue boat almost flip as it came through the rapid we had just swum.

Our boatman had a sheepish smile, almost going over in the rapid he had sent us swimming through, but we all had an adventure to remember as we somehow mustered the strength to pull ourselves back into the boat.

With one day left on the trip we reached flat water, the upper reaches of Lake Mead, where the rapids had long ago been submerged by Hoover Dam. A motorboat brought us engines and we tied our boats together for the last 45 miles over calm water to the place where we could leave the river. Our boats moved faster this way, but somehow lacked the dignity of being powered by oars.

Eighteen days is a long time on a river and in some ways I was ready to return to the real world. I was ready for hot showers and cold drinks, ready for indoor plumbing, desperate for ice cream, and curious about what had happened in the world while we had been completely cut off.

But it wasn't long after I heard my first telephone ring that I longed again to be floating through the Grand Canyon.

The biggest, baddest river I did was the Zambezi in Africa, starting at the base of Victoria Falls, one of the world's biggest waterfalls. I started with a few days at the falls, including a scenic plane ride over them and some safaris, one by boat and another walking safari, where we came across an elephant with a baby. The elephant ripped a small tree clean out of the ground with its trunk and threw it at us. We quickly backed away. Lions can be fierce but make no mistake, the elephant is King of the Jungle.

The Zambezi marks the border between Zimbabwe and Zambia. The river trip was a weeklong run by Sobek, a pioneer of adventure travel, whose founder Richard Banks was the first to run the river.

It was a steep hike down the canyon with local guides carrying the gear and we got on the rafts with the deafening roar of Victoria Falls behind us. There were ten immense rapids on that first day, every one bigger than the biggest on the Colorado through the Grand Canyon. Each could swallow a raft whole.

I had swum a few rapids, some for fun and some when a raft turned over, but no one would have wanted to swim one of these monsters, though I ended up doing just that.

The most powerful oar stroke on a raft is backwards. Since these waves were so big, approaching head-on wouldn't let the guide get into the proper position. The technique was to approach backwards, then swing the boat around at the last minute to power through the waves. Going over the waves, as most river rafters do, wasn't possible.

So the heaviest people were put in the front of the boat and the idea was to just smash through the waves, letting them crash over the boat while holding on tight and hoping to emerge upright on the other side.

We were going through the biggest rapid on that first day and our boat was first. We had four passengers and two guides, one an experienced whitewater expert from California where Sobek was based, and the other a local African guide. So the two other very large men, one woman, and the local guide all were at the front, ready to lunge forward at the right moment to crash through the wave. I was alone in the back. The guide figured correctly that they would have enough weight to push through but didn't realize they were so heavy he wouldn't be able to turn the raft.

As we headed towards the rapid backwards he frantically pulled the oars but couldn't turn. I realized I would hit the wave first with no chance my weight would be enough. When a raft flips it is usually side-to-side. We flipped end-over-end. I wasn't really appreciating the drama of the scene as I went airborne and flew over the raft and was thrown right into the maw of this massive wave. When I emerged on the other side my first thought was, "Wow! My life jacket worked and I survived." I was feeling good and strangely calm.

Then I remembered the crocodiles. The river was filled with them, which was one reason this was considered one of the most adventurous and challenging rafting trips.

I was downriver of my upside down raft with no rafts ahead of me. I swam back and climbed on the bottom of the raft. We quickly got everyone on before noticing one passenger was missing, the only woman on our boat. We scanned the river and there was no sign of her. The guide ran his arms under the water along what had been the top of the raft. River guides always carry knives but this was the first time I'd seen it used to save a life.

During the flip a spare oar tied to the raft somehow pushed inside her life jacket, spearing her and trapping her under the overturned raft. She had a terrifying trip through that rapid, breathing air trapped with her under the raft. The guide dove in and cut off her life jacket and we pulled her up. She had cuts and bruises but remarkably no serious injuries. She was a trouper for the rest of the seven-day trip, but frankly she didn't have a choice, since continuing downriver was the only way out of there. There was no way to call for help and no one who would come.

As the other rafts caught up with us we got to shore and turned our raft back over. The gear was all fine in waterproof bags and my crutches still tied on tight. I wouldn't lose them for a few more days.

While those first-day rapids had the biggest waves, they were not the most dangerous. There were a few we had to portage around because they couldn't be safely run. One was in an extremely narrow and deep section where the rapid had a giant "hole," a whirlpool so strong it would pull a swimmer with a life jacket down so deep and fast his eardrums would burst and he might not be thrown back up to the surface in time to breathe.

So the passenger-less rafts were guided through from the shore with ropes attached, while we hiked around over steep rocky terrain. I reached a point where I had to climb hand over hand, and one guide took one of my crutches and a fellow passenger volunteered to carry the other. I scrambled safely over the rocks but the other man lost his balance and my crutch dropped into the river and immediately sank. This was not good.

I managed with one crutch and some help to finish the portage and get back on the river. I hobbled around at that night's camp with a single crutch but my mobility was severely limited. I had brought an extra rubber crutch tip and an extra metal cuff, since that was the part of the crutch most likely to break under stress. One of our local African guides found a piece of hardwood with a protrusion that formed a natural handle. Using only my Swiss Army knife, he carved me a beautiful wooden crutch, attached the spare cuff and tip and I was back in business. I flew home through London with that crutch, which I still have in my closet.

But this mighty river wasn't done with us yet. Our small group had five rafts and one kayaker who was into some serious adventure. He was shooting video and got great footage of my end-over-end flip, but there is no video of his encounter with the crocodile. We were passing through a quiet stretch of river when we saw a crocodile on a rock and the crocodile saw lunch. He jumped into the water as the kayaker paddled like a madman for the closest raft, where we pulled his kayak straight up onto the raft with him still in the seat. The crocodile was furious and kept circling our raft looking for a way to get our kayaker but eventually gave up.

I felt I had made the right decision the night before the trip began. At the elegant Victoria Falls Hotel crocodile was on the menu but I chose against it, figuring eating a crocodile would sacrifice the moral high ground if one of them wanted to eat us.

The biggest danger in this slower section of river actually wasn't the crocodiles, but the hippos. Not because they wanted to eat us—they only eat plants—but because they are very stupid. If they surface next to a raft they'll bite it and can easily sink it. And you don't want to be in the water next to a pissed-off hippopotamus.

So when we moved through hippo areas we had to make lots of noise, yelling and banging on the raft, hoping that would prevent them from being surprised and attacking us. It seemed to work.

Looking back, it was a wonderful trip and I'm glad I took it, but when I got home I realized I had gotten as adventurous as I wanted to be. I no longer needed to look for bigger, scarier rivers and took a whole different direction in rafting.

My eldest nephew, Ilan, was nine at the time and I asked his parents if I could take him on a rafting trip. We went back to my first river, the Rogue, in Oregon. It was such a different experience and wonderful in a whole new way. There were lots of other kids on the trip and they got as much joy from catching newts (the slimy amphibians, not the Gingrich kind) as going through the rapids. It was like discovering everything for the first time again through his eyes. Though I was surprised by how much I worried about him all the time (after all I was the cool uncle who didn't make kids follow the rules), we both had a great time and ran rivers together every summer well into his teenage years.

I have been lucky enough to snorkel on colorful reefs all over the world and snorkel with many large creatures. The biggest were manatees in Florida, which are sometimes described as sea cows. They are quite gentle, and when snorkeling with them, they will come up and check you out. I've seen a few sharks, snorkeled with dolphins, too, but sea lions were always the most fun. They are extremely playful and sometimes play in the same way dogs do. If you swim in a pattern they will copy the pattern and if you put your hand out to a young sea lion (I am not recommending this), it will pretend-bite like a puppy does.

But snorkeling with sea lions in the Galapagos off the coast of Ecuador things got a bit tricky. I was having a great time playing with a small group of young female sea lions. We were swimming all around and I was oblivious to what was happening above the water. Others in our group later told me a large male sea lion on a rock was getting progressively angrier and was barking loudly in my direction. I first learned there was a problem when I saw a large gray shape swimming very fast right at me. The sea lion approached me at high speed, then turned at the last minute and slapped me with his tail. Not hard enough to hurt me, but hard enough to deliver a message, which could be translated as "stay away from my women!"

I swam away and he returned to his harem.

THE BIG APPLE

I had a nice going-away party when I left Dallas and my colleagues even bought me a real cowboy hat custom fitted to my head. I used to wear it whenever I returned to Texas to cover a story and still have it. And while they were happy for me, more than one questioned why I would leave Texas for someplace as horrible as New York.

Since I was being transferred, UPI was paying my moving expenses and would put me up for a month in a miserable little hotel near the bureau in the Daily News Building on 42nd Street. The office had an iconic lobby with a giant globe that spun around and was the "Daily Planet" lobby in the first Superman movie.

Even in 1976 moving to New York involved sticker shock. In Dallas I had a big furnished apartment with a swimming pool and a large free parking lot. In New York I paid more than twice as much for an unfurnished tiny studio apartment in a high rise. But the location was great, two blocks from the office.

It was stupid to have a car in Manhattan but I grew up in Southern California and life without a car seemed inconceivable to me. Between special press plates issued to reporters by the police and a handicapped placard, I managed to always park it on the street (since I certainly couldn't afford a garage) and on weekends would head out to Long Island or Connecticut or somewhere else with trees.

I arrived on the day of a big going-away party for one of the UPI executives, so my introduction to the managers was when they were plastered. The Hollywood image of heavy drinking, heavy smoking, crusty newspeople was still very much the reality at UPI in those days.

I did a bit of everything in New York. I would take the printed news stories off the wire machine and organize it for the anchors, take in stories from correspondents and stringers around the world, edit tape, do phone interviews, and report on the stock market.

And I made beep tones. Every hour, we would send out batches of stories and sound from newsmakers in feeds assembled on reels of tape. Stations would record them onto audio carts, which could then be easily played in a newscast. Some had automated devices that would record the cart directly after hearing a beep at a certain frequency. So each report was separated from the next by a few seconds of silence, then a beep tone, then one more second of silence.

The stations had the automated devices but we made the beeps by hand. We'd have to cut half a second of pre-recorded tone with a razor blade and, using splicing tape, attach it to a second of white leader tape for the silence. I made thousands of them during my year in New York.

I learned early on it's always good policy to trust your instincts. That paid off one day when I was told to record a story on the phone from a stringer in Florida.

School busing for integration was a big story in those days and this reporter was offering a story the editor wanted about a race riot at a high school. He fed the piece, which included sound of screaming and yelling and was pretty well put together. I took his name, address, phone number, and social security number so we could pay him.

But as I was editing it, something just didn't feel right. There had been no wire copy about a school riot in Miami; I hadn't heard of any racial problems connected with busing there, and I just had a bad feeling about it. We were always in a hurry and I was told to get this piece ready to feed, including, of course, attaching a beep tone.

I told the editor of my unease and asked if I could just make a phone call or two to check this out. I called the local police and school district and both denied knowing anything about a riot.

So I called the reporter back and after quite a few rings someone answered. I asked for the stringer but the man seemed confused and told me I had reached a pay phone in a city park. It was a pretty elaborate hoax by someone who knew a lot about how to sell a radio story to a national network.

I had a similar experience years later at Mutual/NBC Radio. I was in the main newsroom in Arlington, Virginia, when an AP bulletin came over that Bob Hope had died. The source was a member of Congress who had taken the floor in the House of Representatives to announce Hope's death and began to eulogize him.

I had covered Hope for many years in Los Angeles and it struck me as extremely odd that first word of his death would come not from his publicist or family but from a member of Congress who had no reason to know him. I still had a home phone number for Bob Hope. I called it and was told he was in the next room and was fine. I asked the person to just pop in and make sure and they came back to the phone and assured me he was alive and well. We were one of the few news networks that didn't go on the air that day with what turned out to be a totally false story.

On one of my first days on the job at UPI Radio in New York I heard a voice boom over the loudspeaker that was set up as a full-time intercom with the Washington Bureau. The voice said "Hello, New York" and so I answered "Hello, Washington." There was a pause and then the voice asked, "Who is this?" I told him who I was and that I had just started working there that week and then asked who he was. Big mistake.

A longer pause. And then: "If you want to make it to your second week you better learn to recognize my voice!"

And that was how I met Pye Chamberlayne, one of the most talented, difficult, egocentric, and eccentric people in a business that has no shortage of any of those. Pye covered national politics and was one of the leading radio reporters in Washington.

I could write a whole other book with just Pye Chamberlayne stories but here are two of my favorites.

He and fellow correspondent Gene Gibbons were at the train station returning from a Democratic "mini-convention" in Philadelphia (a brief experiment in conventions every two years that fizzled fast) when Pye found his way to the room where the public address system was controlled.

He then in his sonorous radio voice began announcing changes to the schedule, re-routing trains and sending people scrambling to new tracks. I believe the "Orient Express" was leaving from one of them. It was one of several times only some fast talking by Gene (who was equally talented but straight laced and well behaved) would keep Pye out of jail.

Pye covered the Senate and was interviewing California Senator Alan Cranston, a liberal Democrat who made a brief run for the presidential nomination in1984 when he was 69. Cranston ran marathons and, while in great shape, was as thin as a rail and looked older than he was.

At one point in the interview Pye said to Cranston, "Senator, even members of your own staff say you look like a skeleton with skin on it, won't that be a problem for you in running for president?"

Another great character in the Washington Bureau was the White House correspondent Don Folsum, subject of a wonderful story first told in the book "Boys on the Bus." He was at his first radio job at a small station and was being constantly yelled at by the news director for not saying "alleged" in crime stories. He was told he had to use the word every single time and was getting tired of being harangued every time he forgot.

And so assigned to the early morning shift on Easter he opened the newscast with these memorable words: "Millions of Christians around the world are today celebrating the alleged resurrection of Christ." He was fired by noon and went on to a great career.

There were two of us in the bureau who were young and ambitious and wanted to be out covering news. Tom Foty and I would constantly pester the managers to send us out on the street. We lived in the same building and became friends and later worked at CBS News together.

I did get assignments. I covered the Tall Ships coming into New York harbor for the Bicentennial, did some stories at the UN, and even covered the NFL draft; and in the summer went to my first political convention.

The 1976 Republican convention in Kansas City was the last one where there was any suspense about who the nominee would be. There were still lots of uncommitted delegates back then and it was a "brokered convention" of the kind we will likely never see again because parties changed their rules to avoid them.

President Gerald Ford, who came into office in 1974 after President Nixon resigned, was seeking to run for a full term. California governor Ronald Reagan was challenging him, representing a growing conservative movement in a Republican Party that at that time was run by moderates and actually still had liberals.

As the convention opened neither candidate had enough delegates to win the nomination and the back room dealing was intense. The key moment came when the Mississippi delegation moved some of its votes from Reagan to Ford and the president won re-nomination by a narrow margin on the first ballot (only to lose to Jimmy Carter in the general election).

As low man on the totem pole I covered stories during the day, including meetings of critical delegations still being wooed, then at night when the Washington correspondents came in I cut tape and helped them prepare their reports, and later helped put together the all-important morning package (because most people listen to radio news in the mornings as they drive to work).

I remember my time sheets from that convention included one 24-hour day; the rest were over 20 hours and I was loving it. My hours were no shorter at the Democratic convention in New York later that summer, where, with far less drama, Jimmy Carter was nominated.

I would go on to cover more than a dozen other national conventions, at most working as a floor reporter. Convention floors are crowded to a crazy degree and one of the challenges was just moving around. Part of this is deliberate; party officials think it makes a better picture on TV when the party faithful are crowded in so tightly. But it makes it almost impossible to get around and while moving through intense crowds can be more challenging on crutches, they also can provide some leverage if used to help clear a path. As a floor reporter, I would be carrying a fair amount of gear and wearing a headset and would be dispatched to various delegations to find people to talk to. I once managed to convince Moses himself, Charlton Heston, to come down from a VIP section to the floor to talk to me at a Republican convention. In later years covering Congress was a big advantage for my convention work, since I knew congressmen and senators scattered all over the convention floors and I could pull them aside. Still, it was physically grueling work and the conventions that I helped anchor from a comfortable booth high above the action were a lot easier.

Living in New York as a young reporter was great. I tried to check out new neighborhoods whenever I could and loved the food. I became more of a connoisseur of great restaurants later when I had more money, but I tried every kind of food New York had to offer, which is pretty much every kind there is.

Despite all that eating, I was never leaner or in better physical shape than the year I spent in New York, because I walked everywhere.

New York was not quite as safe a city in 1976 as it is today. Times Square had not yet been turned into a family-friendly sanitized place and still had barkers inviting you into seedy strip clubs. It had character.

I sometimes had to go to work in the middle of the night but never felt unsafe because my short two-block walk was along the backside of the Daily News building where the loading dock was, so it was filled with teamsters loading newspapers on trucks. No one fooled with teamsters. My experience with teamsters was less friendly a few years later when I covered one of their conventions in Las Vegas at a time their union president was being investigated for corruption and a variety of felonies. Large men would stand right behind us in the press room listening and reading over our shoulders as we filed our stories.

I had no inkling my time in New York would be so short. I had been working there just a year and was in a motel in Palo Alto, California, for the wedding of my former college roommate Francis Dickerson and his longtime girlfriend Lynne. It was at the beautiful Stanford Chapel and those of us in the wedding party all wore brown blazers and white turtleneck shirts. It was the 70s!

The phone rang and it was my boss Frank Sciortino asking me if I wanted to become the West Coast correspondent for UPI Radio and open and run a new one-man radio bureau. I said sure, and a few days later was in Los Angeles checking out the bureau, meeting the print reporters and photographers who would be my colleagues for the next 15 years in the next stage of my career.

HOLLYWOOD IS A STATE OF MIND

When I arrived in Los Angeles early in 1977, I was UPI's youngest bureau manager at 22 and responsible for all the news west of Texas, along with Canada and Mexico. I would pursue stories by phone and set up a network of stringers and would travel several times a month to all the big stories. My boss was 3,000 miles away and I had pretty much carte blanche to cover half the country any way I wanted.

Covering Congress and the White House later would be exciting, but those years in LA were the best. I covered politics and celebrities, major trials and sports, earthquakes, wildfires, tornadoes and medical breakthroughs. But nothing was more important to the stations than the Academy Awards.

A reporter's reputation is made on big stories. Flub the little ones and no one remembers as long as you deliver on the big ones and for a national reporter in Los Angeles nothing was bigger than the Oscars.

I prepared for weeks making sure I had clips from all the films that might be nominated. Nominations were announced in a small theatre at the motion picture academy's headquarters in Beverly Hills, before sunrise. The hour let the morning news shows, which are on east coast time, carry it live.

Between the nominations and Oscar night I would return to that theatre often for screenings to watch any of the nominated films I hadn't already seen. Then there was the Oscar lunch, where all the nominees came and pretended that being nominated was honor enough and winning would just be icing on the cake. But the key to the lunch was the chance to interview all the nominated actors. Along with the movie clips, that would provide me enough material for a full week of previews I would put out for stations leading up to Oscar night.

I had never worn a tuxedo but you aren't allowed to cover the Academy Awards without one. I figured since I'd change at the office and work most of the night after the show, it would make sense to rent my tux nearby.

The UPI office was on Broadway in downtown Los Angeles in an area dominated by the Mexican American community. It was a busy and crowded neighborhood filled with street vendors and music. And there was a tux rental shop a block and a half away.

I went in and found lots of tuxes in pastel green and blue and some bright red ones. They did reluctantly rent me a black one.

Clearly after a few Oscar shows it was far more practical to buy my own tuxedo but UPI wouldn't pay for it. So I bought one and asked the store for a stack of rental receipts and after a few years UPI had paid for the tuxedo.

It was a strategy I learned from a legendary UPI salesman in Dallas named Pinky Vidacovich. He was on a sales trip to West Texas trying to get some small radio stations there to buy the UPI wire. He knew he would have an easier time if he showed up in a cowboy hat, and bought one for the trip. It worked and he signed up a couple of new clients. But when he submitted his expense account, New York rejected the hat and refused to pay for it.

The next month Pinky submitted his expense account for motels and gas and dinners with prospective clients and put a little note on the bottom that read "find the hat."

When my first Oscar night approached I put on my tuxedo and headed over to the Los Angeles Music Center, where it was held in those days. I set up my equipment to broadcast from the press room, where we would watch the show on TV and interview the winners when they were brought back.

Unlike television, radio reporters are one-man bands and we had to carry, set up, and run all of our own equipment. There was a lot of heavy gear to carry but being a one-man band also is why radio is so much more fun than print or television; you have total creative control over the product you put out. No one helps you but also no one edits your script or changes your story. Every aspect of the product that goes on the radio is under your control.

The trick in covering the Oscars for radio is to have your script written and ready to go before they announce best picture so you can get on the air immediately. To do that you have to try to figure out what film is going to win best picture, which is always announced last. The best director category is the best indicator since most years the movie whose director wins the Oscar gets the top prize. But not always.

I was able to call it right most of the time starting with "Annie Hall" at that first show in 1977. But in 1981 when Warren Beatty won best director for "Reds" and the top acting awards went to Henry Fonda and Katherine Hepburn for "On Golden Pond," I was floored when "Chariots of Fire" won best picture and had to frantically re-write my bulletin story.

The following year I was ready when "Gandhi" won best picture but wasn't happy about it. I thought "ET" should have won.

During the 15 years I covered the Oscars I never was in the actual auditorium or anywhere the TV audience could see me but always had to wear a tuxedo anyway. One year when the awards were held at the Shrine Auditorium we worked in a tent and they had porta-potties for us. Black tie still required.

When I got to Los Angeles I was told I had to do a daily show business feature. That would definitely limit my flexibility to travel and I was determined not to get tied up with too much Hollywood news. (Hollywood, by the way, in the news business is not a physical neighborhood in Los Angeles but a state of mind. Very few "Hollywood" stories actually happen in Hollywood but we sign off "Hollywood" when the story is about show business.)

So one of the first things I did was sign up UPI's Hollywood correspondent Vernon Scott to do the daily Hollywood show. He had never done radio before but was a legendary columnist in the entertainment world who interviewed movie stars every day, usually over lunch in Beverly Hills, paid for by a studio publicist.

Vernon could be irascible at times but he knew everyone and everyone knew him. I taught him how to record his interviews and helped him turn each one into one-minute radio features. We became friends, his daily show was a success, and I only did Hollywood stories when they rose to the level of national news, which was actually pretty often.

I covered the nation's first palimony case, where actor Lee Marvin was sued by his longtime live-in girlfriend; Carol Burnett's successful lawsuit against the National Enquirer for libel; and the trial over the competency of the great funny man Groucho Marx. That case pitted Marx's young female companion against his son and was sordid and sad as a judge tried to determine if Groucho was still capable of deciding who should care for him. At bottom, it was about who would get his money.

For sordid, though, it's hard to beat the rape case against famed film director Roman Polanski. The director of such films as "Rosemary's Baby" and "Chinatown" had more than his share of trouble in his life. Born to Polish parents in Paris, he fled the Nazis, and his wife Sharon Tate was murdered by the Manson family in a brutal attack at their Los Angeles home in 1969.

It was in 1977 that he was arrested for raping a thirteen-year-old girl at Jack Nicholson's house. He pled guilty to a lesser charge of illegal sex with a minor as part of a plea bargain to avoid jail time. The prosecutor went along to spare the teenager from testifying.

Every seat in the courtroom in Santa Monica was filled when the day came for him to be sentenced. He had gotten wind of reports the judge might send him to prison despite the plea deal and everyone was in place but Polanski wasn't there. His defense lawyer stood up and told the judge Polanski had called and said he had fled the country and was in Paris.

It was a scene right out of the movies (fittingly enough) as we ran out of the courtroom and down the hall to the bank of pay phones—there were no cell phones yet—and breathlessly filed our stories. I've covered a lot of dramatic court cases since but never remember a more dramatic moment in a courtroom.

The judge was furious and ordered an arrest warrant but it was too late. Polanski held French citizenship and sex with a 13-year old was not considered a serious enough crime by the French to extradite him. Polanski went on to direct other hit films but was never able to return to the U.S.

Though Vernon Scott did the daily show, I still did my share of celebrity interviews. Bob Hope would invite me to his house for lunch once a year and I'd interview him about his latest project. He'd also send me (and lots of other reporters) little presents at Christmas. I was concerned about the ethics at first but I figured it was just too tacky to send them back.

One of my favorite interviews was with George Burns around his 90th birthday (he lived to be 100). He chomped on a cigar and was sharp as a tack and falling down funny.

Another high point was when Shirley MacLaine told me at the end of our interview that she could see my aura and it was wonderful. I figure if anyone could see my aura, it was Shirley MacLaine.

Long before he took an interest in politics I interviewed Arnold Schwarzenegger. He had ably used his reputation as a bodybuilder to get into show business and was starring in action films that showed off his body. My main memory is that he had a very powerful handshake.

I did have a brief interlude as a movie reviewer. I had contracted with Steve Arvin, who reviewed movies for one of our Los Angeles stations, to do reviews for the network.

After a few years he approached me to see if I would join him in two-man reviews for a new phone-in service. These were the early days of 976 numbers. There was a brief time when people thought this new technology where you paid extra for each minute on the phone could make money by offering weather and sports and movie reviews. Eventually they figured out what worked—and all the 976 numbers became phone sex lines.

But for that brief period companies were spending money on other ideas and one was for people to call the number and then choose one of ten movie reviews to listen to. Siskel and Ebert were big then and so they asked Steve to find a partner.

It was fun and easy and didn't, take much time except I had to watch every new movie that was coming out. I went to three or four studio screenings a week and while it's great to see a good movie at a screening when you know nothing about the film going in, most of the movies aren't great. Or good. Most are awful. And sitting in a small screening room at a studio, you can't walk out on a bad movie, so I sat through a lot of them.

Now truth be told, it is a lot more fun to write a bad review than a good one, but I prefer only going to movies I have some reason to think I'm going to like. Steve and I agreed most of the time on films but there were a few notable exceptions. He loved "Prizzi's Honor" with Jack Nicholson and I hated it, and I thought "Brazil" was a brilliant satire and he didn't. The gig lasted about a year and the extra money paid for my rafting trip to Africa.

The biggest responsibility of covering Hollywood is having the obits ready. I amassed a collection of movie clips, TV theme music, and songs to be ready when a celebrity died. Lots of my obit stories were pre-recorded and standing by in New York.

Another critical tool in obit preparation was a good list of phone numbers to get reaction. One of my best was a home phone for Jimmy Stewart, who appeared with and knew all the other great stars of his generation. I called one day and his wife Gloria answered; I heard her call out "Jimmy, it's Bob Fuss on the phone from UPI Radio, someone must have died."

When John Wayne died in 1979 it was an enormous story. He was an iconic actor and part of American folklore. He was in the hospital suffering from cancer and I would do updates every day, and before I went home at night I would call the UCLA Medical Center to check on his condition.

On June 11th when I called I was told he was walking the halls and joking with the nurses. A few hours later I was rushing to UCLA for a middle of the night news conference, where it was announced he had died. I worked through the night and only later reflected on the time of death and realized that when I was told he was walking the halls, he was already dead.

I've been lied to a lot as a reporter by press secretaries and police, congressmen, senators, and presidents and it happened so often when I covered the second Iraq war at the Pentagon I came to just assume nothing I heard at Defense Secretary Donald Rumsfeld's news briefings was true. But this was the first time I was told a blatant lie on such an important story and it stuck with me. Reporters frequently become cynical but it's often well earned.

When an older movie star or singer died, I was generally ready, but then there were the surprises, like Natalie Wood and John Belushi. Natalie Wood was a child star in "Miracle on 34th Street" and was wonderful in later films including "West Wide Story" and "Bob and Carol and Ted and Alice"; her death was a mystery to be sure. She had been on a weekend yachting trip to Catalina Island with her husband Robert Wagner and their friend Christopher Walken. She somehow ended up overboard and drowned. A dingy was found near her body about a mile from the boat.

To say it was suspicious is an understatement but Wagner and Walken insisted they had no idea what had happened or how she had left the boat. The case was closed, though several decades later police re-opened it and did another investigation, but still couldn't figure it out.

There was no mystery about the death of John Belushi, the breakout star from the early days of "Saturday Night Live" and a brilliant comedian, who died of a drug overdose at the Chateau Marmont hotel in West Hollywood on March 5, 1982, at the age of 33. He was sadly one in a long line of young stars of music, television, and movies whose early success led to the same end.

The death of movie star Rock Hudson in 1985 was sad but also had profound political and social implications. He was the first celebrity to publicly announce he had AIDS, a disease that was still very much looked upon as a "gay plague" and not discussed in polite conversation or dealt with in any meaningful way by the government. Hudson had been such a popular actor that it forced many people to take a new look at AIDS and helped bring what was then a devastating and incurable illness out of the closet.

But it was still a slow process. When Liberace, the flamboyant piano player and uber-celebrity died two years later, his doctor lied on his death certificate to try to hide the cause and it was only when the medical examiner performed an autopsy that we learned he had also died from AIDS.

SEEING THE WORLD

My vacation time in my first two jobs in Dallas and New York was used to return to California to spend time with my parents and sister Lorri. Once I moved back to Los Angeles I no longer needed vacation time to see my family, and serendipity once more intervened to start a lifetime of travel to exotic lands, with more than 70 countries so far.

Danny Brenner was a college friend who was several years ahead of me. He was a teaching assistant in a communications class I took and also worked at KZSU.

He went to law school and had just finished a prestigious clerkship with a federal judge and was taking a little time off before starting his next job. Danny is smart and funny and ended up as a prominent specialist in communications law, a professor, and a judge, but always really wanted to be a stand-up comedian.

We met for lunch and Danny told me he was planning a six-week trip through Asia. I told him that sounded fantastic to which he responded, "Why don't you come along?" I replied that I only had two weeks of vacation, so he told me to just come for two weeks. I said, "Sure." I would join him in Bali and Hong Kong, and then come home as he traveled on. We met a few times and made our plans.

Finding a truly compatible travel companion is very hard. Even people who really like each other (and many who are married to each other) have trouble with the stresses and compromises of traveling together. Neither of us had much money, but I wanted to splurge a bit and Danny not so much. So we divided it up and I chose the hotel in Bali, a beautiful Hyatt resort on the beach, and he picked for Hong Kong: the YMCA.

It was a very funny combination but actually set the pattern for my future preferred way to travel by alternating cheap, interesting hostels, rustic cabins or camping with some of the world's best luxury hotels. They would balance out money-wise to be the same as staying at mid-priced places for an entire trip, but made for much more interesting experiences.

Bali was beautiful and fascinating with its unique animistic form of Hinduism with spirits everywhere. Taxi drivers would stop several times during a short drive to drop off an offering of flowers or food at shrines under a tree or by a rock. We visited villages that each specialized in an art form like carving or music.

The visit to the holy snakes was memorable. We had to wait for low tide, tie a yellow cloth around our waist, and walk out to a rocky island where the holy snakes lived in a cave. They were pretty well behaved, which is more than I can say for the holy monkeys.

When we went to visit them we had special food to give them, but one didn't want to wait. He jumped on my back and ripped the food out of my hand.

A day or so later I got quite sick with a high fever. People at the hotel were convinced I had been bitten by the holy monkey and were very concerned. A doctor came and gave me some drugs. Even though I was starting to hallucinate from the fever I was able to see the pills had expired years before, so just stuck with orange juice and bed rest and got better in a few days. But I learned two important lessons: never go to a developing country without my own supply of antibiotics and steer clear of holy monkeys.

Hong Kong is a great city and that first visit was a fun one. It turns out the YMCA has one of the best locations in the city, right next to the Star Ferry terminal, and we explored at length. In later visits I had developed a more sophisticated palate and enjoyed Hong Kong's culinary delights as well as its spectacular harbor.

A little side trip to Macau, still a Portuguese colony at the time and a mecca for gambling, taught me a lesson about relying on the kindness of strangers. I went over on a hydrofoil, and while I hadn't had a problem with seasickness before, I was turning green. Two local girls saw I was in distress and unwrapped a small baggy and told me to eat what was inside. They assured me it would help. It was a piece of heavily salted ginger and relieved my sea sickness instantly. It wouldn't be the last time I would understand that people know their own places better than we do.

(When I was in Cuzco, Peru, many years later on a visit to Machu Picchu, our group was warned of the dangers of altitude sickness in that city, which is at 11,000 feet. We were told to drink the local coca tea and then lie down. Several in our small travel group wouldn't do it because even though coca tea has no hallucinogenic properties, it is made from the same plant as cocaine. I drank the tea and those that didn't all got sick.)

But back to Macau. It was an introduction to gambling, Chinese style. Sitting at a blackjack table, people lined up behind me and the other players and made side bets on our hands while shouting advice on whether or not to take another card. Everyone was enthusiastic and emotional and it was a lot of fun, though I felt badly when I lost a hand because all those others were losing with me.

I've always enjoyed gambling and though I never went to Las Vegas just to gamble, I covered lots of stories there and always managed to spend time in the casinos. I learned craps when I was maybe six or seven from my grandfather, who used to visit us on Sundays and loved to take the senior citizen bus trips to Las Vegas. He taught me how to play cards and dice, but it was my mother who inadvertently convinced me that gambling could be fun and profitable.

We were on a family driving trip to Yellowstone. Heading through Nevada, we had not made reservations anywhere and pulled late at night into the small town of Winnemucca. The only place we could find a room was decidedly seedy. As we walked through the casino to get to our room, my parents held my younger sister and me tight, but I was enthralled by the slot machines. My mother told me all these people playing were unhappy and losing money; it was not a fun thing to do. She could tell I wasn't buying it, so decided to prove it to me and put a quarter in a slot machine, telling me to pull the handle. I did and I won a small jackpot.

We made it safely to our room, where the locks had shown signs of being jimmied, but it was too late. The lesson had been learned. Gambling was fun and I could win money at it.

I like blackjack and craps, though my favorite game is baccarat, not just because James Bond played it, but because it has the best odds in the casino, or so I've convinced myself. I've probably won and lost about the same amount over the years and never lost more than I could afford (though sometimes lost more than I wanted to). I was very unhappy when ATMs started showing up in casinos because it undermined my strategy of only carrying the amount of cash that I was willing to lose.

I have gambled all over the world and enjoy visiting casinos in other countries. I learned a good lesson playing blackjack once with my father in the Bahamas when the table was hot and everyone was winning. Then they changed dealers and we all started losing.

I lost at a casino in Zimbabwe and blamed it on the money. I figured I just couldn't take it seriously when I was betting currency with pictures of elephants on it.

KIDNAPPED BY NUNS

Popes didn't do this.

They occasionally took a trip out of Rome, but John Paul II was different. He was a rock star pope. He would travel the world in his "Popemobile," attracting immense crowds and preaching not just to the converted but to everyone he could reach. His moral teachings were old school but his style was definitely not.

He likely held the Catholic Church back from the modernizing it eventually has to do, but this first Polish pope changed the world. The Gdansk uprising in Poland that led to the collapse of communism and the breakup of the Soviet Union would never have happened without him and the old line Communist bosses who later tried to assassinate him knew it.

His trip to Mexico in January, 1979, was the first of his journeys and the first of his trips I covered. It was uncharted ground for the pope and for Mexican authorities and it was an adventure for all of us. We began with bribes, the way business is often conducted in Mexico. My colleagues at the UPI bureau in Mexico City began sending bottles of liquor to priests to get credentials and eventually obtained them. It didn't help much because the American TV networks printed up much fancier looking credentials in New York and since most of the security guards couldn't read they often preferred the more colorful credentials and rejected the real ones.

At one event the guards refused to let us in and I joined a small group of intrepid journalists who ended up crossing a field and crawling under a barbed wire fence to cover one of the outdoor masses. I had no religious feelings towards the pope but there was no doubt about the extraordinary personal charisma of John Paul. It was more than just being swept away by the intensity of the emotions of the Mexican people who were beyond thrilled to be in his presence. I could feel a spiritual power in the man that couldn't be denied.

There was no transportation to follow the pope so we all made do. I flew to Oaxaca for the most memorable of the stops. More than 100,000 people representing Mexico's indigenous groups gathered in a field; many had walked there from distant villages. Fear spread as the pope's helicopter approached since most had never seen one before. It was an extraordinary and moving event but after he left, the authorities decided to keep the airport closed, so a whole group of us ended up having to stay the night and try to catch up with the pope the next day.

The final, big event of the trip was a parade in the new Popemobile through Mexico City. I had covered big crowd events before but nothing like this; there were over a million people lining the route. The general chaos of the trip continued and while there was supposed to be a flat bed truck for reporters to ride on in front of the pope, no one knew where we were supposed to go to get on it.

I joined a group of my UPI colleagues in a taxi and went to where we thought the meeting point was, but we couldn't be sure, so I stayed with the car while the others went to find out where we were supposed to be. Remember, this was before cell phones so they were going to have to come back to find me or get back in the car if we were in the wrong place.

I waited a long while outside the car and was starting to get nervous when a woman came up to me, looked at the credential around my neck and told me to come with her. Now I took Spanish in high school and could say hello, order dinner, and ask where the bathroom was, but that was about it.

I figured my colleagues had found the right spot but couldn't come back out (which would have been typical for this trip) and sent this woman, who had all kinds of official tags, to get me. I paid the driver and off we went, my confidence growing as we sailed through one security checkpoint after another.

Then we entered a courtyard, which seemed odd, and she left me there. As I looked around I saw Mexicans in wheelchairs and on crutches and with all manner of afflictions. It hit me like a ton of bricks. My friends hadn't sent her. She saw me standing on the street and brought me to a courtyard where the sick and disabled had gathered under a balcony to be blessed by the pope.

In full-blown panic I started to rush back to where the taxi had been and where the other UPI reporters would go to find me.

But nuns stood in my way.

My distress and poor Spanish prevented me from explaining or understanding what they were saying, but figure it was along the lines of "You idiot! You obviously need the pope to bless you, so where are you going?"

I pushed my way out and back to where I had left the car. I never found my colleagues or the flat bed truck but covered the parade, sent back my broadcasts, and later that night explained what had happened to my fellow reporters, who found it much funnier at the time than I did.

Later, of course, as a more seasoned reporter, I realized how foolish I had been and what a great exclusive, colorful story I would have had if I stayed in the courtyard. But not as colorful as the exaggerated story about me that grew out of that day. Thirty years later reporters who meet me still ask about the story they've heard that I was "kidnapped by nuns" in Mexico.

I covered several more trips with Pope John Paul II, which were far more organized. There was a huge mass in Central Park in New York, a memorable trip in San Francisco, and a fun excursion in Canada.

John Paul had a special affinity for indigenous people and in Canada scheduled a visit to a small isolated Inuit village in what was then the Northwest Territories.

I flew first to Edmonton, where I spent a day doing a feature on the world's largest shopping mall, complete with an indoor water park. That afternoon I had to go to a hotel ballroom for credentials for the next day's trip by charter plane to follow the pope. It was a fascinating display of different approaches to security. The Secret Service, which protected the pope in the U.S., relies heavily on technology, with lots of metal detectors and computer background checks.

At the hotel waiting for my credential a man came up to me and started chatting, just asking where else I had been and what my job is like. I noticed he seemed to be making small talk with everyone. The next morning as we boarded the plane he was there, in charge of security for the Royal Canadian Mounted Police.

Metal detectors and high-tech credentials can be helpful, but he had made a personal connection with every reporter on the trip and would have immediately known if someone didn't belong. The people in the Inuit village weren't Catholic, of course, and seemed a bit perplexed by the visit from this man in a funny hat, but it was a colorful and memorable story.

The last papal trip I covered was to Cuba in 1998, when I was working for Mutual/NBC Radio. Cuba was still off-limits to American tourists, so I was anxious to see it and the trip interested me from an historic point of view. Fidel Castro was one of the last communist leaders left; Pope John Paul II had helped bring communism down. These were two of the most intriguing figures of the last half of the 20th century, on opposite sides of an epic struggle, meeting as old men in a nation Castro had declared atheist that was still Catholic to its core.

The Treasury Department had issued a blanket approval for journalists covering the pope to go to Cuba and flights had been laid on from

Miami. It was still complicated, though, because of the embargo. No checks or credit cards could be used, so bigger news organizations had to send people in with suitcases full of cash to pay the bills.

Havana is a fascinating city and not what I had expected. While there was certainly political repression, the atmosphere was nothing like what I had seen in Warsaw or Moscow under Soviet domination. It was more like the Bahamas. People were open and friendly and not afraid to talk about the man they all called "Fidel" and seemed to genuinely admire. There was a lively street life, music everywhere, and it was anything but somber.

But the economy was a mess. Basic food and other necessities were bought with government issued scrip, but anything worth having required hard currency like U.S. dollars. Cab drivers were often professors or physicians whose salaries didn't help them buy what a few tourist dollars could.

Havana was beautiful but falling apart and it was right out of a time machine from 1950s America. The architecture and the cars were all American but frozen in another era. It was amazing to see all the cars from the 1940s and 50s, which they somehow managed to keep running with homemade parts.

I spent a few fun days doing feature stories on Cuba before the pope's arrival, including heading out to a beach resort to report on the effect of the U.S. embargo on tourism. I found a bunch of happy vacationing Canadians dreading the day the embargo might be lifted, confident if Americans came in large numbers the price of everything, especially beer, would go up.

The government owned all the restaurants, which were pretty bad, but had just started an experiment allowing very small private restaurants in people's homes with limited menus. With the help of our local Cuban "fixer" my colleagues and I had some good meals and met some interesting people. At one place I asked if they had any of the local lobster and they said, "no, it's not allowed." Later the owner invited me into her kitchen, where away from prying eyes she could show me all the good forbidden things they had that I could order.

It was a huge story and all the TV network anchors were there and then—they all left. The pope arrived as the story of President Bill Clinton and Monica Lewinsky broke and an Oval Office sex scandal took precedence.

It shouldn't have, of course, and the exodus from Havana demonstrated so much of what is wrong with the media. Sex and scandal sell but that doesn't mean we should sacrifice substance to cover it. I stayed and covered the rest of the pope's visit, but knew it wasn't getting the play it should have.

Traveling with the queen of England was less adventurous but certainly had its moments. Queen Elizabeth II visited the west coast in 1983, arriving in San Diego on the royal yacht Brittania. She doesn't like to fly. The reporters who would cover her trip were invited to meet her at a reception and the dress code was "leisure suits." A quick check with British press officials was needed to determine that meant a suit and tie, not the synthetic pastel-colored outfits of the disco era.

It was kind of fun to meet the queen and chat with her husband the Duke of Edinburgh, who was a bit more sociable. There was a furor afterwards when an article came out about the small talk, since the British have very strict rules about never quoting the queen in informal settings, but it was all kind of silly since she certainly didn't say anything worth reporting.

The trip included stops in Los Angeles, where she spoke before the City Council; San Francisco, and a visit with President Reagan at his ranch outside Santa Barbara. It had been raining heavily; the road to the ranch was in bad shape and there were some safety concerns. But the queen who didn't like airplanes was certainly not going to take a helicopter, and so she and her entourage piled into four-wheel drive vehicles and headed up the muddy road.

A small group of reporters drove up in the motorcade and later filed pool reports on what they saw for the rest of us. The American reporter described the poor condition of the road and the bumpy ride from his vantage point several cars behind the queen's vehicle, while the British journalist reported the queen bounced on the road "giggling like a schoolgirl," which he couldn't possibly know and had simply made up out of whole cloth. The Brits have a slightly different attitude about "journalistic license."

We visited Yosemite National Park, which was beautiful in the winter. I then had to drop a rental car at the Fresno, California, airport to fly to the final stop in Seattle. The rental car company was closed when I got there so I just left the car. It was one of several times I've had to abandon rental cars while covering a story and let the company know later where to find them.

The Alaska oil pipeline was controversial and promised (wrongly as it turned out) to dramatically reduce America's dependence on Mideast oil. Its construction created a boom in Alaska, paying people absurdly large salaries to work at the end of the world. The people of Alaska were convinced to support the pipeline the old fashioned way: they were bribed with an annual oil bounty sent to every resident as long as the oil was flowing.

The opening of the pipeline was set for the summer of 1977 and I went up to cover it. The North Slope is a truly otherworldly place. Permanently white with snow and ice, no trees, no shrubs, flat as a pancake and nothing that would suggest people could live there except the small city constructed for the pipeline workers. Roads were a challenge because in the summer the tundra gets soft and you can sink right into it, as I soon learned.

After being shown the impressive living, dining, and working facilities, it was time to go out to the pipeline. I would put my microphone next to the raised pipe to record the clanking of the "pig," an object sent through the pipeline ahead of the first oil. I would record my stories standing by the pipeline. But first we had to get there on the old school buses used by the workers.

As my bus trundled along the roadway that was just wide enough to hold it, something went wrong. The driver veered too far and two wheels dropped off the road and began sinking into the tundra. Photographers, who are just different from the rest of us, grabbed their cameras and stood in the aisles taking pictures of the reporters as our bus sank deeper into the tundra. After much screaming we convinced them they had enough pictures of the "victims" and it was time to clear the aisles and get off the damn bus.

We left through the back emergency exit and as each of us got out we had to move through a phalanx of the same photographers documenting our escape. I have made many good friends with news photographers over the years but it wouldn't be the last time being with them proved slightly hazardous to my health.

Another bus came along and we all got there in time for the clanging of the pig.

It would take several weeks for the first oil to travel 800 miles to the terminal at Valdez, where it could be loaded onto ships. But the oil consortium that flew us all to the North Slope to publicize the long-delayed opening of their pipeline didn't want us in Valdez because they didn't want us to see that even as the oil started flowing, they hadn't finished the terminal yet.

However, that terminal was an amazing feat of construction, and the company that built it, Fluor, was proud of it and wanted some credit too. So their PR man invited a UPI photographer and me to come see it.

We got down to Valdez where he had chartered a boat and brought along some incredible, freshly smoked salmon (a good PR person knows a well-fed reporter is a happy reporter). We cruised by the terminal and got a good story no one else had, and as we got closer (for the photographer, of course) oil company security guards yelled at us to get away from the terminal. Our host yelled back that his company built this terminal! That's when they pointed their rifles at us and we decided we had enough pictures.

The pipeline would bring me back twice more to Alaska, to cover an explosion at a pumping station near Fairbanks and for a follow-up story after the Valdez oil spill.

The pump station explosion, that killed one worker and injured several others, came less than a month after the pipeline opened. My sister Lorri and her soon-to-be husband John were at my home for dinner when the phone rang. There was only one flight left from Los Angeles to Anchorage and Lorri threw some clothes in a suitcase for me while I made travel arrangements. I left them in my condo to finish the nice steak dinner I had made and headed to the airport. Lorri naturally packed warm clothes for Alaska and Fairbanks's hot summer days and giant mosquitos took me by surprise.

In those wonderful pre-TSA days you could still run through the airport to catch a flight and I made it with five minutes to spare. I was able to find a commuter flight from Anchorage on to Fairbanks and rented a car to head out to cover the accident. I used to carry portable hand controls that were just two connected rods that fit on the gas and brake pedals tightened with some screws. They weren't the safest things; I tightened them every time I got in a car and they did pop off once or twice over the years. They were also hard to find, since everyone who made them quickly had understandable trouble keeping their insurance.

It wasn't until after the Americans with Disabilities Act passed in 1990 and the big car rental agencies were sued by the Justice Department that I could rely on being able to get a car with hand controls anywhere I needed to go. Interestingly, over all those years and more than a hundred times renting cars there was only one time anyone at a rental car counter ever asked me how I was going to drive their car. I had a driver's license and a corporate credit card and the question would have seemed insulting.

But one day at an Avis counter at the San Francisco airport a woman asked and I honestly told her I would use portable hand controls and she said she couldn't possibly let me do that. I just smiled and took my license and credit card ten feet away and rented from Hertz.

These same companies that now have hand controls everywhere because they have to, generally don't offer them in other countries where there is no law requiring them to. So if I'm renting a car overseas, the portable hand controls come along.

During my 15 years as the West Coast correspondent for UPI Radio I had a weekly feature called "View from the West," a two-minute piece about anything I wanted to report on. Often when I traveled to a story I would add on a day to find a fun feature.

After covering an NAACP convention in Portland, I took a great scenic drive along the Columbia River Gorge and stopped at the Bigfoot Information Center. After keeping a straight face through the interview I took a hike with my recorder in hand looking for Bigfoot. I didn't find him, but it made for some fun radio.

When in Alaska on a story I took a day to drive to the town of North Pole, which every December receives thousands of Christmas cards and letters for Santa, which they re-send with the much-cherished North Pole postmark.

I took a boat to the Channel Islands off the Southern California coast to report on the little known but striking national park there. Then there was the "Bubblegum Alley" in San Luis Obispo, which for reasons I've long forgotten people decorated with used chewing gum. I had fun at the annual hot air balloon festival in New Mexico and took a long drive to the isolated California town of Boonville, where residents had their own unique language that somehow had survived.

That was an excursion during a break in two weeks in Salinas covering a parole hearing for Sirhan Sirhan, who assassinated Robert Kennedy in 1968. The law said he was due for parole but it would have been impossible politically to let him out, so the hearing was a big news story. We all knew in the end they would have to find a reason to keep him in prison. And they did.

I like animals and enjoyed a few feature stories with them. One was at Shambala, a preserve outside Los Angeles for lions, tigers, leopards, and all variety of big cats run with love by Tippi Hedrin, the actress who was frighteningly pursued in Alfred Hitchcock's film "The Birds." I also visited Koko, the gorilla who speaks sign language and lives in Woodside, California, south of San Francisco. We had a short but still amazing conversation.

There were quite a few perennial stories in Los Angeles: the Oscars, Grammys, and Emmys of course, and the Rose Parade on New Year's Day, and the return of the swallows to Capistrano every March.

New Year's Eve was not a big night for me over those years because I had to head out by about 4 am to get into position for the Rose Parade. Covering a parade for radio is actually kind of dumb but I still had to do it every year. I would sometimes take friends and family members because it was fun the first time. By the tenth time, not so much.

But there was a special VIP reviewing stand for the media where we installed phones and had coffee and hot chocolate and donuts waiting for us and more importantly, we had parking. We would pass the thousands of people who camped out all night and were huddled along the route with their blankets and thermoses. I must say I would not have been out there in the pre-dawn cold if I weren't being paid for it.

The swallows were actually more fun and came at a much more reasonable hour. The missions of California are wonderful historic sites, a series built all up and down the coast by the Spanish and most still maintained in good shape.

The mission at San Juan Capistrano is one of the prettiest and every March 19th, St Joseph's Day, they celebrate the return of the swallows to the mission, where they spend the summer. Now, the swallows don't really know what day it is; they migrate the way they always have and when swallows show up before March 19th they are simply declared to be "scouts."

Other perennial California stories were not so fun, including wildfires. There is an actual wildfire season in the late summer and early fall, and there were fires every year. One of the biggest I covered was in Santa Barbara, where the Sycamore fire in 1977 burned 200 homes in an expensive and beautiful area. I spent many happy summers in Santa Barbara covering President Reagan's extended vacations, but those wildfires are frightening.

The western wildfires are whipped by fierce winds and if the wind is blowing 40 miles an hour, then sparks from the fire are traveling miles from the main fire line. There is no way firefighters can get ahead of it or stop it until the wind dies down. The best they can do is get people out of the way and try to protect neighborhoods where they can make a stand.

What people want to hear on the radio in coverage of a wildfire is a description by the reporter on the scene, which requires going to the middle of things. I remember at one fire I stopped on a canyon road and described what I was seeing with the roar of the fire and wind behind me. When I finished I realized the fire had jumped to the other side of the road where I was parked and made a very quick exit.

The other thing I learned at the Sycamore fire is how to interview people after a tragedy. It is a difficult and emotionally draining thing to do and I didn't want to be one of those obnoxious reporters who sticks a microphone into a crying woman's face to ask her how she feels about her house burning down.

But what I learned is that most people not only are willing to talk but want to. I would approach as sympathetically as I could and simply ask politely if they wanted to talk and expected most of them to say "no." A few did, but most not only wanted to talk but seemed to need to. Once they began to answer questions about what they lost and how they felt and what it was like when the fire was coming through, it just seemed to open the floodgates and they wanted to keep talking. I was still always uncomfortable in those situations but time after time I found the same basic reaction: most people truly wanted someone to care about what they were going through and seemed to have a need to talk about it, and wanted others to hear about it.

This is very different from the standard and in my mind silly "man on the street" interview, where reporters walk up to people and ask about some political or social issue. Most of them tell you to get lost and if I were in their place I would do the same.

Like most reporters, I hated to do man on the street interviews and thought they generally added nothing to a story. You are asking people who don't know anything about an issue for their opinion on it. How does that help educate anyone else? But managers love it. One otherwise creative manager in New York, Lou Giserman, was especially fond of man on the street interviews and asked for them all the time. When he moved on to another job, UPI Radio reporters around the country were asked to record a little taped greeting to be played at his going away party.

I walked out to the neighborhood just outside the Los Angeles bureau and asked people on the street, most of whom only spoke Spanish, "What do you think of Lou Giserman?" The hysterically funny answers, from "No hablo Inglés" to "Who the hell is Lou Giserman?" to those who figured they should know him and said "He's OK" contributed to what was by far the best man on the street piece I ever produced.

My interview technique evolved over the years, but I found as a general rule that harsh questions that are so popular with TV reporters because it makes them look tough rarely produce good answers. I almost always began interviews with a few softball questions to put the interview subject at ease. Asking a tough question right at the start is a sure way to get a useless, defensive answer. While interviews sometimes produced surprising information, most of the time, especially in interviewing politicians, what I was really after was to get them to give their point of view in a clear and concise way that would help the radio audience get a better understanding of what they believed. When the answers weren't clear or concise, which of course was often the case, I would circle around and ask the same question five or six times in different ways until I got a better and more useful answer. When there were tough questions to ask, they came later in an interview and if the person I was interviewing was more relaxed, there was a much better chance of getting a meaningful answer.

I also ended almost every interview by asking if there was anything I didn't ask that they felt was important to say and every once in a while that was when I got my best material.

Of course there are circumstances when a more confrontational approach is called for. I remember one time covering Bill Clinton's campaign in 1992 when an embarrassing story about him had just come out and he was avoiding reporters. We were being held away from him and were told he wouldn't answer any questions, so I just shouted at him "Why are you afraid to talk to us?" I knew that would make him mad, and it did. He came over to me and answered the question and I got the tape I needed.

When a story allowed me to eat really good food in the service of journalism, it was a special treat. A fine opportunity came when the Los Angeles County Health Department got into a major tiff with the restaurants in Chinatown over Peking duck. Now Peking duck is one of my favorite dishes, with its fantastically crisp skin and tender duck wrapped in small pancakes with duck sauce and a few green onions. Awesome!

The health department rules said that when preparing meats, they must be either hot enough to kill any bacteria, or refrigerated. Before cooking, Peking ducks are coated with soy sauce and spices, then left out to hang at room temperature. The county said that had to stop.

The restaurant owners countered that Peking duck had been made this way since the 1300s; they served these ducks every day and no one ever got sick from them. It was a perfect story in so many ways: well-meaning but overreaching bureaucrats, tradition versus modernity, and an opportunity to eat Peking duck on an expense account.

I felt I couldn't research this story alone so I took several of my UPI colleagues to Chinatown, where we happily consumed some Peking ducks and interviewed the chefs and the patrons. The story even had a happy ending when the county backed down and the ducks could still hang in Chinatown.

Another time eating Peking duck I received my favorite fortune in a fortune cookie. It read: "Next Time Order the Shrimp."

GREAT LAKES 2009

I began my August road trip to see the Great Lakes camping out at a three-day music festival in West Virginia. Kind of like Woodstock but we're a lot older, and with better food.

I was surprised to see windmills on the hillsides in southwest Pennsylvania and a covered bridge too.

Driving the rather boring Ohio turnpike it struck me how peculiar it was to be visiting Ohio in an odd numbered year, having covered more presidential campaigns there than I care to count.

I got to Cleveland as a thunderstorm began but after three nights of camping a hotel room was nice and it looked out on a Great Lake. It looked eerie in the storm but Erie is the first of the good and great lakes I will be visiting.

While I'm sure there are other reasons to go to Cleveland, I only had one and spent seven hours at the Rock and Roll Hall of Fame. I got a kick out of seeing Jim Morrison's Cub Scout uniform and the first guitar James Taylor got from his parents, which stood out because his brother painted it blue.

An excellent display on Woodstock 40 years later was interesting, watching the long-haired, stoned, half naked youngsters railing against the man, which they now are. Tickets to Woodstock by the way were $7.

Always a treat to find great food in the "middle" and I had a fine three-course feast at One Walnut, including an interesting onion soup with fried potato puffs and other treats in it. Another good find was a Hungarian restaurant, Balaton, in an out of the way neighborhood with

Wiener schnitzel and spaetzel like in the Old Country, and potato pancakes like mother still makes.

Relaxed by a lake (a good one but not a great one) near Union City, Michigan, and for the first time in a long time was in a town where the restaurants, both of them, allow smoking.

Visited Douglas and Saugatuck, two cute touristy beach towns along Lake Michigan (the second Great Lake of the journey, for those playing along at home.)

Lots of art stores. One with imported French glass sculpture had price tags on everything, except the piece I liked. The owner explained he kept it hidden so as not to "scare the customers," and it was indeed a very frightening number.

All along Lake Michigan there are beautiful beaches with perfect sand and lighthouses and fudge but what's missing is the smell. The Great Lakes look like oceans, but I keep sniffing for that sea salt smell.

Kudos to Michigan for a 70 mph speed limit in between construction zones. My car really likes to go fast.

Kudos too to Yelp an app that finds good restaurants in towns too small for Zagat.

A stop at P.J. Hoffmaster State Park gave me my first view of the famous Lake Michigan sand dunes which are very impressive and unusual. The biggest ones are all sand in the front, but heavily forested on the back side, which makes them a lot easier to climb.

Ludington had a nice lighthouse and pretty beaches, but the highlight was lunch at the "House of Flavors," celebrating 60 years of ice cream making and serving a fresh roasted turkey sandwich that melts in your mouth. Plus they had WiFi! Of the 36 ice cream flavors, I had chocolate almond truffle and caramel caribou, which were wonderful, but not enough to earn one of their coveted pig buttons. In my younger days perhaps I could have handled it—four scoops, four toppings, and whipped cream.

The best scenery along the Lake Michigan coast was Sleeping Bear Dunes, with a great scenic drive that climbs the back of a 450-foot sand dune with glorious views at the top. A number of younger folks scampered down the dune to the beach in about five minutes, then spent 45 minutes slogging their way back up.

I cannot imagine why a small college museum in Traverse City has one of the country's best collections of Inuit art from the Canadian arctic, but they do and it was great. They were also having a once-a-year sale of Inuit sculpture, but recession or no, the prices were still a bit high.

After two very nice nights camping in the northern Michigan forest, I headed to Mackinac Island (on the "Arnold" ferry line), a very genteel resort out in Lake Huron (number three) where no cars are allowed and transportation is by bicycle, foot, and a fleet of horse-drawn carriages.

It has a very colonial, tropical feel with green-blue water and tons of tourists in t-shirts and shorts and grand, over-large houses, so I started out with a piña colada overlooking the harbor.

At the next table a woman complained to the waitress that the lime in her drink wasn't fresh enough but clearly the island atmosphere made her forget she is well over a thousand miles from the nearest lime tree.

Judging by the number of shops, fudge seems to be the main cuisine on the island; another specialty is cheesecake on a stick.

Toured Mackinac Island by horse drawn carriage and wandered through the historic Fort Mackinac, first built by the British worried during the Revolutionary War that the Americans would attack. Needless to say, they never did, since George Washington had bigger fish to fry.

Weather is pretty hot, but better than winter, when if you want to get here you ride your snowmobile across the ice bridge that forms when the lake freezes.

A visit to the Grand Hotel had some déjà vu. As I walked in, the place was way too familiar, down to the color of the chairs and the pattern of the floor tiles. It turns out the interior design was done by the same woman who designed the Greenbrier Hotel in West Virginia, also built in the age of the robber barons, where I had stayed a few months before. But the Greenbrier, stuffy as it is, wasn't tacky enough to charge $10 for non-guests to visit the lobby and sit on a rocking chair on the porch.

I paid, and must say the porch was very nice, the longest anywhere they claim, and I spent a good chunk of the day reading and looking out at Lake Huron, with a break for the tasty but overpriced $40 lunch buffet.

After three days with the horses I'm back in my car again, crossing the Mackinac Bridge, the longest suspension bridge over fresh water (they need to add that last part because of that little Golden Gate thing).

That brings me to Michigan's upper peninsula known for forests, moose, bears, and the rough shoreline of Lake Superior, the biggest, coldest, and deepest of the Great Lakes, and number four on our hit parade.

Driving through Paradise (the cranberry capital of Michigan) I head to Whitefish Point because of Gordon Lightfoot. I really like his song, "The Wreck of the Edmund Fitzgerald," which went down off this coast and is remembered in the Great Lakes shipwreck museum. Its prize possession is the Edmund Fitzgerald's bell, recovered by a Canadian navy mini-submarine in the 1990s.

This area is also filled with waterfalls, the largest of which is the color of tea, due to all the tannic acid from the hemlock and other trees.

They sell smoked whitefish everywhere here, the highest concentration this side of Zabar's.

The Australian theme restaurant in the very small town of Munising seemed odd, but the fresh fish was great.

Then it was off on a sunset cruise of the "pictured rocks" shoreline on Lake Superior. A three-hour tour, shades of Gilligan.

The sheer cliffs are "painted" with minerals leaching reds, greens, blues, browns, and black along with giant caves and coves and waterfalls. Altogether a very striking shoreline with crystal clear water.

I also took a very unusual cruise on a glass bottom boat that went to three shipwrecks in shallow water. One only six feet down was completely intact and you could even see some of the iron ore it was carrying in its hold. At another, the captain's bathtub and toilet sat on the rocky bottom.

At about the halfway mark on my road trip (2000 miles or so in a leisurely two weeks), I crossed the International Bridge at Sault St. Marie (known here as "the Soo") and went into Canada where the donuts at Tim Horton's are always fresh, the moose are plentiful, and the people are nice.

It was a long rainy drive down the east shore of Lake Huron accompanied by a few Amish buggies and what seemed like every truck in Canada before calling it a day in the old mining city of Sudbury.

Visited a tourist attraction that tells you everything you ever wanted to know about nickel and copper mining with a tour through an underground mine.

South through Ontario on two-lane roads there are a plethora of pretty lakes, rivers, and wildflowers and only a handful of towns.

Hotel most in need of a marketing expert: "Yesterday's Resort."

Cutest billboard for a small motel: "One location all across Canada."

Had an unplanned day of research into the Canadian health care system, which works far better if you are Canadian. I suddenly started seeing lines and dots and shapes like tentacles swimming frantically in front of my right eye. It turned out to be floaters, which are not uncommon, but are seriously weird. The ophthalmologist who examined me found all was well but had to make up a fee and since none of his other patients pay him, had no way to take credit cards. I took a trip to the ATM.

Arrived in Toronto on Lake Ontario, which makes five Great Lakes by my count. A very multicultural city with a vibrant street life. Hit the tourist highlights and walked the neighborhoods, rode the street cars, and saw "Jersey Boys." Toronto is a great city for theater and tickets are a lot cheaper than on Broadway.

Had some Canadian elk for dinner one night—quite rich and a tad tough. Tastes like emu.

Favorite signs: "Sin and Redemption," the name of a pub opposite a Catholic church, and "Back to School Sale" at a strip club.

Stopped in the very charming town of "Niagara on the Lake" on the way to the larger and remarkably tacky town of Niagara Falls. Niagara on the Lake is known for its not quite world-famous annual George Bernard Shaw festival. I had lunch at the grand and oh so stuffy "Prince of Wales" hotel, where the unusual dish of french fries covered with lobster, melted cheese curds and béarnaise sauce was delicious, but not what I would describe as a light lunch. Before taking the slow, scenic route to the falls, along the Niagara River in an area filled with vineyards, I made a stop at my new favorite Canadian ice cream chain, "Cows."

Just across the river is New York and it's close enough for my iPhone to think it's home and stop charging me outrageous international roaming rates.

As for Niagara, it's a darn big waterfall, two of them actually, and riding right up to them on the Maid of the Mist was very scenic and very wet. The view from the bottom via elevator was also amazing, as were the double rainbows that form in the mist when the sun comes out.

Looked for a barrel rental store but they all wanted really big deposits. Lest you think I exaggerate in calling the tourist center of town tacky, I counted three wax museums in one block, one dedicated just to wax figures of infamous killers and other criminals.

After being questioned by one of our always-surly border agents, I returned to America over the Rainbow Bridge and meandered around the Finger Lakes region of New York, where wine is made and the lakes are long and skinny.

I pulled into a little out of the way motel in the woods at Seneca Lake and sitting outside, I see a Porsche drive up, then another, then a four-by-four towing a Porsche on a trailer. By the time I walk to the restaurant for dinner I count at least 20 Porsches, all up for a "driving school" at the nearby Watson's Glen race track. They come to drive really fast without getting a ticket.

Finished up my trip with four days in New York City. Stayed in Tribeca on a nice street with a wonderful smoked fish emporium and an old-fashioned soda shop with egg creams and lime rickeys.

TRIALS OF THE CENTURY

I spent a lot of time in courtrooms over the years, covering more than a few "trials of the century," since a pretty universal failing among journalists is a lack of historical perspective.

My first trial of the century was the case against John DeLorean in 1984. He was a legendary figure in the auto world and gained his reputation at General Motors, where he developed the Pontiac GTO. After he left GM, he started his own car company with a futuristic product he named the DeLorean. It gained fame as the time-traveling car in the "Back to the Future" movies, but while the cars were very cool looking, hardly anyone bought them. DeLorean was losing money hand over fist and was desperate to raise some cash to save his company when a neighbor, who just happened to be an FBI informant, came to him with a plan to raise money by smuggling cocaine.

DeLorean was probably one of the least likely people in all of Los Angeles in the 80s to be involved with cocaine, but he was convinced that was the only way to save his car company, so he agreed to the rather serpentine smuggling plot that his neighbor proposed in conversations he was secretly recording.

DeLorean was arrested and charged with conspiracy to smuggle drugs and the case was a huge story, the OJ trial of its day.

And it was one wild trial. At one point a good citizen came forward to help, Hustler Magazine publisher Larry Flynt. He, of course, was a major character in his own right and interjected himself into the case when he claimed he had evidence that DeLorean had tried to back out of the deal but the FBI informant threatened to hurt his daughter if he did. Flynt played a tape for reporters he claimed contained the threat.

When the federal judge, Robert Takasugi, ordered Flynt to appear in court and produce the tape, Flynt said he had lost it and when he was ordered to appear the next day to say why he shouldn't be found in contempt of court, came to the courtroom wearing an American flag as a diaper.

Often in a trial (or at least the ones on television) there are clear villains and sometimes heroes too. In this trial they were all villains. DeLorean had, in my view, clearly ripped off his investors and committed all kinds of fraud as his car company began to collapse, but he wasn't charged with any of those crimes. The informant was clearly trying to set DeLorean up and get him involved in something he never would have done on his own so he could show the FBI what a good informant he was. And of course Flynt was just being his usual crazy self.

In the end DeLorean was acquitted, which struck me as the right verdict, since if there was ever a textbook case of entrapment, this was it.

Another memorable trial was the espionage case against Christopher Boyce and Andrew Daulton Lee, which was the basis for the book and movie "The Snowman and the Falcon."

These were two young men from wealthy families who became the most unlikely spies you could imagine. Boyce, through his father's connections, inexplicably was given a job at government contractor TRW with access to some of America's most sensitive secrets, including detailed information and codes for spy satellites the government wouldn't acknowledge it even had. In a case that, looking back, seemed to foreshadow the episode decades later of the NSA leaker Edward Snowden, Boyce was furious at what he learned about how the U.S. government was abusing its technology and spying on friendly governments.

But unlike Snowden, who leaked the information to the public, Boyce and his childhood pal Lee, who was spending his time selling drugs, would decide the best response was to try to sell the secret satellite codes to the Russians. To say they were amateur spies would be a vast understatement; their first contact with what was then still the Soviet Union was when Lee knocked on the front door of the Soviet embassy in Mexico City and told them he had secrets to sell.

These kinds of cases rarely come to trial. The government is loathe to bring them into open court because that would reveal many of the secrets they were trying to preserve, and other major espionage cases usually ended in plea bargains. But Boyce and Lee felt what they had learned justified their actions and so wanted to make their case in open court.

The trial was pretty amazing, with new details every day about who the government was spying on and how easy it was for these two kids to steal America's most closely guarded secrets. It was also the only trial I've ever covered where the judge limited who could bring paper and pens into the courtroom. Accredited journalists like myself who were covering the trial had to show ID and sit in only certain rows of the courtroom and no one else was allowed to take notes. A fun game at that trial was to pick out the KGB agents and the CIA agents in the courtroom and it was usually a pretty easy task.

Some trials were newsworthy strictly because they were tawdry. That was certainly the case with the rape trial in West Palm Beach, Florida, of William Kennedy Smith, a nephew of Senator Ted Kennedy. He was in a bar with his uncle and cousin Patrick Kennedy (who later was elected to Congress) when they met a young woman who went back to the Kennedy compound with them. She accused William of rape, while he said they had consensual sex after a walk on the beach. The trial was televised and under orders from the judge the defendant's face had to be blocked out with a kind of orange blot to protect her privacy.

Senator Kennedy was called as a witness. It was fairly humiliating all around and the younger Kennedy was acquitted.

Then there was the trial where I ended up being called as a witness, which is a position no reporter ever wants to be in. In 1986, Steven Livaditis entered the fancy Van Cleef & Arpels jewelry store on the most famous shopping street in America, Rodeo Drive in Beverly Hills. He came to rob the store, but the police interrupted the robbery and it ended up as a long and terrifying hostage situation. One of our UPI wire reporters had been instructed to call Van Cleef & Arpels to double check the spelling of the store's name. He dialed the store in Beverly Hills and the robber answered the phone. He said he wanted to give us an interview and since I worked in radio and had the equipment to record the call, it was transferred back to me. During the recorded interview he described how he had killed the store security guard by stabbing him with a knife because he didn't follow instructions and had "kept talking." He said it had been the right thing to do and he had no regrets.

Livaditis threatened to kill the rest of the hostages and a short while later shot one of them to death. He tried to escape by walking out in a tight circle with the hostages and he was caught, but in the ensuing chaos police accidentally shot and killed another of the hostages. It was a horrible situation all around. We turned the tape over to police since it was clearly evidence (and there was no question of protecting a source as we had already broadcast the tape).

I was called to testify simply to confirm that I had indeed made the tape recording of the conversation and we had turned over an unedited version of it. The defense didn't cross-examine me because there really wasn't anything to ask. Livaditis was sentenced to death.

I covered a few Supreme Court cases, an anti-trust case that pinned the National Football League against the Oakland Raiders, and plenty of other trials of mass murderers and assorted celebrities. Quite a few got to be named the "trial of the century"—at least until the next one came around.

PATAGONIA 2008

I began my South America sojourn in Santiago, Chile. It's a pretty city, flush up against the Andes, quite sophisticated with wonderful parks, sidewalk cafes, and very nice people.

The weather was in the eighties and on the first day in the central square I ran across unhappy government workers protesting with whistles and signs. Quite colorful, but when I noticed the riot police massed on a nearby street I moved on. A young man later explained they have democracy in Chile but it is still a "work in progress."

Because of my complexion and mustache I can easily pass as a local as long as I don't speak. Once I open my mouth it is clear I am either an imbecile or a gringo, since my high school Spanish has gone from rusty to pathetic. Hopefully in a few weeks here it will work its way back to rusty.

The people are very friendly and men and women always greet each other with a single kiss on the cheek. Men greet men and women greet women the same way. To be safe, I'm just kissing everybody.

This is a long way from Italy but for some reason no one says "adios" or "hasta la vista." They all say "Ciao."

I love the fact that at every major intersection there are jugglers who run into the middle of the street and juggle for tips until the light turns green. So much better than squeegee men.

I visited the giant fish market with every imaginable thing that swims in the ocean. It's filled with small restaurants, each with aggressive barkers assuring you their place has the freshest seafood (two feet rather than four from the market) at the best price. I ended up at Donde Agusto, which was recommended, and had wonderful razor clams parmesan and grilled sea bass in a room with towering wrought iron ceilings reminiscent of a 19th century European train station.

The tour of the home of Pablo Neruda was very interesting. Every schoolchild in Chile knows he is a Nobel-prize-winning poet and famous communist, things I learned when touring the amazing home he designed for his mistress and future third wife. It looked like a ship perched on a hill overlooking the city. The collection of items from around the world was quite impressive, as was his "Stalin Peace Prize," which is not something you see every day.

Street vendors sell everything from slightly used socks to TV rabbit ear antennas, though my favorite was a lady with gallon glass jugs of perfume. Customers picked the perfume they wanted and the size and she poured it into smaller containers.

Took a bus to Valparaiso, a coastal city with a dramatic look. The houses, in pastel colors, hang along extremely steep cliffs overlooking the city. There are a dozen funiculars, made of wood and built around 1900 to help carry you up where you climb even higher into the neighborhoods. You pay your 50 cents and hope you make it to the top. At the top the streets are so steep they make San Francisco seem like Kansas. In some neighborhoods every wall is covered with wonderful murals, some by Chile´s best-known artists.

Though the town was interesting and I enjoyed my time there, it was not what I expected. The upper reaches were fun, but the main part of the city was sprawling and falling apart, a decrepit and dirty port town overflowing with stray dogs. It did have a very impressive headquarters for the Chilean Navy, though, which I suppose is keeping the coast safe from Peru.

I hopped on a commuter train one day and took it to the end of the line to check out a small town in the countryside. It was very pleasant and as I sat in the town square watching high school kids throw water balloons at each other, I realized how small the world is getting. There was free WiFi there.

My trusty restaurant guide was no help, so I followed the smell of roasting chicken up some rickety stairs and had a wonderful lunch. The french fries were so good, they had to have been fried in gobs of trans fats.

People here are crazy for seltzer. Bottled water without bubbles can be hard to find, as folks here very much favor the fizzy water.

After a quick night in Buenos Aires, where I will return in a few weeks, I flew to Bariloche, a stunning mountain town high in the Andes. At the top of a chairlift the view is breathtaking. There are dozens of lakes, some snaking as far as the eye can see, all surrounded by deep forests and encased by a near 360-degree ring of snowcapped Andean peaks. It is an incredibly beautiful place and has lots of chocolate. Apparently dating from Swiss settlers, the main part of town has a chocolate shop about every half block, each making its own fine chocolates. Dedicated as I am to consumer education, I was compelled to try them all before buying a box for the road, or more precisely, for the short bus ride back to my hotel.

Following the theory that if the economy is collapsing, I should go out in style, I am spending several days here at the Llao Llao Hotel, which deserves its reputation as the most luxurious resort in South America.

Favorite spot: in the infinity pool looking out at the lakes and mountain peaks.

Oddest drink offered at the bar: Gatorade (two flavors).

Coolest over the top gadget: the in-room safe operated by fingerprints.

I took a boat tour of the national park that surrounds the city with many more wonderful views. One stop had Arrayanes trees found nowhere else. The bark was a mottled light brown and white and the trees were tall but not straight; instead, the trunks split into branches that bent and curved and became intertwined with each other and nearby trees, creating a truly enchanted forest.

My three days in Bariloche ended with a gourmet dinner at Patacón, which still brags of once serving dinner to my old pal of big appetites, Bill Clinton. On the 20-minute cab ride back to my hotel I took turns with my 20-something cab driver, who didn't speak any English, singing the words to his Creedence Clearwater Revival tape.

After an appropriate breakfast of waffles smothered in chocolate sauce and fresh whipped cream, it was time to cross the Andes again back to Chile, this time without a plane

The two-day journey is by boat, using a string of beautiful lakes that cover this part of the Andes ending at the Pacific coast of Chile. The lakes are clean and cold, fed from the snow still topping every peak, and a deep green color due to mineral deposits.

After the second lake we reached the end of Argentina with a small customs office and a snack bar. A short bus ride led to an overnight stop in Peulla, just over the Chilean border. That is when things started getting strange. Peulla is a kind of Potemkin town, with two hotels belonging to the tour company that runs the lake to lake crossing, and literally nothing else. Except, that is, for the Chilean customs office, and that was trouble.

Chile and Argentina don't like each other very much, with several ongoing border disputes and bad feelings going back to the Falklands War where Argentina fought Great Britain over some tiny islands near Antarctica and Chile didn't take their side. The Chilean customs officials claimed there was an outbreak of German measles in Argentina and so they had to give us all shots of vaccine. There was no way to return to Argentina at that point and thus no choice. But while they said everyone could get the shots, they only required them of males aged 16 to 39. I was very glad to be over the hill but couldn't figure out how they got to the odd conclusion that women don't get measles.

I shared some nice meals with two interesting couples who live in Paris: a Frenchman married to a British woman and an American man married to a French woman and they kindly kept the conversation in English.

I did realize any language problems I had paled in comparison to a large family from Budapest on the lake to lake crossing. No one could speak even a word of Hungarian.

The last lake in the crossing was the most scenic with fjord-like passages, huge waterfalls, and several large volcanoes, some of the more than 2,000 in Chile.

I ended up in Puerto Varas, a lovely little town on a beautiful lake, founded in the 1800s by German immigrants, that looks out on two huge snow-covered volcanoes.

I stayed at a little guesthouse on a quiet street owned by a guy from Indiana who came to start a cranberry farm. He married a Chilean woman and has three young children and half a dozen guest rooms. They provided a great breakfast, taxi service, and even did my laundry.

Wandering through the small town I sampled their chocolate and visited a casino. It was just too much of a temptation and I had to go up to the roulette table and throw down 50,000 pesos, a definite James Bond moment, even though it came to only about $75. I celebrated the fact that I left the casino with a few more pesos than when I entered by enjoying a local delicacy of king crab, which is very sweet like Dungeness.

I took a local bus to Frutillar, a smaller, cuter town that has kept its German heritage. There was a little museum explaining how the Chilean government recruited German immigrants in the mid 1800s to settle in this fertile valley that looks very much like Bavaria, as a way to establish control over the indigenous population.

Many generations later the residents all look Chilean, speak Spanish, and are Catholic, but eat German strudel and great breads and German is taught in the schools. The downside is the town is filled with large, loud German tour groups.

Just as a heavy rain began to fall, I passed the "German Club" and ducked inside, sat by the fire and ate Wiener Schnitzel.

I then flew to Punta Arenas at the bottom of Chile. The central square is very nice, with musicians and craftsmen selling their wares. There's also a big statue of Magellan, who found his strait and discovered Patagonia, which was of course quite exciting for the Indians who already lived here.

I arrived on a sunny day, which is rare, so I went right out to see the penguins about an hour away. The terrain is pretty desolate with only low shrubs. Trees of any size can't survive here because of the incessant winds blowing in from the Magellan Strait. I experienced that first hand in the one-mile walk to the penguins with gusts so strong at times I was stopped in my tracks.

But the penguins were seriously cute, and while smaller than those in Antarctica, they still march and dress in formal wear. There were also local flightless birds called nandu, like an ostrich but smaller.

A six-hour drive into the wild took me to one of the highlights of the trip, four nights at the Explora Lodge in the heart of the Torres del Paine National Park. There are bright turquoise-colored lakes flowing from glaciers and peaks carved into amazing and improbable shapes, including the towers by which the park gets its name. From outside, the lodge looks dull and ordinary, but inside is elegant with finely polished wood, incredible food, a pool and spa, and views to die for, along with an expert staff of guides. Each room had perfectly situated bathroom windows allowing the view to be enjoyed from the toilet seat and the bathtub.

The hikes were challenging, with steep, narrow trails but every turn brings astonishing views of lakes, waterfalls, and peaks, as well as glaciers making thunderous noise as they calve.

There are guanacos, which are like llamas, giant condors, puma, pink flamingos, black-necked swans, those nandu ostrich things, and rabbits of unusual size.

One hike brought me to a natural scene unlike anything I've seen before. After a short walk through a forest with wild orchids in bloom, crossing a swaying suspension bridge I dropped down to a large beach on a slate gray lake. It was a warm spring day but house-sized icebergs were floating just off the beach. There is a huge glacier at the far end of the lake and pieces break off from there and float to the beach. I took a boat right up to the glacier with its otherworldly spires of ice rising right out of the lake with crevices and caves, and looked into the deepest blue there is.

Back in Punta Arenas my journey takes me in a few days on a boat trip through the Straits of Magellan and I will hope for calm seas since you may recall Ferdinand and his friends had a pretty rough trip.

The town's top tourist attraction is the cemetery, with extravagant mausoleums and groves of bizarrely sculpted Cyprus trees. The names reflect the variety of Europeans who settled here, mostly Croatians, and of the huge wealth the port generated until the Panama Canal was built.

There was a stiff Antarctic wind blowing, but a lunch of king crab and spit-roasted lamb warmed me right up followed by a visit to Cohen's candy store. Walking through town there were vendors selling individual cloves of garlic, along with several stores selling "El I-Phone."

I was excited to head out on my cruise through Magellan's favorite strait and around Cape Horn, but also a little sad to leave Chile, which is a wonderful and welcoming place. On the same dock was an American science ship readying to go to Antarctica, since this is the closest port.

There was a very international crowd on the ship of 118 passengers from 16 countries, only eight from the U.S. My table companions were French, Belgian and Dutch.

We sailed through misty fjords with lots of ice, boarded Zodiacs for shore excursions to hike on beaches and through forests, and visited elephant seals, sea lions, and of course, the penguins.

Hikes always ended with whiskey served over ice chipped from an iceberg.

At dinner on the second night we passed through a narrow channel with a hanging glacier topping the cliff on one side and more than a hundred waterfalls coming down.

I was awakened at 4 am with a reminder of how this stretch of water got its reputation and why thousands perished here in the days of sailing ships. The sound was the bow crashing down against giant waves as the boat rocked not at all gently and the wind howled and suddenly I was less anxious to find icebergs. Things calmed as a group of albatrosses followed the ship.

We landed the next day and climbed to a lookout point on smooth rock just a few hundred yards from a large glacier and sat for about an hour listening to it crack and crash as pieces broke off and tumbled down to the water.

Later that day came the perfect scene, sitting on the uppermost outdoor observation deck, where champagne was served as we sailed past a dozen huge glaciers, each named for a European nation for reasons that seem a bit obscure. But since we had people from each of those countries we toasted each glacier.

We stopped at Cape Horn where the Atlantic and Pacific oceans meet but they kind of look the same.

Ushuaia, where the cruise ended, is the southernmost city in the world, and very pretty with the snow-capped southern edge of the Andes just behind it. The city started as Argentina's Devil's Island at the end of the world, but ended up a nice town built by convict labor.

The first inhabitants of Patagonia were Yamana Indians. Magellan thought they were giants and Darwin thought they were part animal and part human, and used them to try to prove his wacky evolution theory. Odd thing about the Yamana is they were always naked, which would be fine for Indians in Arizona or the Amazon, but even in summer here it is darn cold.

A short way out of the city I took a 15-minute chairlift ride over a rushing river to another glacier with great views of the Beagle Channel, named for the boat Darwin sailed on. My favorite spot along a trail was where the river flows under the ice.

My solitude was briefly disturbed when a busload of tourists took the chairlift and walked my trail. My touring would be better without tourists.

The top restaurants in Ushuaia were more expensive than elsewhere on the trip but perhaps that's because I kept ordering the luscious king crab.

A taxi driver who just took his final exam in an English class took me on a tour of the nearby national park with lakes and short hikes and a stop at the "end of the road," the place where the Pan-American highway that begins in Prudhoe Bay, Alaska, 30,000 miles to the North, ends at the sea.

I ate at "Aunt Elvira's" restaurant for a final hit of seafood before heading north to Buenos Aires to eat mass quantities of meat. It struck me how much easier and more pleasant it is when you walk with metal crutches to go through security at airports in a place where they don't care if the metal detector goes off.

Buenos Aires is a big, sophisticated, warm city and my five days there were delightful. I stayed at a little boutique hotel called "Home" where President Bush's twin daughters famously partied when they were here. My morning began with breakfast in the garden, which was exceedingly hip, with a shot glass of apple juice mixed with basil and chocolate blended into the butter.

Riding the subway I took the "A" train with classic old cars with all-wood interiors and benches, light fixtures hanging from the ceiling, and open windows. At the end of the line there was a great little neighborhood off the tourist track where I visited a barber shop with chairs and décor from the 1890s. Had a haircut and a shave. It was the full "Godfather" treatment with scalding hot towels, shaving cream whipped up on the spot, and a frighteningly sharp blade.

Later, I visited Eva Peron's tomb and hummed "Don't Cry For Me Argentina" the rest of the day. I hung out in the neighborhood of Recoleta, which feels more like Paris than South America. The tango show, mandatory for all tourists, was great, which is not something you can usually say about a performance featuring several accordion solos.

After a month of nearly perfect weather I flew in a driving rainstorm into Iguazú in the jungle where Argentina, Brazil, and Paraguay meet. Even the monkeys were diving for cover and mosquitos plotting to give me a host of tropical diseases. But this is where one of the world's most spectacular waterfalls is.

As we headed down a flooded dirt road into the jungle and away from town, the cab driver tried to convince me my choice of a tiny family-run inn was a mistake and I should stay at a real hotel where the other

Americans go. When we pulled up just as lightning knocked out the power that thought crossed my mind, but when an 11-year-old grabbed my backpack and the family dog came out to greet me, I knew this was the place to be.

The falls were wet, crowded, and awesome. From about half a mile away you can see the immense size of the horseshoe-shaped falls, but hiking the trails along it you see it is made up of dozens of separate enormous waterfalls and hundreds of smaller ones and the power of the water is incredible. As a trained observer of men and events, I can report Iguazú is a damn big waterfall.

Back in Buenos Aires I realized how well I've adapted to two-hour lunches with wine followed by siesta, but fear it is a pattern that will be difficult to maintain after I return to work.

SPACE, SCIENCE AND SPORTS

I started covering space stories soon after I got to Los Angeles and they were among my favorites.

The two little Voyager spacecraft were launched in the summer of 1977 to explore Saturn and Jupiter. They would later go on to Uranus and Neptune and become the first man-made objects to leave our solar system. Though they were launched from the Kennedy Space Center in Florida, they were designed, built, and run from the Jet Propulsion Laboratory (JPL) in Pasadena. It's a campus setting filled with NASA engineers and scientists and I loved covering stories there.

Each Voyager spacecraft had a golden phonograph record with images and sounds of earth: whales singing, a picture of the Taj Mahal, a selection of music including Beethoven and Chuck Berry, and greetings in every language that was designed to be played by any aliens that may come across Voyager after it left our solar system. On the back was etched a little map showing where Earth was, stick drawings of a man and a pregnant woman, and an illustration of how to play the record. The pictures and sounds were chosen by a committee chaired by famed astronomer Carl Sagan, who was convinced there were aliens out there to find it.

There is a scene in the movie "Starman" in which Jeff Bridges plays a visiting alien and the record from Voyager is found in his spacecraft. During an argument over what to do about this visitor from outer space wandering across the country, a scientist tries to convince the military he is not an enemy by declaring, "We invited him!" That is precisely what we did with that gold record.

It took two years for Voyager One to reach Jupiter and another year to get to Saturn and it was thrilling. For days at a time at JPL we watched as amazing pictures came down, appearing on the monitors one line of pixels at a time showing things no one had ever seen before.

A lot of science and medical stories involve translation and this was no exception as I would listen to hours of briefings by the scientists about what they were finding about magnetic fields and the gravitational pull of Saturn's rings and try to explain in simple language what it all meant. I would always try to talk to Ed Stone, the chief scientist who had a wonderful way of explaining the findings while conveying the sense of wonder and awe.

And it was awesome to realize that what I reported each day was not only changing the scientific understanding of these planets—Jupiter's wildly varied and utterly strange moons and the complexity of Saturn's rings—but also our basic knowledge of how many moons and rings there were. Every time Voyager reached a new planet it would require our astronomy textbooks down to the elementary school level to be rewritten.

I covered Voyager's fantastic voyages for a dozen years, returning to JPL each time one of the little spacecraft reached a planet, ending at Neptune. I was also at the Ames Research Center in Mountain View, California, which tracked Voyager One after it finished exploring planets as it left our solar system, heading out to unexplored space where maybe, someday, some being would listen to its gold record.

I didn't get the same thrill from covering the space shuttle, which even NASA described as a "space truck" that sent astronauts back and forth to orbit. I covered all the early flights starting with the testing of the "Enterprise," which never went into orbit but was named for the "Star Trek" spaceship, and whose first landing was a pretty exciting event, since no spacecraft had ever been built before to land like a plane and be re-used.

In 1977 the Enterprise was flown atop a modified Boeing 747, then released by explosive bolts for two astronauts to pilot to a landing on the dry lakebed at Edwards Air Force Base.

Edwards is in California's high desert. Palmdale was the closest town and not much of one. It had long been the site for experimental planes and was where the sound barrier was first broken. The advantage was that a pilot could miss the runway by a mile, literally, and still land safely on a dry lakebed with nothing to get in his way.

We were set up in the middle of the desert to watch that first landing test. Driving there before dawn I got lost and was driving around on runways and the lakebed before finding the right spot. They don't have lights or signs out there, but they do have police, who in later years seemed to take special delight in ticketing visiting reporters for speeding on the wide open desert roads.

My ability to do live broadcasting was sorely tested that day at Edwards. A small company called IDB had just started offering portable satellite services for radio and it was set up with a small satellite truck out in the desert. We had not ordered a line from them but I knew the people running it and asked if they had any spares. They did, so I arranged to buy one.

I called UPI Radio on a phone we had put in some distance away and told them about the line. But there was a small problem. It was only an outgoing line and no return line was available, so there was no way I could hear a cue or an introduction.

So when the action began and the shuttle left the 747 and began gliding down piloted by the astronauts I just went on that line and started broadcasting. I had no idea if I was on the air or how long they were staying with me, so I just kept talking and describing everything that was happening for as long as there was something to describe.

When I was later able to get back to our phone I found out I had indeed been on the air for the entire time.

I returned to Edwards many times over the years because that's where the space shuttles landed after the early flights. Eventually there was enough confidence to bring them back to a regular runway in Florida, but until then the wide-open, dry lakebed of Edwards provided a good margin of safety.

I would often help cover the missions from Edwards, sharing the day-to-day coverage with my colleague in Florida and then handling the landing.

I remember one day when a small group of us were hungry and hoping to find something to eat without the long drive off the base. We went to the officers club where reporters were allowed to eat during space missions, but they had just closed.

A freelance reporter who was more than a bit odd, a likable fellow named Chuck Cohen, was with us and when we were told the dining room was closed he insisted that we be served and began introducing us as military officers, referring to me as "General Fuss." I was appalled but also amazed when the young man brought us in and fed us. He couldn't possibly have believed that we were really Air Force officers, but I guess he couldn't take any chances.

The thing about dry lakebeds in the Mojave Desert is that sometimes they're not dry. It doesn't rain much in the desert, but when it does it can cause flash floods and the lakebeds turn into lakes.

That happened in March of 1982 when the third manned shuttle mission was in orbit. They stayed up as long as they could but there was no dry place to land at Edwards. So the landing was switched to the "emergency" landing spot at an even more remote desert in New Mexico at the White Sands Missile Range.

It was not NASA's first choice and for good reason. Massive amounts of equipment had to be moved there and quickly set up and we in the media had to rush in our equipment too. And because White Sands was mostly used for weapons testing it was filled with unexploded ordinance. For safety reasons we had to be brought out by bus to the landing area and had to be extremely careful where we walked.

And then there was the sand. To call it sand is to be generous; it was more like talcum powder and whipped by the wind, it got into everything. The landing was delayed one final day because of the wind, and when the shuttle did land everything went fine for the astronauts, but millions of dollars of equipment, including a lot belonging to news organizations, had to be replaced afterwards because that blowing sand got inside it.

NASA never landed another shuttle at White Sands.

I did cover one space shuttle launch at the Kennedy Space Center in Florida and it was a lot more exciting than the landing. The trailer we broadcast from shook wildly when the shuttle took off and the noise was so loud I couldn't hear what I was saying into the microphone, but presumably the people listening to the radio could. Florida's Space Coast also is a lot more developed than the desert at Edwards and during what had become the normal days of delay before the launch, I enjoyed a lot of Florida's excellent stone crabs.

My Los Angeles bureau was made into a two-person operation with the arrival of Rob Navias, who worked with me until he moved to Miami to open a Florida bureau, where he mostly covered space shuttles. Rob, who was known to his colleagues as "the dude," fell in love with the space program from the first day. He had been working in Washington and was transferred to Los Angeles only with the condition that he could still go to Florida and cover all the shuttle launches.

And so over the years he covered the launches and I covered the landings and we shared coverage of the middle of the missions. In between shuttles he worked with me in the bureau covering all the rest of the news. He applied to become a "journalist astronaut" when NASA was considering that and got pretty far in the competition before the program was cancelled, but ended up working for NASA in their public affairs operation after he left UPI.

He was replaced in my bureau by Bob Brill, who worked with me until I left UPI Radio, and stayed on until that network closed. Bob became a good friend and we covered a lot of stories together.

The biggest challenge in writing for radio is getting a lot of information in an easy to understand format into just 30 or 35 seconds. The writing has to be simple without big words or complex sentence structure. Not because listeners aren't very bright but because they aren't paying close attention. Most of the time people who are listening to news on the radio are also driving a car or cooking dinner. So the key is to keep things simple without being simplistic and to keep it short.

While that is difficult with all kinds of stories, the hardest are medical stories. When researchers have a breakthrough in treating cancer or Alzheimer's disease, their publication in a medical journal is filled with caveats, making clear the limits of what they've found and all the reasons it will take longer before it can actually be used to cure patients. The problem with reporting them for the general public is not only that there isn't room for all those caveats but that for the most part people won't pay attention to them.

If you hear on the radio or TV or see a newspaper headline about some important breakthrough in a disease you care about, or research that some vitamin or other may help prevent disease, you often don't get any further. And though I always tried as hard as I could in medical stories to make sure the listener understood the limits of what was being reported, I knew there would be people out there who would get false hope and rush to their doctor to ask for something that wasn't ready to be used.

Two big medical stories stand out and both had to do with hearts. The first was in 1982 when I traveled to Salt Lake City where the first artificial heart was put into a patient at the University of Utah. It was the "Jarvik" heart, a huge machine tethered to a patient who had no other options, a retired dentist who lived just over three months. It was an experiment, and an important one.

The second, far more controversial experiment I covered was at Loma Linda Medical Center in California two years later, when a doctor did the first heart transplant with a non-human donor. A baboon heart was put into an infant named "Baby Fae" in a procedure that became a big national story. It sounded like science fiction and in many ways it was. The doctor and hospital were very proud of being the first to try this but less clear about why they had done it and whether it was a wise thing to do. It turned out the baby's mother had no health insurance and couldn't afford a human heart transplant and so agreed to an experiment that researchers at the hospital had been anxious to try. The baby rejected the heart and died after three weeks.

I have never been much of a sports fan but have covered a lot of big sporting events. The first baseball game I ever covered was a World Series and over the years I covered Super Bowls, major golf tournaments, boxing championships, a World Cup sailing race and two Olympics.

That first baseball game came when I was still a stringer just out of college living in Mountain View, California. I used to do some work for a little outfit called Radio News West, which provided news to California radio stations. One of the editors I would file to on the phone was Dana Rohrabacher, a surfing party dude whose career in radio would be short lived.

I would run into him again in 1980 when I was covering Ronald Reagan's presidential campaign and he was a deputy press secretary and one of the "true believers," who would only give you a straight answer if it made Reagan look good. He later became a speechwriter in the Reagan White House and ended up being elected to the House of Representatives, where I would run into him from time to time when I covered Congress.

Radio News West called me one day and asked if I could cover one of the World Series games in Oakland, where the A's were playing the Los Angeles Dodgers.

I said sure and managed to get a second press pass and invited one of my roommates, Francis Dickerson, to join me. Francis actually knew a lot about baseball and so he would tell me what was going on and I would go on the radio and report it. It was an early lesson that I could cover pretty much anything. In broadcasting, sounding like you know what you are talking about can often be more important than knowing what you are talking about.

I didn't know a whole lot about football either, but ended up covering a couple of Super Bowls, more than a dozen Rose Bowls and some playoff games, and it wasn't all that hard, either.

I covered several heavyweight boxing matches in Las Vegas. The first championship I covered at Caesar's Palace taught me a lesson that close isn't always best. I had a press seat right at ringside, not far from Frank Sinatra, and when the fight began I started getting splattered with sweat and blood. I quickly retreated to the press room for the rest of the fight.

Golf was among my favorite sports to cover because it was incredibly easy, there was no blood, and it was always played in really nice places. I covered the U.S. Open in Pebble Beach and used to cover a PGA tournament every year at the La Costa Resort near San Diego. It was wonderful in part because ethics rules for sports reporting are, shall we say, lax. We would get rooms for a fraction of their cost, free meals, drinks and presents.

And covering golf is not exactly a challenge. In fact my feet never touched grass. I would go to a press room and watch on TV while runners would update giant boards showing what every golfer had shot on every hole, and who was ahead, and would bring in a steady supply of drinks and snacks. When the tournament was over you didn't even have to ask any questions. The PGA brought in the winner and one of their representatives asked the questions at the news conference. It was a nice break from real news.

The Olympics, though, were real news and took a lot of work. The work for the 1984 Summer Olympics in Los Angeles started months ahead of time. Besides preparing for the Games and producing dozens of special preview reports, I also had to make the logistical arrangements for coverage, which would include half a dozen other reporters who would come out from New York to help.

I oversaw construction of a second studio at the UPI bureau in Los Angeles and got a major upgrade of all my equipment, including my first cell phone, which at the time were big and bulky and not very good.

I interviewed dozens of track and field athletes, gymnasts, shooters and archers leading up to the games and it was an opportunity to learn about all the sports I would be covering during the games themselves.

The opening ceremonies at the Los Angeles Coliseum were spectacular as they have been for most Olympic Games and the Games are a blur of constant work. There was so much to cover and so much to coordinate, but it was an exciting two weeks. The most memorable moment came when I was covering what was expected to be the gold medal long sought by American runner Mary Decker, who had set more than a dozen world records but lost her opportunity for an Olympic medal four years before when the U.S. boycotted the Moscow

Olympics to protest the Soviet invasion of Afghanistan (seems a tad ironic now).

Decker was heavily favored to take gold in Los Angeles in the 3,000 meter race and as we watched her running next to barefoot Zola Budd, the South African runner who was competing for Great Britain to get around sanctions against apartheid, they bumped each other once and recovered, but then a second collision took Decker out of the race. She initially blamed Budd for tripping her and the controversy raged for years.

I covered the Winter Olympics in 1988 in Calgary and they were a lot more relaxed. There are fewer sports, fewer athletes, and less pressure and it was a great time. We all lived in a "journalists' village," with accommodations similar to college dorm rooms. They were comfortable enough, though the organizers didn't have everything quite organized. They arranged laundry for us in the unit but forgot to separate out the clothes. So when the laundry was done they ended up putting clothes from scores of reporters from dozens of countries out on a giant table and we had to try to figure out which were ours.

One of the UPI Radio sports reporters who covered the games with me was Bob Berger, who actually knew a lot about sports and with whom I became lifelong friends and frequent travel companions. Though we didn't get off to a great start at those Games.

A day or two before the Games opened I decided we should go take a look at the downhill ski course, and so we went to the mountain and took the chairlift up to the top. I then thought it would be fun to walk a ways down the course just to get a feel for what it was like. It was an incredibly stupid thing to do but I managed to convince Bob to come along.

Needless to say, after a very short way it became obvious there was no way we could possibly walk back up the ski slope to the chairlift and so proceeded to walk, slide, and fall our way down the mountain. Bob came down with a terrible fever the next day and was confined to bed the first few days of the games and was convinced our little adventure was the cause (and it may very well have been).

I, on the other hand, decided right then and there that when these Games were over, I was going to learn to ski.

I took part in a lot of outdoor sports, but had always avoided skiing because it wasn't something I could do myself. Unlike hiking, river rafting, kayaking, or snorkeling I couldn't just go out and learn to ski. I would need special equipment and special instruction and it just always seemed like a lot of trouble. But after covering the Winter Games and sliding down that mountain, I decided it was something I needed to do.

My first effort was at Winter Park, Colorado, which has the nation's most prominent school for disabled skiers. They said they could teach anyone to ski and so I booked a week at a wonderful little lodge called the Woodspur, with home-cooked meals and two outdoor hot tubs, and set out to ski.

They evaluated me and decided I should ski sitting down in what is called a monoski. It is basically a metal capsule mounted on a single ski that you are strapped into and ski on using two little "outriggers" on your arms, which are half-sized crutches with skis on the bottom that can flip up and down.

The chairlift is terrifying on a monoski because you are strapped into this big, heavy device that sticks way out over the edge and are held in by a little safety line and your arm gripping for dear life.

But skiing in one is exhilarating and I learned quickly. That's good, because an out-of-control monoskier is incredibly dangerous since it is very heavy; with such a low center of gravity it just flies down the mountain. As I started out I had at least two instructors at a time and one of them would "tether" me by skiing behind me with a rope attached to make sure I didn't lose control and plow into anyone.

When I fell I would just roll over and be thankful I had a helmet and then use the little outriggers to get back upright and start heading down the mountain again. The learning curve was fast (especially since falling when you are sitting doesn't hurt nearly as much as it does when you are standing), and by the end of the week I was doing moguls.

But there were some downsides. No matter how warmly I dressed and how many toe heaters I used there was no way to keep my feet and legs warm because they didn't move the entire day of skiing. And I knew that no matter how good I got, I would never be able to just pop by myself up to a mountain to go skiing, if for no other reason there was no way I could lift a monoski or put one on my car.

And so I decided later that year to try to find a way to ski standing up and did it by pitting one handicapped ski school against another. There was a school at Heavenly Valley in Lake Tahoe, California, and I booked a week there and stayed at a great little ski lodge run by the Stanford Alumni Association. I told them the instructors at Winter Park had not been able to figure out a way that I could ski standing up and basically dared them to do better. And they did.

It took a lot of experimentation and an awful lot of falling but they finally came up with a way I could ski standing up. They basically treated me like a one-legged skier. They mounted a binding up a few inches off a single ski and angled the binding so my left foot, which points left, could go in and the ski could still point straight. I put my left leg, the one that has a knee that can bend a little, in the binding, and then they built a shelf off the raised binding and my right foot, which points out at a dramatic angle, sat on that. Initially it was attached with a Velcro strap, but it later turned out to be much better if that leg was free. I then used two full-length outriggers, crutches with skis at the bottom that flipped up to walk on the snow and I was set.

The chairlift was the most challenging part. They would slow the lift down for me to get on at the bottom, but when they did that at the top I didn't have enough momentum to ski off and got smacked by the chair. And then there was the problem that when my ski first touched the snow it was at a sharp angle, because that's the way my foot pointed when I was sitting down. I used to fall every time I got off the chairlift, but eventually figured out how to make it work as long as the lift was going fast enough.

It was a lot more work than skiing sitting down and I was exhausted at the end of each day. I would go back to the lodge and enjoy some après ski snacks and then go take a little nap. I didn't manage to stay awake until dinner once that week. But by the end of the week I could ski standing up.

I then joined a disabled ski club in Los Angeles called the Unrecables and started skiing every chance I got. I met some wonderful people in that club, including Richard Wu, an amputee who was a great one-legged skier. He brought me from a novice to a decent skier who could handle most any blue run and some black diamonds too. The club had trips to Mammoth Mountain in Central California every few weeks in the winter and into the spring. The group would rent condos and we would cram in there, sharing rooms and occasionally sharing beds, and would ski like maniacs all weekend long, then drive back to Los Angeles.

I also returned often to Winter Park since it was such a welcoming place for disabled skiers and I loved the lodge I stayed in when I first went there. Many years later I would return to Winter Park and that same lodge every year during the Christmas school break with my nephew Jeffrey for ski trips, starting when he was seven.

My first experience with Jeff on skis was when his sister Jenna and my sister Lorri and brother-in-law John all met for a little ski weekend at a small resort in southern Utah called Brian Head. Jeff had no fear. We were on a bunny slope and he was with his parents; I skied down a little ways and then told him to ski to me. He did exactly what I told him and skied straight to me and straight into me and knocked me down in the snow. It was a great beginning to our skiing years together.

During our trips to Winter Park he wanted no part of the ski school and so I taught him and tried to adapt my techniques on one ski to a kid on two skis. It wasn't long before he was skiing far better than me and would head through the trees and wait patiently for me at the bottom. Those ski trips with Jeff were wonderful and we kept them up until he was well into his teens.

I decided one year to attend a "learn to race" clinic for disabled skiers at Breckenridge, Colorado. I had no interest in becoming a racer but thought it would be fun and make me a better skier. Despite the embarrassment of watching kids with one leg whip past me without even trying and losing consistently to blind skiers, I did indeed become a much better skier after that week of racing.

A small group of us from the disabled ski club became friends and we started heading out on our own to ski. We skied every major mountain in Utah and California and were crazed skiers who started with the first run in the morning and didn't quit until the chair lifts closed.

Over the years I skied at most major mountain resorts in Colorado, Utah, Montana, California, and Idaho. After moving East I would sometimes ski at the little local resorts in Pennsylvania and West Virginia but never went skiing in New England. It took the same amount of time and money to get out West and the snow there is so much better. I especially enjoyed Sundance, Robert Redford's resort in Utah. It was small and uncrowded, and the only place quiet enough that I saw deer and other wildlife while skiing down the slopes. Steamboat Springs in Colorado was terrific, in part because of the wonderful hot springs in town. Big Sky in Montana was hard to get to, but a treat with no lift lines and long, beautiful runs.

I got to be a pretty good skier who could handle all but the toughest runs on any mountain. What I couldn't handle was deep powder. Most skiers live for it, but the problem with skiing with outriggers is that the single ski on your foot will move through the powder at a different speed than the outriggers held with your arms, meaning as soon as you put the outriggers down into the snow, they pull you over.

I have seen one-legged skiers in powder but they have the strength and balance to stand on their one leg without using their outriggers at all and I couldn't handle that for more than a minute or so at a time.

I never set out to be an example for anyone; I was just having fun. But I know from the people who came up to me all the time that I helped inspire others to try things on the slopes they didn't think they could do, and that was nice.

My niece Jenna never caught the skiing bug but we took many trips together over the years and she was the one who gave me my very best writing assignment. When she got engaged to her longtime boyfriend Duncan they shocked me by asking me to perform their wedding ceremony. I was incredibly flattered but also a little nervous about the responsibility.

First I looked into the law, and found pretty much anyone can perform a wedding. There are different ways to do it but the easiest was to go on line and sign up as a minister with the Universal Life Church, which exists for the purpose of letting people perform weddings. It was free and I became a "minister for life" and paid extra for a very fancy looking certificate. I don't think I ever spent more time writing, re-writing, and editing anything than I did on that wedding ceremony. I know nothing I've written was more rewarding, as I married them on a beautiful sunny day at a beachfront hotel in San Diego.

I'm not much of a prankster and joking in the news business can be dangerous, as I learned one April Fool's Day. Each night in Los Angeles I would send a description of the pieces I was filing for the morning so the overnight editor in New York knew what the material was and could put it out. Along with the description we would always include the "outcue," which are the last few words spoken in a piece of tape because, it is important for the news anchor using the sound on the radio to know when it was time to start speaking again.

So I sent a description of a piece for the morning of April first saying that it was me with Quartas5 reporting on aliens landing in Los Angeles. Now, I didn't think this was very subtle. The outcue I used on the tape from Quartas5 was "take me to your leader." I thought it would produce nothing more than a little chuckle by the overnight editor. Instead he called and woke me up in the middle of the night in a panic, apologizing profusely for waking me but saying he couldn't find my pieces with Quartas5.

I asked him if he had read the descriptions and he said, "of course I did." I then asked him to read them out loud to me and he got partway through and then started saying words even aliens wouldn't use.

That was the last time I tried an April Fool's joke at work.

THE AMAZON 2009

The Amazon always held a kind of mysterious allure for me, and so I decided to take a small group cruise on the mighty river and chose a stretch in Peru.

Flying to Lima, I changed planes in El Salvador, where they save everyone a lot of trouble by just using U.S. dollars and had a wonderful airport shop that just sold chips: potato chips, corn chips, and yucca chips. We began the trip with a few days in the upscale Lima district of Miraflores right next door to a casino. My favorite sign: a pistol with a red line through it, indicating no guns allowed inside.

There were a dozen of us in the group, led by a man who spent his childhood in a small village in the Amazon rain forest before his parents came to the city so their children could go to school. His kids are all now headed for college.

I had a fantastic dinner at a wonderful restaurant called Huaca Pucllana, with three women from our group who shared my interest in a gourmet meal. We ate on a porch that overlooked a 1500-year-old adobe pyramid lit at night and shared a variety of interesting and delicious appetizers including guinea pig, which oddly tasted nothing like chicken.

Downtown Lima was packed with thousands of people pressing to get into the main cathedral and surrounding old churches for Good Friday. Many walked to each church carrying flowers. At the presidential palace and other government buildings flags flew at half-staff for the death of Jesus. Then on Easter Sunday flags are put back up to celebrate the resurrection.

No separation of church and state here.

Miraflores is very upscale but still cheap by U.S. standards. Not sure why, but it's also filled with Chinese restaurants and proves it has reached the pinnacle of culture with a beachfront mall with movie theaters, a bowling alley, and a "Hooters."

We saw an excellent folk dance show (not at "Hooters") that had one very unusual dance in which the men and women held candles and tried to light each other's backsides on fire. It was kind of like a flaming version of pin the tail on the donkey, in which enough shaking could put your fire out, so to speak.

We went to a market that had a dozen kinds of potatoes, black corn used to flavor pudding, and some very tasty bananas that were purplish inside. We bought lots of groceries including a chicken sans feathers but con feet, and brought them to one of hundreds of shanty towns on the outskirts of Lima filled with poor people basically squatting on public land with no sewers or running water, but building working communities with communal kitchens, schools, and little stores

There we had an interesting visit with warm and friendly people proud of what they've built and with little kids following us everywhere. The one question the adults had for us was, how was President Obama doing? It always amazes me how little we know about other nation's governments and how much they know about ours.

We flew to Iquitos, a city of almost a million people on the Amazon, and the biggest city in the world with no road access. It's over 2000 miles from the Atlantic and the farthest west large ships can navigate the Amazon. It has the look of a fading frontier town but is extremely lively, with a huge market for local products arriving by boat. I wandered a bit and spent a few minutes at the biggest church, which was crowded on Easter Sunday and had music from a guitar and a children's choir.

Then it was time to journey up the Amazon and we boarded our small boat with 11 cabins. We began with some typical and tasty Amazonian food, including salad of fresh hearts of palm, which they shred to look like coleslaw.

I've never been to a place where such a large percentage of the creatures seem determined to harm me: from the yellow fever- and malaria-carrying mosquitos to flesh eating bees, poison ants, frogs so deadly just holding one can be fatal, stinging plants, gigantic snakes, electric eels, and man-eating fish. Though to be fair, swimming with the piranha is still probably safer than crossing the street amid the crazed traffic in Lima.

Sailing up the Amazon, which is light brown here, we pass lots of little villages with makeshift soccer fields and volleyball nets. People fish and grow crops and move around in hand-carved wooden canoes. No cannibals or giant Amazon women (actually all the people here are pretty short), but lots of friendly kids swimming and waving from the shore.

By nightfall the last cell phone signal from Iquitos is gone and we tie the boat to a tree for the night. Even through cabin walls, we go to sleep to the sound of some of the more than a thousand species of insects in the rain forest.

Touring the next day we visited a small village. No electricity and thatch houses, lots of banana and mango trees, and of course, plenty of fish. We brought a present of salt, one of the few things they can't provide for themselves.

Later we pulled over at small still making moonshine rum by squeezing sugar cane with a machine run by a gasoline engine and using wood fires. At the little bar and store we sampled straight moonshine, then mixed with ginger root, and finally mixed with molasses, which was quite good. Their dogs provide security and they feed the leftover squeezed cane to the water buffalo.

Just like the earliest adventurers and explorers, when we get back in the skiff we get cold towels and ice water, and on the boat take off our muddy shoes so the crew can clean them for us.

So far, no giant snakes or headhunters.

We took our small skiff through tiny canals and into a small tributary to fish for piranha. We put a bit of raw meat on a hook attached to a cane pole and they immediately attacked. The trick was hooking them before they ate up the bait; we got the hang of it and caught 19 before our bait ran out. Piranha were flying all over the small boat and we were dodging their nasty teeth.

On the way back, local folks found us and pulled their canoe along side and the store was open with baskets, beads, and other handicrafts. We saw some spider monkeys and lots of parrots and came back at dusk for the chef to start cooking up our small man-eating fish.

The next day we took a hike in the rain forest along a wet, muddy steep trail accompanied by a local villager carrying a machete, which was lighter than I expected but quite effective. Saw only one snake and one itty-bitty poison frog, but lots of giant "24-hour ants," so named because the severe pain and fever from one bite goes away the next day.

We also saw plants used to make blow darts with curare-dipped tips, plants used for medicine, and the hallucinogens used by the shamans and visiting hippies. I'm estimating the temperature was 120 degrees with 300% humidity but that's only a guess. The hike seemed much more fun looking back on it after a shower and lunch.

We also saw the world's largest water lilies, which are enormous. Pink dolphins swam nearby. Indians consider them sacred but didn't feel that way about the manatees, which have been pretty well wiped out from hunting.

We had fun paddling our own dugout canoes through narrow back tributaries and passed several canoes of children paddling home after school.

Our destination was a village of about 100 people and our visit to the school. It is a one-room schoolhouse for the first through sixth grades. The kids taught us a Spanish song and we taught them the hokey pokey, which, after all, is what it's all about. We delivered pencils, notebooks, crayons, and other supplies we had brought from home. The central government is supposed to send books but they haven't arrived yet.

We had lunch in the village, providing the bottled water for our drinks but otherwise eating their food, which was scrumptious: a local fish cooked in banana leaves, plantain, yucca, some roasted local nuts, and delicious barbecued salted meat from an animal similar to a wild boar our host hunted for. When we asked what he used, expecting to hear about poison blow darts or a bow and arrow, he said he shot it with a rifle.

We also had an extraordinary visit with a shaman who showed us her cures for snakebite, diarrhea and headache, and showed us ayahuasca, which is similar to LSD, for getting in touch with the spirits. She says most local people go to the doctor first, and then come to her when his medicine doesn't work. She also explained that local witch doctors are her enemies because they use spirits to hurt people. We took part in a ceremony that included incantations with leaves and her blowing cigarette smoke in our hands, which we then pushed over our heads and down our bodies. It was for good luck, happiness, and prosperity—so I hope it works for the lottery.

A night ride in our little skiff up a narrow tributary in pitch-blackness with no moon or running lights was exciting. The sounds were amazing and using a hand-held searchlight we found some critters including nighthawks, bats, and two kinkajous, cute tree-climbing relatives of the raccoon. At one point I was smacked hard across my face and knocked over and dragged a bit. It wasn't a 20-foot anaconda, just a tree branch the pilot couldn't see in the dark. The bruise on my cheek is impressive though, so we'll call it an anaconda.

We actually never saw the giant snakes, but did run into several species of monkeys, three-toed sloths, parrots, toucans, and lots of leaping pink river dolphins.

Our last stop on the river was at a good-sized market town and the guide gave us each one sole, about 33 cents, to buy fruits, vegetables, and other items that looked interesting for our lunch. It was a wonderful way to both get us interacting with local people and get a sense of how they lived. The only rule was you had to spend it all—and no live chickens. We came back with bags full of fresh produce and got a sense of how cheap things are here (and how rich we are).

It was the last full day of our trip and wandering away from the market a bit I found a one-room radio station and stopped in to say hi. They were completely computerized and were playing music. I was told they do news at 6 pm. There is no traffic to report and the weather is either hot and raining or hot and about to rain. They were very nice and glad to meet a gringo radio reporter but they had no openings.

COUPS AND EARTHQUAKES

Ferdinand Marcos was one of many dictators the U. S. government supported because they opposed communism. He stole millions from the Philippines and stashed it away in Swiss bank accounts. He was brutal and ruthless but finally went too far when he had a leading opposition figure who was gaining strength, Benigno Aquino, gunned down at the airport as he stepped off a flight with an American reporter watching.

Marcos was pressured to have an election in February 1986, with international monitors, led by former President Jimmy Carter. His opponent was Corazon Aquino, the widow of the man he had ordered killed.

I've covered many elections but nothing like this. The Catholic Church was powerful in the Philippines and a hotbed of opposition to Marcos. (An interesting tidbit was that many of the priests there were married. They had always believed it was fine for priests to marry and the Vatican just pretended it didn't notice.) The leader of the Church in the Philippines was the wonderfully named Cardinal Jaime Sin.

One of the best quotes I've ever had came from Cardinal Sin. When I and other reporters met with him and asked his view of the election, he said the Church was neutral and could not take sides but in general terms he would describe the contest as "between good and evil."

The Philippines was one of several countries where UPI made a profit, but because of local laws could not send any of that money back to the U.S. UPI was always short of money at home but had more than it could spend in the Philippines. So the bureau in Manila paid all my expenses. I stayed at the city's top hotel, had a car and driver when I needed one, and was given cash for everything else.

The election was a fiasco. Marcos stole it and everybody knew it. There were protests, but the U.S. seemed to be standing with Marcos and I was sent home. I stopped in Bangkok on the way, a busy, dirty, fascinating city, which I returned to a few years later to tour Thailand in a more leisurely way.

I wasn't home long before the military coup that would bring Marcos down was launched and I was back on a plane to Manila. What a difference, soldiers guarding the hotel and tension everywhere. The coup leader (and a future president) General Fidel Ramos was held up with other rebellious officers inside a big military base in downtown Manila. Cardinal Sin went on the Catholic radio station "Veritas," which Marcos had never been able to control, and urged the people to go to peacefully surround the base and protect it.

A hundred thousand or more men, women, and children displaying yellow, the color of the Aquino campaign, surrounded the base and blocked an attack. It was one of the bravest and most extraordinary things I've ever witnessed.

Soldiers loyal to Marcos were held back by these unarmed civilians, though the crowd was happy to let western journalists in. I found an office with a phone and broadcast live from inside the base, just down the hall from where Ramos and the others were running the coup. There were some other Americans there who wouldn't talk to me who I've always assumed were with the CIA.

Marcos fell within days, the U.S. government flying him out to Hawaii. People entered the Presidential Palace, finding Imelda Marcos's famous closet with thousands of pairs of shoes.

I was in the room when Corazon Aquino, on a wave of people power with not a single shot fired, took the oath as the new president. I never felt in danger, even when my crutch got caught in the strap of an AK47 in a crowd. But I should have. A day or two later I was sitting in a flower-filled courtyard with a few other reporters interviewing the head of the army at his home. He was providing lots of inside detail on how the coup proceeded and told us how after the army refused to attack the civilians surrounding the base where General Ramos was held up, Marcos ordered an Air Force wing outside the capital to bomb the base. He said the planes were in the air headed to the target but in the end the pilots wouldn't drop their bombs. A chill went down my spine as I realized the timing of that planned attack was when I was there.

Reporters cover lots of natural disasters, though most of the time we wait until they happen. The exception are hurricanes and I was always a little disturbed by the idea that when being sent to cover a hurricane I was heading into an area everyone else was trying to escape and was actively working to put myself directly in harm's way.

Television reporters often like to be seen right in the worst of it, holding onto a tree or some other crazy stunt, but for a radio reporter what we want is the sound of the wind. One discovery I made while covering a hurricane on the Texas gulf coast was that the sound was just as dramatic holding my microphone outside my motel room door as it was actually standing outside and the risk to life and limb was less that way.

Floods can be frightening, too, and I remember one of them in a mountainous area around Los Angeles where mudslides had cut off a number of small communities. A photographer (they always seem to be around in the most dangerous places) and I were flying in a helicopter over one of the worst hit areas when we saw a group of people stranded on a bit of high ground and signaling to us for help. The helicopter pilot landed and for the next hour or so we ferried people to safety, doing a good deed while being able to get all the interviews we needed.

What is striking about covering a tornado is that the area of destruction is often quite limited, with houses completely destroyed surrounded by neighborhoods that weren't touched. An exception was a tornado that wiped out a small town in West Texas I covered. It was an amazing site because if you didn't know there had been a town there, you couldn't tell by what was left. There was nothing but rubble and most of it was flat.

It was another of those times when I wasn't sure I wanted to be hanging out with photographers because when in the car with one we heard another tornado was spotted nearby and instead of taking cover like normal, sane people, we rushed towards it. Luckily we didn't find it.

But the worst, at least for me, were the earthquakes.

On September 19, 1985, a massive earthquake struck Mexico City, measuring 8.1 on the Richter scale and blamed officially for 10,000 deaths, though the true number is likely higher.

I was on the next plane to Mexico City, not the first time I would be flying into a place where others were trying desperately to leave. The damage was extensive and the phones were out.

Some of the American networks used private planes to send reporters and their tapes to Texas to file their stories each night, but I used a taxi to go to Querétaro, a town about 150 miles north and the closest place with reliable phone service. I would gather material and do interviews and record stories and then twice a day hire a car for the three to four hour drive to Querétaro. I would find a phone, usually by paying someone to let me use theirs, file my pieces to New York and then head right back to Mexico City to keep covering the story.

I was having dinner in one of the few restaurants operating in the Zona Rosa when an aftershock struck and it wasn't a small one, 7.5 on the Richter scale, a giant quake in its own right. When I got back to the hotel I got off the elevator on my floor and walked down a hallway connecting the central section where the elevator was, to the wings holding the rooms. As I walked through the narrow hallway I noticed there was light coming through the wall and then saw it was coming through the other side too. The building was completely cracked open.

I decided to change hotels and moved to the El Presidente, the nicest hotel in the city and one that was still in one piece. It was a great scene in that luxury hotel because many of the canine rescue teams from different countries that had come to help were there and they would bring their dogs into the lobby and the restaurant for breakfast. The dogs were incredible. One of the most memorable stories was how, more than a week after the quake, the dogs discovered babies in a hospital that had been buried under tons of rubble and somehow managed to survive, some with no injuries at all.

Mostly though, the scene was one of devastation and sadness. Bodies had been piled up in a stadium being used as a makeshift morgue. It was a horrendous scene as I walked through it wearing a mask, describing into my tape recorder the sights and smells of the row upon row of bodies.

It was also a place where I learned a sad lesson commonly known by foreign correspondents that the American Embassy was often the least helpful, least welcoming place for journalists in difficult circumstances. Those in the know always sought out the British or Canadian Embassies instead.

There was an almost comical moment on the day I and other reporters finally did get into the American Embassy for a news conference with the American ambassador to Mexico. John Gavin had been an actor and a friend of President Ronald Reagan, who appointed him for no apparent reason other than he spoke Spanish. Just before the news conference the press assistant came in and instructed us that when the ambassador came into the room we were all supposed to stand. We told him that was absurd, and having been covering horrors for days at this point, none of us were in a very conciliatory mood for officious embassy flacks. The man explained that the ambassador represented

President Reagan and it was like the president entering the room. When he came in, none of us stood.

A few days later first lady Nancy Reagan came to Mexico City to survey the damage and offer condolences from the United States government and to show the people of Mexico we would stand by them. I was lucky to have a taxi driver who knew how to get things done.

I hired the driver and told him I needed to go where the first lady was going and to stay as close as he could to her motorcade. He pulled over at a stationery store and bought a piece of white cardboard and some markers. He drew an American flag and a Mexican flag and then wrote "official vehicle" in Spanish. I couldn't believe that would work, but when we found the first lady's motorcade at the airport we were welcomed right into it and stayed with her through the day.

There was a cholera scare, as there often is in these types of disasters in developing countries when bodies start piling up. I used one of my trips to a phone to check with my doctor, who advised me that he thought the chances of developing cholera were lower than the risks of getting a vaccination in a place where sterile needles could not be guaranteed. I took the advice and all was well.

Earthquakes are profoundly disturbing because we just don't expect the ground to move. They can have a real impact on your psyche and after covering them I would sometimes wake up back home in the middle of the night, thinking I was experiencing another earthquake.

There was one quake I risked contempt of court to cover. It was a big quake in San Francisco in October 1989, that hit during the World Series there. There was substantial damage, deaths, and injuries and thousands of people were left homeless. One of the worst hit areas was a neighborhood in Oakland just at the end of the Bay Bridge, which suffered severe damage. One of the most disturbing scenes there was caused by reporters. A poor neighborhood that had suffered a lot of harm, it was where the networks decided to anchor their evening newscasts after the quake. Just doing what they do without thinking, the network anchors arrived in the neighborhood in limousines. It was an embarrassing moment to be a member of the media.

The earthquake struck in the late afternoon and I immediately flew to San Francisco to cover it and after working all night I had a phone call to make. The day before I had been serving jury duty and was supposed to report to the courthouse where a jury was being chosen for a criminal trial. We had filled out questionnaires and the next day was when they would start choosing jurors. I had my boss in New York call the judge and explain where I was and what I was doing. The judge was very understanding and even excused me from jury duty after I had returned from the quake.

San Francisco is one of my favorite cities but I've covered a lot of bad stories there and there was one stretch when the city truly seemed to be cursed.

It was November of 1978 and the horror began 4,500 miles south in Guyana on the coast of South America, where Jim Jones, whose People's Temple had been a longtime fixture in San Francisco, had moved his flock.

Following up on reports that some members of what had clearly become a cult had been prevented from leaving and returning home, San Francisco Congressman Leo Ryan flew down with several members of his staff and NBC reporter Don Harris to check things out. On November 17th he went to the compound and about a dozen people told him they wanted to leave and he took them back with him the next day to a small airfield.

As they were preparing to depart, a group of Jones's followers drove up and began shooting, killing Ryan, Harris, and several others. It remains the only time a member of Congress has ever been assassinated on the job. But things were about to get much worse.

Jones gathered 918 men, women, and children at his People's Temple compound, and while some were murdered, most appear to have willingly taken their own lives and those of their children at Jones's direction by drinking poison. When authorities reached the jungle compound everyone was dead.

It was so beyond reason and so beyond explanation—and struck so hard in San Francisco, raising questions that could not be answered. Then, just over a week later, with the city still reeling, another inexplicable tragedy struck that had people truly asking if something in San Francisco had gone terribly wrong.

Former firefighter Dan White had been elected to the Board of Supervisors and was more conservative than most of those in the city government. He had a bitter political feud going with Harvey Milk, another supervisor, who was the first openly gay elected official in San Francisco, or anywhere else for that matter. White had to give up his job with the fire department when he won the election and was having financial difficulties, and so resigned his seat.

It was up to Mayor George Moscone to appoint a new supervisor, but when it became clear he would choose a more liberal politician, White changed his mind and asked Moscone to appoint him and give him his old job back. Milk was among those who strongly lobbied Moscone not to do that and the mayor decided to appoint someone else.

It was the kind of dispute that happens all the time in local politics but what happened next would reverberate for decades. White walked into Moscone's office at City Hall and said he wanted to talk. The mayor was pouring them drinks when White took out a gun and shot him. He then left Moscone's office, walked down the hall to Harvey Milk's office, and killed him too.

Though most of the attention then and since focused on the killing of Milk, a hate crime and a sad marker in the history of gay rights, this was also a political assassination, the second in a week of a major San

Francisco politician. Amid the horrible emotions of that day and all that followed, I always felt that critical point had been lost.

Dan White hated Harvey Milk because he was gay but he killed George Moscone because of a political decision that went against him. This struck at the heart of our democracy and thankfully is rare at any level of government. Moscone died cradled in the arms of another San Francisco supervisor, Dianne Feinstein, who took over as mayor and later, during a long Senate career, never stopped trying to toughen gun control laws.

That night, covering a vigil outside city hall with tens of thousands of people holding candles and Joan Baez singing "Amazing Grace," I was sad for those gunned down, but also for a wonderful city that would take many years to emerge from the dark shadow of that November.

THE KINDNESS OF STRANGERS

When people see me on crutches their first instinct is often to offer to help me. I rarely need help and as a young man would occasionally get into heated arguments with elderly women who were insisting on giving up their seat for me on a bus. But as I got older, I realized while people offer help because they are generous, it also makes them feel good. I eventually matured enough to understand that by refusing them I was denying them a good feeling, which is kind of the same thing as making them feel bad. So now when it's a small thing, I let someone open a door, or give up their seat, or take my carry-on down from the overhead bin on a plane. And on those few occasions when I actually need help, I ask for it.

Sometimes a friend or relative would intervene to assure a well-meaning stranger that I didn't need any help. Those who know me well stop seeing the crutches and more than once a friend driving with me would start to chastise me for pulling into a handicapped parking space before remembering I was allowed.

Things do change as you get older, though, and my younger self would surely be appalled that I routinely use my status as a disabled person to go to the front of long lines at airport security.

The pattern of people responding to my crutches with offers of assistance is why it was noticeable on a visit to Israel when I tripped a few times on uneven cobblestones in Jerusalem, one of the world's most fascinating cities, that no one offered to help. I didn't need any help, but I was struck to realize I'd fallen in all corners of the globe and this was the only place people looked but made no effort to approach.

There is a saying that just because you are paranoid doesn't mean people aren't out to get you. And while the people of Israel have plenty of reason to be suspicious of all strangers, it still saddened me.

An odd tendency some people have with a disabled person is to turn to someone else to speak for them; for example, asking a friend or companion if the disabled person needs something, as you might ask a parent if it's all right to offer their young child a cookie. It's quite rude and insulting but pretty common, and led to one of my favorite stories from Rio De Janeiro.

I was there covering the first U.N. Earth Summit on the environment and global warming in 1992. After a long day of listening to boring speeches, I was walking one night along the outdoor cafes of Ipanema beach with my colleague Jon Bascom of ABC Radio. We were approached by two ladies of the evening and one asked Jon if he would like some female companionship. Then the other young lady asked Jon if I would like to partake as well. As I chuckled, Jon told her she could ask me herself and we both declined their kind offer.

MR FUSS GOES TO WASHINGTON

UPI was always short of money, and while set up as a for-profit company (unlike the Associated Press, which is a cooperative), it never made money. Scripps-Howard, a major owner of newspapers, used it as a tax write-off and the family that owned the company also felt it to be a trust and an obligation to good journalism. At its peak it served thousands of newspapers and radio and television stations; the intense competition with AP kept both companies sharp and focused.

Things started to change with a new generation of owners at Scripps-Howard, who had no interest in subsidizing a money-losing wire service and sold it in 1982, beginning its slow demise. The first bankruptcy came in 1984, right after our paychecks bounced. The company went through multiple sales; each time new owners would bring in cash and things would get better for a while, then worse again.

The next big cash crunch hit in 1988 when I was traveling with the Dukakis presidential campaign. We were told the company could no longer afford overtime and were asked to take comp time instead for the rest of the campaign, with its 15-plus-hour workdays and seven-day workweeks. My colleagues who were writing the print stories refused, but I did some quick calculations and told my boss I would finish the campaign as long as I'd be able to take the comp time off all at once. He agreed and I helped out the print side as well as covering for radio.

On the morning after Dukakis was creamed in the November election, I sat in a Boston hotel room and happily tallied up my comp time, which added up to a two-month paid vacation. It also happened to be a year United Airlines was offering triple frequent flier miles and so I started planning. In the spring I flew first class to Tokyo and spent six weeks exploring Japan and Thailand, then flew to Hawaii for a week on the beach in Maui. The two-month vacation was wonderful but three years later, after the second bankruptcy at UPI and a salary cut, it was clear this great job wasn't going to be around much longer and it was time to move on.

In large part due to the help of my good friend Peter Maer, who was the White House correspondent for Mutual and NBC Radio, I moved to Washington in 1991.

I arranged other interviews in Washington when I flew in to talk to the managers at Mutual/NBC, including one at NPR, whose newsroom at the time was being run by a former newspaper reporter who I covered stories with for years and knew well. NPR also was a client of UPI Radio to supplement its hourly news updates and so I had been heard on their network for years. But NPR had a longstanding prejudice against commercial radio reporters, preferring to hire from public radio stations or take on print reporters and teach them radio. The interview was not going well and it was apparent that I was not going to get hired. So after the third time I was asked if I really could do longer pieces of the type NPR likes, I finally told the interviewer the truth no one at NPR likes to hear: that writing a radio story that can run four minutes long is a lot easier than trying to write the same story and get it into 30 seconds.

Things went much better at Mutual/NBC, two of the country's oldest and largest networks, which had been combined and were run out of the same newsroom in the Virginia suburbs by a company called Westwood One.

They had two openings: one, to cover Congress; the other, to cover the Pentagon. I was nervous about the Pentagon job because my old college roommate Pete Williams was then Assistant Secretary of Defense for Public Affairs, the Pentagon spokesperson. While it certainly would have given me an edge, it would have also been awkward. Sometimes journalists need to report things that press officials don't like and covering a close friend would have been uncomfortable, I think, for both of us. Happily they offered me the job covering Congress. I took it and would work in the Capitol building for the next 23 years.

I covered one final Oscar show ("The Silence of the Lambs" won best picture), then left UPI after 16 years. I left the Los Angeles bureau I had started in the hands of Bob Brill, who stayed until the network shut down a few years later.

As frustrating as it was later, after Congress became so bitterly partisan and incompetent it lost the ability to perform the most basic duties of government, the feeling of coming to work in that grandest of Washington buildings with so much history never faded. Hurrying back and forth between the House and Senate sides covering late night negotiations on a big bill, I would sometimes stop for a moment and stand alone in the rotunda and soak in the wonder of it all.

I was certainly no stranger to national politics. I had already covered conventions, spent time with five presidents, and traveled on presidential campaigns.

But Washington was different. Politics is the city's lifeblood and reporters don't only cover politicians but also socialize with them in what always struck me as a bit too incestuous a manner. There was no conversation without spin and the city has its own customs and language. Things weren't just on or off the record; they could be "on background" or "deep background" or "not for attribution."

There is also a massive industry of press secretaries, communication directors, and media consultants whose only job is to influence reporters, and they vastly outnumber us. Most were pleasant enough and helpful when it served their interests, but if you said good morning to someone like Ari Fleischer, who worked on the Hill before becoming President Bush's press secretary, he'd likely tell you it certainly *was* a good morning because Republicans were keeping the nation safe and prosperous.

Washington reporters also had to have a thick skin. No matter how tough you think you are, it is hard to hold your ground when a White House press secretary calls you in and starts berating you.

While the Senate has an overabundance of millionaires and in those days was almost exclusively male, white, and old, the House was more vibrant and far more reflective of the nation as a whole. There were lots of lawyers and successful businessmen, but there were also some farmers and small shop owners and teachers. They came from rural areas as well as cities; they were more diverse in their backgrounds and their views. Some were smart and dedicated, some were slightly corrupt, others more so; some were genuinely stupid.

But overall most members of Congress I got to know were committed to trying to help the people who elected them. They cared about their constituents and worked hard. Though sadly, a huge portion of the work they needed to do was fundraising for the next election.

Members of Congress spend remarkably little time debating issues. In fact, unless a vote is underway there are rarely more than a handful of members on the floor during debates of even the most important bills. A key reason the cameras in the House and Senate chambers are controlled by employees of the Congress and not C-SPAN is to make sure they never take a wide shot to show the debate is taking place in an empty room.

In many ways Capitol Hill is the best beat in Washington, in part because it is the easiest place to get information. At the White House information is tightly controlled and there are guards to make sure you don't wander anywhere you might run into someone who knows something. At the Capitol you can wander anywhere and frequently bump into senators and House members at a cafeteria or in the hallway.

There is only one president and the balance of power is lopsided. Reporters on that beat find if difficult to learn anything the president doesn't want them to. But on Capitol Hill there are 435 House members and 100 senators and thousands of staff members, and if one person won't talk to you, there are plenty of others who will. One reason there are so many nasty fights between the executive and legislative branches over sharing of classified information is because people at the Pentagon, CIA and White House believe the Capitol leaks like a sieve. And they are right.

Tom Foley of Washington State was Speaker of the House when I first started covering Congress. He was a Democrat, as every speaker since the mid 1950s had been. He was a friendly if not overly garrulous man, and every day the House was in session he would have reporters gather in his office to tell us what was coming up that day and answer our questions. There were no cameras at these sessions and they were extremely helpful.

The Republican Leader was Bob Michel of Illinois, a nice man who believed in civility and compromise; someone who fought for his beliefs but who always put the needs of the country above the needs of his party. I had no way of knowing he would be the last of his kind.

The Democratic Leader was Richard Gephart of Missouri, a strong pro-union liberal but like Michel, the kind who would regularly meet with people of the other party to try to work things out. When they left Congress both became lobbyists.

At the start of each new Congress there would be separate gatherings of Democrats and Republicans to discuss issues, plan strategy, and socialize. They were generally held at resorts in Maryland or Virginia within a few hours' drive of Washington. I attended a few and they were helpful to get to know members in a less formal setting. I remember one where a group of reporters joined a group of members at an evening of karaoke. Thankfully that was long before the days of YouTube.

In later years, reporters were seen as the enemy. Security guards would chase us out of the lobbies of the hotels where the gatherings were held and bar us from the grounds, except for official briefings. I didn't bother to go anymore.

While I could generally set up an interview with members of Congress when I needed them, it was often easier to just go to what is called the Speaker's Lobby during a vote. A lounge-type area just off the House floor, it was open only to members, a very small number of senior staffers, and reporters. We could go and talk with members as they walked through, or ask the staff to go into the chamber during the vote and tell specific members we wanted to talk to them, and they would come out. It's a great arrangement and an easy way to talk to members of Congress; the only downside was men in the Speaker's Lobby have to wear ties.

Whether run by different parties or the same, the House and Senate never got along with each other. Though they share a building, in many ways they live in separate worlds. They have different telephone systems, different cable TV systems, separate staffs, and separate parking stickers. The Senate side of the Capitol is fancier and its offices far more plush. Walking from one side to the other on any floor you can immediately see when you've crossed over.

The restaurants and coffee shops are run separately, too. In fact, the vending machines in the basement sell the same cookies and candy, but you will pay more for them if you are on the Senate side of the building.

An extraordinary display of the silliness this can bring came when there was a shooting at the Navy Yard about a mile away from the Capitol. The shooting was over and the situation contained, but there was still concern a shooter might be loose when the Senate Sergeant at Arms, who is in charge of security, decided as a matter of caution to "lock down" the Senate. So the Senate went out of session, thousands of staffers were ordered to stay in their offices, and the doors were all locked. But the House Sergeant at Arms saw no reason to take such drastic action and so for about two hours the Senate office buildings were locked down while the House ones were operating normally. In the Capitol building itself there were tourists freely moving in and out of the House side of the building, while police were posted at the midpoint to make sure no one entered or left the Senate side.

The House and Senate as legislative bodies also operate in dramatically different ways.

The House is basically a dictatorship of the majority. Whichever party has a majority has complete control through the Rules Committee and determines what bills come to the floor, how long the debate is, what amendments are allowed to be offered, and how the votes will be structured. The minority party has virtually no power at all.

In the Senate, not only the minority party, but every individual senator has enormous power to influence legislation. That's because the complex rules of the Senate allow individual senators to hold up nominations and bills, and because of the filibuster can tie the Senate in knots for days or weeks at a time. No bill can pass without 60 votes and there was only one very brief time during my 23 years there when one party had that big a majority. And so in the Senate nothing can get done without compromise and consensus. While the majority party has substantial power to set the agenda, any senator can offer an amendment and change the debate.

So as long as the majority party can control its members, the House operates efficiently, rolling over the opposition and passing lots of legislation that may or may not become law, while the Senate can sit around for weeks unable to do anything until compromise is reached that allows a bill to pass.

One critical thing reporters needed to do was get some good guidance on votes that were coming so we would know when they would happen and get a sense of how they would come out. In the same way as figuring out ahead of time who would win best picture helped me do my job better covering the Oscars, I could be better prepared to quickly file my stories on a major vote if I had a good idea before the vote which way it was going to go.

A key job in the Congress is that of whip. Democrats and Republicans each have one; their job is to figure out where their members were on a particular issue and work to get them to vote the way their leaders wanted them to. They would tell other party leaders which members needed some extra persuasion (though usually not with an actual whip) and they needed to be able to accurately count the votes. Some were better at it than others and some were more willing to share their information with reporters. Some would just flat out lie to us on occasion in order to try to generate stories that they weren't worried about a vote when in fact they were, but the whips and their deputies were important people for their party leaders and for us.

One of my favorites was Bill Richardson, who served as a deputy Democratic whip while a representative from New Mexico. An extraordinary man and always incredibly nice, he was one of the few leaders in Congress who always told reporters the truth. I could count on him to tell me exactly where the votes were, even when it may not have helped his party for me to know. One of the most important leaders in the Latino community (despite having a profoundly un-Hispanic name), Richardson for a while developed an amazing sideline as a freelance diplomat. President Bill Clinton sent him on a number of sensitive missions and he had a great track record, including freeing American captives from Iraq and North Korea. I missed him when he left Congress, first to be the U.S. Ambassador to the U.N., and later serving as the Secretary of Energy and Governor of New Mexico.

Another of my favorites was Illinois Republican Ray LaHood. Elected in 1994 to the seat held by the retiring Republican Leader Bob Michel, LaHood had worked for Michel and like him was a moderate Republican who liked to work across party lines to get things done.

Though he did look a little bit like Dracula, he was not only one of the most decent members of Congress but actually launched a campaign to try to get others to be nice too. At a time in 1996 when Democrats and Republicans had pretty much stopped talking to each other, much less working together, he and Colorado Democrat David Skaggs decided to launch an effort to restore civility and would start by simply seeing if they could get members of Congress to spend time together. They put together a "civility field trip" at a resort and asked members to bring their families and go out of town for a long weekend, Democrats and Republicans together, to just get to know each other. They traveled by train, which would also help them to spend time together, and I remember covering their departure at Union Station. It was a good idea but sadly didn't work.

One of the Democrats LaHood was nice to in 2004 was the newly elected Senator Barack Obama. LaHood told me once that Obama was surprised when LaHood called him soon after his election to congratulate him and ask him to come visit LaHood's district in Peoria, so they could work together on issues that could help the people of Illinois. When he became president, Obama surprised LaHood by naming him Secretary of Transportation.

There are a number of reasons for the increasing nastiness in Congress and the lack of civility, including the growing partisan divide in the country generally. Some of it is also frankly deliberate. Political consultants understand that making people angry and convincing them to hate the opposition is good for business because it gins up voter interest. Creating anger and mistrust is also sometimes in a more blatant sense good for business. Political fundraisers bring in more money and so make more money for themselves when they make people angry. It's why the National Rifle Association has a political and pecuniary interest in trying to increase paranoia and make people believe in the fiction that the government is out to take their guns away.

Sometimes it has to do with nothing but money. Political opinion shows on radio and television get higher ratings and both the hosts and the station owners make more money when viewers and listeners are angry at someone. There is a profit motive to try to increase the anger and thus make reasonable discussion of issues harder for everyone.

But a few smaller factors in the growing divide specific to Congress have to do with the culture of the capital. When I first came to cover Congress most members lived in Washington. They had to maintain residences in their home states, but spent most of their time in the DC area and raised their families there. That was true of almost all senators and a sizable percentage of House members.

As that started to change more members would come to Washington three days a week for votes, then immediately head back home where their families lived. As a result they never had any social contact with members of the other party.

This is not a small thing. Members of Congress who spent time together at the gym or had kids in the same schools or on the same Little League teams got to know each other. If you were a Democrat who met Republicans at church or at the neighborhood bake sale, you were more likely to become friends—or at least it would be harder to be full-time enemies.

Reaching compromise with someone at any level requires a certain element of trust and it is very difficult to trust someone you don't know. So the growing trend for members of Congress to view themselves as commuters made it far more difficult for friendships to develop, even between members of the same party. That in turn made it harder for the kind of back and forth that is required for Congress to function.

When Bob Michel decided not to seek re-election in 1994 he complained many of his fellow Republicans were more interested in picking fights than passing laws. Nipping at his heels and taking over after his departure was Newt Gingrich of Georgia. Working together quietly was not Gingrich's style. He didn't do anything quietly.

Gingrich was a street fighter of a politician who never talked when he could shout and who was always on the attack. From a reporter's point of view he was a dream. He always made news and was never shy about sharing his views. Sometimes his "facts" were dubious and he seemed to make false accusations with as much vigor as true ones, but he made great copy and things were never boring. His background was academia and he was never short of proposals on absolutely everything. A joke told often by members of his own staff was that there were five large filing cabinets in his office labeled "Newt's ideas" and one labeled "Newt's good ideas."

I always had the feeling that an awful lot of what Gingrich said and did was for effect. He struck me as someone who was far more interested in power than ideology and would take whatever position would get the most attention and get him ahead.

Democrats had controlled the House of Representatives for forty years and had become complacent, too comfortable with their power, and a bit corrupt. Not the "normal" type of bi-partisan corruption where members of Congress raised money from large corporations and interest groups and then did their bidding, or the flagrant kind where members took direct bribes, but the stupid, small kind, like ordering the House bank to cash bad checks for members. There was also widespread corruption at the House post office, with ghost employees, flat-out embezzlement, and blatant fraud: members exchanged stamps, intended for official mailings, for cash.

That scandal brought down Dan Rostenkowski of Illinois, the powerful Chairman of the House Ways and Means Committee, who ended up in jail. And both scandals helped Republicans take over the House in the 1994 elections.

The first two years of the Clinton Administration had been rocky and the President's enormous popularity was fading. A task force headed by first lady Hillary Clinton had come up with a plan for universal health insurance, something Bill Clinton had promised in the campaign, and it had been a disaster. The political groundwork hadn't been laid; the health insurance industry vigorously opposed the bill, and it died in the Democratic Congress. It is no coincidence that when universal health care finally passed during the Obama administration it was written in a way that added billions of dollars to the coffers of private insurance companies.

Newt Gingrich, whose own brushes with scandal would later help end his congressional career, saw an opportunity. Though congressional elections are usually decided by local issues and local personalities, he helped put together a national campaign that knocked Democrats out of power in Congress for the first time since 1954. There were several other factors, including gun control. In 1993 Congress passed the Brady Bill, named for Ronald Reagan's first press secretary, James Brady, who was shot and severely wounded in the assassination attempt on the president. The new law required background checks to buy a handgun.

Then in 1994, Congress passed and President Clinton signed the assault weapons ban, which tried to stop military-style weapons, which are designed to kill people as quickly as possible, from being bought by individuals. It was intensely controversial. One of the difficulties was defining an "assault weapon," since some of these weapons could be used for hunting, and of course any gun could be claimed to be purchased for self defense.

The National Rifle Association, which represents the interests of gun manufacturers as much or more than those of gun owners, vehemently fought against both measures and managed to water the assault weapons ban down substantially. Still, it had been defeated, and set out in 1996 to send a message. It poured money into the election, and wielded its substantial ability to mobilize the votes of gun owners, playing a major role in helping Republicans gain control of Congress. There has been some debate over how much of a role the NRA played in that election, but clearly politicians of both parties believed it was critical, because in the 20 years I covered Congress after that election the NRA never lost a vote. Members of both parties quaked before them and even after increasingly horrendous school shootings, Congress never passed another major gun control law and the assault weapons ban was allowed to lapse in 2004.

After so many decades in the wilderness, the Republicans' first order of business upon their takeover was revenge. Bottled up anger over the way they had been treated for so long boiled over, and the Democrats were marginalized in small and petty ways. Key Democratic leaders were kicked out of their plush offices and in one case sent to the basement; thousands of staff members hired by Democrats lost their jobs, and suddenly parking places for Democrats started disappearing. Beyond this, a program led by the new majority whip Tom DeLay (a nasty but very effective politician who would later have his own ignominious downfall), set out to make sure Democrats lost their jobs in other places. He pressured major lobby groups and associations to get rid of their Democratic lobbyists and staffers and replace them with Republicans, making clear if they didn't do that they wouldn't be welcome anymore. And being welcome was important, because during the Gingrich years Republican lobbyists wrote much of the legislation.

The Senate had a very different history and changed party control a number of times over these same years, including one strange period of a few months when they were evenly split 50-50 and tried to share power. By the time I retired in 2014, the Senate had become much more like the House and its partisan divides would become more personal and bitter but that hadn't happened yet in the 1990s. In fact after changing offices following a couple of elections, Senate leaders decided it was a silly waste of time and money, and so permanently assigned one set of offices to the Democratic leader and another to the Republican leader, regardless of who was in the majority.

The Republicans got the better offices but that was because everyone liked and respected Republican Leader Bob Dole, who loved to sit out on his office's generous balcony and sunbathe, and no one wanted to take that away from him. To this day it is known as the "Dole Balcony."

The first few years of the Gingrich speakership was a heady time in Congress and a great time to be a reporter there. Gingrich would hold court almost daily with televised news conferences and would always make news. The focus of news in Washington shifted dramatically and instead of most stories originating from the White House with members of Congress reacting, it was the opposite, and the House Republicans were setting the agenda.

That's not to say they were getting very much passed into law, but they were certainly changing the conversation. They came in with a specific agenda they called the "Contract with America," which had provided a unity and focus that was rare for either party. House Republicans proceeded to pass one major bill after the other, including a Balanced Budget Amendment to the Constitution, the line-item veto, and bills to shut down various government departments. Almost none of their contract became law.

One interesting fight was over the funding of public broadcasting. PBS and NPR had long been favorite targets of conservatives, who could rile up their base with the claim that tax dollars were being used to fund news organizations with a liberal bias. But when Gingrich tried to strip funds away from public radio and television, he made an interesting discovery. It turns out that while Washington Republicans love to hate public television, out in the country things were quite different. Not only was there huge support for "Sesame Street" and other children's programming, but some of the biggest supporters of local PBS stations were business leaders in their communities, the same people who contributed to local orchestras and cultural groups— and many of them were Republicans.

It was the first issue on which Gingrich ran into serious opposition from within his own party in the House. He had to eventually back down and PBS kept its funding.

As Gingrich set about trying to re-make the government, the Senate was also under Republican control but Bob Dole, while also a conservative and strong believer in fiscal responsibility, was a realist and a more seasoned political leader. He was also wonderfully honest with reporters. Every time the House would pass some new bill to shut down a department or stop funding an agency, we would ask Dole what he thought and often his answer when there were no cameras or microphones around was a wry smile and the line, "They really need some adult supervision over there."

We didn't report that because getting Bob Dole in trouble for his candor was the last thing any of us wanted to do. He was able to be honest because he knew we wouldn't use that type of quote. But his opinion was extremely helpful, letting us accurately report that the Republican Senate was "unlikely" to take up the House-passed measure. There is no question Gingrich got the message.

It was no surprise that when it came time to agree on a budget, Republicans were demanding spending cuts that President Clinton wouldn't agree to, and the crisis grew through the fall of 1995. The Republican Congress passed several spending plans that President Clinton vetoed and when the last temporary spending measure expired on November 14th, the government had to shut down all non-essential services.

There was a brief, temporary fix but then the government shut down again and stayed shut down for almost a month. Federal workers stopped getting paid and besides causing a lot of grief for people needing government services or just wanting to go into a national park, it ended up costing the taxpayers a huge amount of money and the economy billions in lost tourist dollars and contractor payments. Politically it helped President Clinton and hurt the Republicans, who had been riding high for most of the year.

That's because polls showed the public overwhelmingly blamed Republicans for the shutdown. That perception was solidified when Gingrich told reporters that part of his problem in dealing with President Clinton was that the president had "snubbed him" when he rode on Air Force One to Israel for the funeral of Yitzhak Rabin. Gingrich complained Clinton hadn't come back to talk to him about the budget impasse and then made him leave the plane by the back stairs with reporters, staffers, and other guests, instead of walking down the front steps with the president.

I don't believe the shutdown was really caused by Gingrich throwing a temper tantrum because he had to leave Air Force One by the back stairs, but it wasn't completely out of character either, and probably did contribute to the length of time it took for the two sides to finally sit down and resolve their differences. The political fallout from the shutdown actually led to some good things, as Republicans in Congress realized they were hurting themselves. They started seeking compromise and there were some important accomplishments.

The budget picture had started improving after President Clinton, with only Democratic votes, pushed through a large tax increase for the wealthiest Americans in 1993. As the economy boomed during these years, tax revenue increased. When that was combined with substantial spending cuts that were pushed by the Republicans in Congress, including a major welfare reform measure, the deficit started dropping dramatically and for each of his last three years in office President Clinton presided over surpluses, in which the government took in more money than it spent and started paying down its debt. That all ended under President George W. Bush, who cut taxes in 2001, then sent the deficit into the stratosphere with the wars in Afghanistan and Iraq.

Dick Armey of Texas who, like Gingrich, played a key role in the Republican takeover of Congress, was majority leader, Gingrich's number two. A plainspoken conservative, he was friendly and gruff and fun to cover; he always made news and was wonderfully quotable.

Once a week he would sit down with the half-dozen or so network radio reporters for an on-the-record roundtable interview. A memorable one was when we asked about an effort to raise the minimum wage and he told us that would only happen "over my dead body." An even more memorable line came in what would be his last interview with the network radio reporters who covered Congress. He was assailing Democrats including Barney Frank, a liberal from Massachusetts, who as the Democrat's best debater and an expert on House rules, often caused grief for the new Republican majority. It was only later as we were listening to the tape that it registered that he had called Frank, who is openly gay, "Barney Fag."

We were pretty sure he hadn't meant to say that out loud, but it was newsworthy and as Frank said later it "can't slip off your tongue if it isn't on your mind." It certainly didn't seem out of character that Armey and other House Republican leaders referred to him that way in private.

We decided the fairest thing to do was to give Armey a chance to explain it before any of us put it on the air, and called his press secretary, Ed Gillespie. He immediately accused us of lying and insisted Armey never said it. We invited him to come to our offices in the Radio-TV Gallery, where he listened to the tape, which was clear as day. He again said it wasn't true and then began to threaten us. He first told us if we reported what Armey said they would accuse us of making it up, despite the fact it had been taped on six different recorders. When that didn't work, he told us if we reported it Armey would never talk to any of us again. He then returned to his office and began calling our bosses at CBS, NBC, ABC, NPR, and the rest, making the same threats and thus forcing our hands. With threats like that, there was no choice left and we had to use the tape.

Later that day Armey took the House floor condemning liberal reporters "twisting his words," blowing a "slip of the tongue" out of proportion, thus turning a little story into a big one and guaranteeing the tape would play on radio and television for days.

Armey, who was majority leader until 2003, never held another interview with network radio reporters and when I'd pass him in the hall he would say "hi," then smile and declare, "I'm not supposed to talk to you," and walk away.

Gillespie went on to be Chairman of the Republican Party, then co-founded a lobbying firm with a top Democrat and made millions in Washington's rarified world of bipartisan influence peddling, before running and losing in a Virginia senate race.

When Armey left Congress he cashed in too, and became an important player in the conservative groups that raised millions of dollars in the name of the Tea Party.

ICELAND 2010

After more than a month of hot steamy weather in Washington I was more than ready to head to Iceland. The more ice, the better!

Reykjavik is a small capital in a very small country of only 300,000, all of them tall and blond (not counting the elves and trolls who seem to be widely believed in).

In a land with no trees to speak of, and lots of rain and wind, many of the buildings use corrugated iron siding, which is very practical if not very attractive. For a city known as a party and music center it appears at first glance more dowdy than hip, but is a pleasant place.

Though the economic collapse here cut prices in dollars in half it is still a very expensive place. They also have a language filled with absurdly long, unpronounceable words but everyone speaks English. They only use first names, even in the phone book, because last names aren't family names, and in most families they all have different last names. If your father was Sven your last name is Svenson, and your sister's is Svendóttir. Your mother's name didn't change when she married.

The whole country is sitting on hot water. The power is mostly geothermal and the hot water that gushes out of the ground, literally boiling at 212 degrees, heats all the homes, and more importantly, all the pools and hot tubs.

I walked to a large hot pool complex near my hotel and it was a trip. It was clearly the place to be on a Saturday afternoon, with hundreds of people in the huge lap pool, giant children's pool with water slides and six hot tubs ranging from warm to scalding, and one with heated sea water. At $3.50 for the day, it is far and away the best bargain in Iceland.

They are sticklers about hygiene, with a requirement to shower without a bathing suit before entering the pools. Monitors make sure you do and hysterically funny illustrated signs show you the dirty parts of your body where you have to wash with soap.

The food has been very good with lots of seafood, fish, and lamb, with wonderful fresh breads everywhere. I was also happily surprised to learn they make excellent chocolates and very rich ice cream.

On the other hand they eat puffin, whale, horsemeat, and petrified shark.

After a day on my own, I joined my 16-member Overseas Adventure Tour group for my trip around Iceland. As we headed out, the landscape was green and lush, without any trees but with fjords and rivers and hundreds of waterfalls.

At the site of an ancient convent, we climbed what our guide described as a "small mountain," which was somewhat steep and wet from the very frequent rain. But if you climb it in complete silence, then circle a large rock structure at the top and face east (towards the fjord, not Mecca) you can make a wish. I'll let you know how that turns out.

Arriving in Stykkishólmur, we find a picturesque little town on a fjord filled with islands. Every town and village in Iceland has a Lutheran church and a hot springs public pool. I take in the church from a distance and walk straight to the pool for a pre-dinner soak. Less fancy than in Reykjavik, but very nice with hot tubs, a big pool, and a water slide.

The scenery is wonderful as we tour the west coast with lava fields and sandy beaches and more waterfalls than I can count. After one hike, we end up on the deck of a small cafe enjoying the first sunshine so far. It's a tiny, out of the way place, and there are only a few other people there. Some in our group greet a friendly lady named Amy, who says she and her husband and teenage daughter are from Minnesota. I wait until they are alone before I go over and chat with Senator Amy Klobuchar about how small a world it is, and she is surprised to have run into the only person in all of Iceland who would recognize her.

There is only one road around the island and we are going the same direction, so run into each other three more times.

We get the skinny on the petrified shark. It is the Greenland shark, which is poisonous if simply cooked and eaten, so they seal it in boxes and bury it for three weeks, then hang it outside in the air for three months, ending up with what they (and no one else) considers a delicacy. It smells awful but a small piece eaten with bread isn't so bad, especially when followed by some local schnapps, which we buy at a store that only sells liquor and baby clothes.

The day ends with an evening cruise on the fjord with puffin and some rare white-tailed eagles. The crew drops a net and drags up crabs, clams, sea urchin, scallops—and some starfish that we throw back. The rest we open up and eat. I'd never had a raw scallop straight out of the sea like that and it was delicious.

On the long drive to the far north of Iceland, some of it on a gravel road, the landscape was barren but dramatic. Green, treeless expanses between mountains and the sea and fjords with sheep wandering about and the occasional farm or village, always with a church. Some, oddly, are painted black.

We visited the re-constructed Viking home of Erik the Red and his son Leif Erikson, who, as every Icelander is happy to tell you, discovered America almost 500 years before that pretender Christopher Columbus.

I noticed something nice about the showers. Because the hot water comes straight out of the ground, there is no need for water heaters, and the water is hot as soon as you turn it on and stays that way as long as you want.

A whale-watching trip yielded a few whales and lots of seasick people in very rough seas and cold weather.

We visited one of Iceland's most beautiful waterfalls, Godafoss, or "waterfall of the gods," so named because in 1000 AD the leader of Iceland, who made the nation Christian to keep the peace, threw his sculptures of the pagan gods into that waterfall after the decision. It has two magnificent wide falls with a rushing narrow chute between them.

Lake Myvatn is in a stunning, steamy, desolate landscape of lava fields, green hills, and steaming hot springs, steam vents and bubbling mud pots. Took a hike through an other-worldly lava field with cliffs, spires, caves and shapes like animals, and of course the trolls who are said to live here.

We had lunch at the "Cow Shed," with glass walls between the dining room and the barn where the cows are being milked. I have no idea why they would think that's a good idea.

The public hot springs pool in Akureyri was the best yet, with multiple indoor and outdoor pools and hot tubs, a steam room, hot waterfalls to sit under, great kids' pools, two water slides, and an ice cream stand.

The food with the tour group has been very good, including a home-cooked meal with a salty, retired fishing boat captain and his wife. But on my own one night, I tried the Icelandic lobster, which while smaller than our crustaceans in Maine, was very tasty. At the next table I saw a hamburger with béarnaise sauce served with a fried egg on top of the bun.

While the food here is expensive, people in Iceland don't tip and tax is included in the menu price, which helps.

Crime is not a problem here. Bikes are never locked, farm stands are all on the honor system, and last year there were two murders in the whole country.

We flew from Akureyri International Airport, which has a duty-free shop but none of that bothersome security, before boarding our twin engine prop plane back to Reykjavik to explore the southern sites.

We visited a field near a large lake where the Althing, Iceland's parliament, widely advertised as the oldest continuous legislature in the world, first met. It is a questionable claim since the parliament was dissolved for a few hundred years when the King of Denmark ruled Iceland, but it's still a lot older than our Congress and not nearly as crazy. We watched steam shoot into the air at Geysir, another active geothermal area, from which all other geysers get their name.

Visited Gullfoss, one of the biggest and most dramatic waterfalls. It featured an incredible volume of water cascading into a steep narrow river canyon.

Our guide, a retired banker who would occasionally break into song and recite long Icelandic poems, made a stop at a little rural church to show us the grave of chess champion and renowned crazy person Bobby Fischer.

We stayed two nights in the small town of Selfoss at a modern hotel right on a river, only a ten-minute walk from the hot spring pools. They let me in free and I wasn't sure if it was because of the crutches or because I hadn't shaved in a week and looked like a vagabond without a króna to my name.

Drove along high cliffs with lots more waterfalls and volcanoes, including Eyjafjallajökull, the one that not long before had spewed out enough ash to shut down all the European airports. If anything, the landscapes are even more dramatic in the south than they were up north.

We visited a black sand beach with towering rock formations and saw a dog barking furiously at a swimming seal.

We did a short paddle raft trip on a glacial river that flowed through a pretty gorge and was fun, though even with a full wetsuit was very, very cold. The paddling gear came from Idaho and the guides from Nepal.

Our final stop on the group tour is the famous Blue Lagoon, a huge turquoise hot springs pool created by the runoff of a geothermal power plant.

After two hours or so the sun came out, so I abandoned my group and just stayed for the rest of the day soaking in the lagoon, putting white silica mud on my face, sitting in the sun, standing under the powerful hot waterfall, eating ice cream, and sharing a lava cave sauna with tourists from many lands.

Back in Reykjavik I hit some museums and stopped at the city's most famous hot dog stand, reputed to be the best in a nation that takes its hot dogs very seriously. Bill Clinton, a man of many appetites, ate here. All they sell are hot dogs and Cokes and I had one of each. I'm not particularly a hot dog aficionado but it was very tasty (they mix lamb in with all those other assorted parts).

I sampled some of Reykjavik's finer restaurants and was not disappointed. The halibut was superb at Fjalakötturinn, and if I could pronounce it, I'd recommend it. After dinner, I headed to a local square where kids were skateboarding, and had a chocolate-dipped ice cream cone. It was barely 60 degrees but that's summer here.

Visited Reykjavik's oldest hot springs pool near the city center. No fancy water slides, but a great old building with private changing cabinets with chairs and mirrors, and big hot tubs outside on a deck overlooking the city.

On my final day in Iceland I went to the amazingly pronounceable "Fish Market" for an extraordinary seven-course tasting menu with overly large portions of calamari tempura, short ribs, watermelon salad, monkfish, cod, salmon topped with lobster sauce, salmon roe, cucumbers, and nuts. And for dessert, piña colada mousse with pineapple sorbet.

Always nice to leave a country with a blast of gluttony.

THAT WACKY CONGRESS

The accomplishments of the Republican Congress under Speaker Gingrich and President Clinton on the budget and other issues didn't change the partisan nastiness, which reached its zenith in 1998.

That was also the year that I moved to CBS News. There had been a lot of consolidation in the radio news business and the company that ran the combined Mutual and NBC Networks was gobbled up by CBS's parent company in a very convoluted business deal. Both networks were shut down at the end of the summer (though a much smaller version of NBC Radio was later re-started and lasted a few years before it too went away). These two defunct networks traced their history to the birth of radio; NBC was the first radio network, founded in 1926, and Mutual began in 1934.

Just before the meeting at which all the talented people working at these networks were told they were being laid off, I and my friend and colleague Peter Maer were taken aside and told we would still have jobs and were both being moved over to CBS Radio. We would later meet with CBS News Vice President Harvey Nagler, who would formally offer us jobs as correspondents at CBS News, keeping the same beats.

When I started with CBS in September of 1998, I stayed in the same office at the Capitol and my first big story came right away with the impeachment of President Clinton. His administration had foolishly agreed to appoint a special prosecutor, Kenneth Starr, to investigate a variety of allegations of scandals Republicans had been hammering away on, mostly dealing with some shady land deals in Arkansas. But Starr couldn't find any crimes there, so focused instead on the charge that Clinton had an affair with a young White House intern named Monica Lewinsky. Anyone who knew Bill Clinton at all knew he had a wandering eye, and in fact one of his previous episodes of adultery had come out during the 1992 campaign, when a young woman named Gennifer Flowers sold her story to the tabloids, backed up with recordings of phone calls.

What supposedly escalated this latest affair into a scandal that so threatened the Republic that impeachment was called for, was that he lied about it under oath. As a general rule men who cheat on their wives lie about it. Lying is indeed an intrinsic part of adultery. But this was a set-up.

Lewinsky had foolishly confided in an older co-worker Linda Tripp, clearly not the right person to trust. Tripp secretly recorded their conversations and fed the information to Clinton's political enemies and later to Starr.

In a deposition in an unconnected case of a lawsuit by another woman who claimed to have had an affair with him, Clinton was asked if he ever had sex with Monica Lewinsky and said he didn't. He would later claim he answered truthfully because oral sex didn't count, but in fact had no idea, nor could he have, that those lawyers already knew about Lewinsky, and knew there was proof in the form of a semen stain on a blue dress Lewinsky for some bizarre reason had never washed, and had told Tripp about.

When Starr issued his public report summarizing his findings it was less a legal document than pure pornography. He included every salacious detail he could find and there were plenty, which provided great fodder to Republicans, whose only goal was to humiliate and embarrass a popular president who had gotten the best of them in near-constant battles.

Not that Clinton was innocent—far from it—but we briefly became the laughingstock of the world as our Congress set out to impeach a president who presided over a booming economy and a balanced federal budget because he had an affair.

The Starr report posed a unique challenge to broadcast reporters since there was enormous competitive pressure to immediately report on what was in it. I was in my booth ready to get on the air as I was handed the report and started to read it. There was yelling in my ear that CNN and others were already reading it live and I had to get on the air.

So I did, but kept trying to read ahead as I read out loud, and several times just stopped because I wasn't going to read salacious details of sex acts live on the radio. Not all news is appropriate for children but radio news is heard in cars and kitchens. I knew kids were listening and did my best to skip over the most obscene parts. The description of Lewinsky performing oral sex on Clinton while he was on the phone with a member of Congress was memorable, but the detailed description of him wetting a cigar in his mouth and putting it in her vagina, then back in his mouth, was too much, and despite requests I never reported it on the radio.

The story was enormous and Republicans in the House decided they had enough to move forward with impeachment. They knew there was no way they could ever get a two-thirds vote in the Senate to actually convict Clinton and remove him from office and didn't really want to, since that would make Al Gore president. But they could try to hurt Clinton politically and hurt Democrats in the process.

Despite the high and mighty talk about perjury and obstruction of justice, the bottom line was they were going after a president they didn't like because with the semen stain on the blue dress they could prove he lied about an affair.

The hypocrisy was off the scale in a city where power is an aphrodisiac and adultery is as common as lunches with lobbyists. Though there were some quiet warnings of the Pandora's box being opened, they were ignored, and more than a few prominent Republicans fell victim to the sexual witch-hunt they began.

The Speaker of the House Newt Gingrich, who railed endlessly about Clinton's moral failings, was at the time having an affair with a staff member in his office, cheating on his second wife, who he had an affair with before divorcing his first wife. The staffer, Callista Bisek, would later become his third wife. Gingrich was ousted from the speakership in November of that year, after a poor showing for Republicans in the midterm elections and amid growing uneasiness about him from the religious right.

As Republicans continued to pursue impeachment, Larry Flynt, the publisher of Penthouse Magazine, offered one million dollars for evidence of adultery by Republican leaders of the impeachment drive and it was open season. Rumors abounded, fear was palpable, and as tabloids and news organizations found out about various affairs, Republican members of Congress would go public with mea culpas, apologizing but stressing their adultery wasn't as bad as President Clinton's because they never lied about it in a deposition.

My favorite was from Henry Hyde, the chairman of the House Judiciary Committee, which took the lead on impeachment. Hyde was a nice man of deep principles, best known for his tireless efforts to restrict abortion. I always enjoyed dealing with Hyde and he was generally liked and respected. His admission of adultery in the middle of the impeachment process was memorable for one great line. After "Salon" published a story of his affair with a married woman (broken up when the woman's husband confronted Hyde's wife), Hyde issued what by then had become a regular flow of "I was wrong, but not as bad as Clinton" statements but then added a new justification, that his was a "youthful indiscretion."

A quick bit of arithmetic showed the affair occurred when Hyde was 41, which led to a good story, some much needed comic relief, and great news for everyone in their 40s that the clock for "youthful indiscretions" was still running.

After the judiciary committee took its party line vote for impeachment, the process moved to the House floor. With Gingrich's ouster there was a power vacuum that Republican whip Tom DeLay, one of the meanest, most ruthless and effective political leaders I've covered, quickly filled.

A group of moderate Republicans and Democrats began pushing for a censure resolution, a way for both Democrats and Republicans in Congress to clearly express they felt President Clinton's behavior was unacceptable (which it clearly was) without having a partisan vote for impeachment. As the House vote approached they had a bipartisan majority for censure but Delay maneuvered through the House Rules Committee to make sure that vote wouldn't take place. He would thus force Republicans who thought impeachment was not warranted to vote for it anyway, since the only alternative would be voting for no punishment at all.

And so on December 19, 1998, in a rare Saturday session, the House voted almost entirely along party lines to bring two impeachment charges, one for perjury, the other for obstruction of justice. Two other charges were rejected.

The debate was intense and led to another incredibly dramatic moment. Bob Livingston, a Republican from Louisiana, had been selected to replace Gingrich as speaker and was set to be formally elected when the new Congress convened the following month. He was a popular fellow who chaired the House Appropriations Committee. He was a good choice. DeLay was the power player, but was way too divisive a figure to ever be speaker. But like so many others who were behind the impeachment train, Livingston too had committed adultery and learned he was about to be exposed. And so on the House floor at the height of the impeachment debate, Livingston announced he had also had an affair and would not run for speaker and would resign from Congress. It was a stunning development and highlighted the hypocrisy of the whole proceeding but didn't change the outcome. For only the second time in American history the House had brought impeachment charges against a president. And just like the first time against Andrew Johnson after the Civil War, it was less about misconduct than about politics.

When the new Congress convened in January, Republicans in the house decided to go with a safe choice for speaker, Denis Hastert of Illinois. An affable fellow who'd been a high school gym teacher before coming to Congress and went by the nickname "Coach," he was generally seen as a pick who wouldn't make waves and would be a figurehead while Tom DeLay called the shots (though in the end that didn't work out so well for DeLay, who was forced out after being indicted in a scheme to violate Texas campaign finance laws).

Meanwhile, over in the Senate, they had to conduct an impeachment trial and were none too happy about it. The House appointed a group of Republican members as "prosecutors," and Clinton would be defended by the White House counsel and other lawyers. Supreme Court Chief Justice William Rehnquist would preside (wearing his custom-made robe with the ostentatious yellow stripes on the sleeves) but the Senate would decide the rules. And while House Republicans wanted a show trial with Monica Lewinsky marched onto the Senate floor to testify, it was not to be.

The Senate had a Republican majority and plenty of partisan rancor towards President Clinton, but also was more steeped in history and tradition. Though in later years it would become increasingly more like the House in its partisan nastiness, it wasn't like that yet. There was an extraordinary closed-door meeting of all the senators in the small and ornate Old Senate Chamber (where the Senate met from 1819 to 1859) to decide how to handle this trial.

The verdict was of course pre-determined, since it takes a two-thirds vote to convict and remove a president and no Democrat would vote that way and in the end not all Republicans did either. But in that meeting, West Virginia's Democratic Senator Robert Byrd, who literally wrote the book on the history of the Senate (several of them, actually), argued passionately that the reputation of the Senate was at risk and was more important than any political considerations. So in the end, furious House Republican prosecutors were only able to take videotaped testimony from Monica Lewinsky and two other witnesses who had no meaningful information, and play some short excerpts. No live witnesses ever appeared and the short "trial" consisted mostly of long speeches. The Senate, most concerned about maintaining its dignity, deliberated in private, took its anticlimactic votes, and ended the whole sorry chapter.

Not a good day for the country, but a wonderful day for me going on the air with Walter Cronkite. He was of course a hero to me and most every other broadcast journalist, but by that time had already been retired as the CBS Evening News Anchor for 17 years. His relationship with CBS News had soured. There was no love lost between Cronkite and his successor Dan Rather, and he was never called upon to appear on CBS TV again. But Mike Freedman, the general manager of CBS Radio news at that time managed to convince Cronkite to appear on CBS Radio in a series of special historical broadcasts.

Cronkite happened to be in the studio in New York that day taping when Mike asked if he'd like to open the CBS Radio newscast at the hour of the historic Senate impeachment vote. He agreed and Mike decided not to tell stations in advance (one news director at a local CBS station later said he nearly ran off the road). And so the sounder went off, and on came what was still all those years later the most recognized voice in America. Cronkite read a few lines on the historic vote just getting underway then said, "and now with more on the story here's Congressional correspondent Bob Fuss, live on Capitol Hill."

Now we had a rule in those days that correspondents didn't say each other's names on the air when we took a handoff because that really could get a bit out of control and wasted precious seconds. But there was no way I was going to follow that rule that day and I proudly said

"Walter" before launching into my report. I knew I'd never have another chance to take a handoff from the legendary Walter Cronkite and indeed I was the last person at CBS News to do so.

After President George W. Bush was elected in 2000, he had a Republican Congress and moved quickly in his first year to reverse the tax increases passed during the Clinton Administration. He passed a massive tax cut bill in 2001 that slashed rates for top earners. Many Democrats went along since everyone likes tax cuts; there was no substantial opposition from Republicans who fought so hard for deficit reduction when there was a Democratic president but seemed perfectly happy to see deficits rise again with a Republican in the White House.

Then came September 11, 2001.

I had been out sick suffering with kidney stones and that Tuesday was to be my first day back. I was driving into work when I heard about the attacks on the car radio. I quickly realized I wouldn't be able to get into the District and instead headed for the Pentagon. I parked the car and walked as close as I could get and spent the rest of the day covering the Pentagon attack.

Washington, like the rest of the country, was in a state of shock and disbelief that an attack like this could happen here. The point of terrorism is to terrorize and in that regard the terrorists behind the September 11th attacks did exactly what they set out to do. The first response involved a lot of panic including shutting down the entire air transportation system for two days.

Partisanship evaporated for a while as Congress and the whole country united. But the panic was still strong and just three days after the attacks Congress passed a law authorizing the president to take "any military action" against those behind the attacks or thought to be planning other attacks. Congress hadn't declared war since World War II and didn't declare this war either, instead simply handing over its constitutional authority to the president. The vaguely worded measure not only allowed President Bush to invade Afghanistan but was also used to justify military and CIA activities against terrorists or perceived terrorists all around the world. Since "terrorism" is a method by which weak groups attack stronger governments, a "war against terrorism," pretty much by definition, can never be won since there is no way to decide when such a war is over. Congress ended up, with very little thought to the consequences, giving extraordinary power to the president and all future presidents to wage war whenever and wherever they wanted.

Then, still in the midst of the panic created by the reprehensible attack, Congress passed the USA Patriot Act in October. There were a few legislators who warned this was an overreaction and the government was being given too much power to spy on Americans and toss aside constitutional protections. For many years those debates went on over this law, often focused on the government using the power it had been given to force libraries to turn over lists of what books Americans were reading. Few people inside or outside the government knew the extent to which those powers would escalate to the point where a dozen years later it was revealed by the Edward Snowden leaks that the massive security apparatus that had been created was in fact tracking every phone call made every day by every American and reading our e-mail too.

Everyone agreed airport security had to be tightened up and the most obvious things, like hardening cockpit doors and putting air marshals on planes, were done fairly quickly. Security at airports was at the time the responsibility of airlines and airports and they used private contractors to do the work. There was substantial debate over whether the federal government should take that over, but eventually the TSA was created and the government re-organized with the creation of the Department of Homeland Security. The intelligence agencies were basically given a blank check by Congress and spent uncounted billions of dollars on often-duplicative programs to try to make America safer.

For reasons that remain unclear to this day President Bush decided in 2003 to go to war against Iraq. Congress voted to authorize military action (again declining a declaration of war that would imply actual responsibility for the decision) and when the war began I was temporarily assigned to the Pentagon, which we were staffing 24 hours a day.

The Pentagon is a strange place to cover and extremely frustrating. The best reporters there, including David Martin of CBS and Jim Miklaszewski of NBC, spent years building up sources all over the building to bypass the large press operation most of us had to rely on.

I was working 12-hour shifts seven days a week. At least once a day, there would be reports that someone might have found the weapons of mass destruction, the reason given for the war, along with the patently absurd suggestion that Iraqi strongman Saddam Hussein was somehow cooperating with the Al Qaeda terrorists, who were his enemies long before they became ours.

The Bush administration came down hard on any reporters who expressed doubt that the weapons were there or would find their way to terrorists. It took years for most Americans to reach the conclusion many of those covering the story came to fairly early on: that the weapons of mass destruction never existed.

One interesting thing that happened at the Pentagon was a split between the political interests of the Secretary of Defense, Donald Rumsfeld, and those of the services—the Army, Navy, Air Force, and Marines. They each had their own public relations operation and the Joint Chiefs of Staff had its own small press shop too.

The administration's goal was to make the war look easy and successful and to keep alive the idea that they were looking for the WMDs. But the services wanted those fighting the war to get the attention and respect they deserved, and that meant the public knowing about the sacrifices they were making.

We would often take information from one press office and then run it by the others and try to find something closer to the truth. Frankly it was not easy and I pretty much started each day assuming I was being lied to, which frequently turned out to be the case. Of course politicians lie, too, but I was very happy when my assignment at the Pentagon was over.

A lot of my time covering Congress was spent watching congressional hearings. They fall into several broad categories. There are hearings to gather information and create a record for legislation, investigative hearings into real problems, investigative hearings to try to embarrass a president of the other party, and the most common, hearings to put on a political show.

One of the most memorable hearings was called by California Democrat Henry Waxman in 1994. Waxman, who at times seemed to relish his role as a pugnacious battler against special interests, played a major role in some of the most important consumer protection issues undertaken by Congress. He fought and won many battles over clean air and water and was a key player in the health care debate.

He was also a tireless opponent of the tobacco industry and that day, called the heads of all the tobacco companies in to testify. After they were sworn in, he asked each of them to say, under oath, if cigarettes were addictive. Every one of them answered "no," and insisted the science is still out over whether their product causes cancer and other diseases. They did acknowledge they manipulate the amount of nicotine in their cigarettes, though claimed that was only for taste, not to get people hooked.

While there were calls after that hearing for perjury charges, they were never brought and weren't needed. The point had been made and it marked a significant turning point in the growing public sentiment against smoking.

While that hearing was only a few hours long, the confirmation hearing for Supreme Court Justice Clarence Thomas in October of 1991 was a lot longer and far more dramatic affair. For the first few days Thomas, who would turn out to be one of the most consistent and reliable conservatives on the court, took a careful course saying he had no opinion about abortion rights or other key issues that would come before him.

But then came Anita Hill, a law professor who had previously worked for Thomas when he ran the Equal Employment Opportunity Commission. She had told Senate staffers that Thomas had sexually harassed her on the job, and not in a subtle way. She said he repeatedly pressed her for dates, talked about sex and his own sexual prowess, and once pointed to what he said was a pubic hair on a soft drink can.

The testimony was electrifying and Republicans on the committee went after Hill with a vengeance, accusing her of being a "scorned woman" and making it all up. Thomas denied it all and made headlines by saying he was the victim of what he called a "high-tech lynching." There were several other women who told Senate staffers that Thomas had sexually harassed them on the job too, but they were never called as witnesses.

One of the hardest things to explain to people in covering the Thomas hearings was that there was no one involved in the process whose interest was getting at the truth. Democratic senators were interested in trying to embarrass the nominee and President Bush, while avoiding charges of racism and satisfying those who charged them with sexism. (It didn't help that there was not a single woman on the Judiciary Committee.) Republicans' interests were in discrediting Hill and anyone else who attacked Thomas, especially Democrats, and to clear his way to confirmation. None of them was interested in simply getting to the bottom of it and finding out what actually happened; the hearings never conclusively did.

Debates in newsrooms are common. News judgment can be very subjective and there are frequent disagreements and arguments over which stories are important and which ones aren't. Very often these come down to finding the right balance between telling people what they want to hear and telling them what they need to know. You do need a balance because the best newscast in the world is of no value if no one is listening to it. So there are constant debates over whether to lead the news with the latest developments in Afghanistan or the latest arrest of actress Lindsay Lohan. Sadly, Lohan sometimes wins out.

Sometimes the debates got heated and sometimes they broke along age lines. I recall the day in 1977 when the news came in that Elvis Presley had died. The younger members of the staff at UPI Radio argued strenuously that we needed to send a reporter to Memphis immediately, while some of the older managers felt it was a story that would die down after a few hours. Thankfully the reporter got sent.

Some arguments were just plain silly. A manager at CBS in New York one day told me I should do a story on a group of beer distributors who were coming to Capitol Hill to meet with their members of Congress to oppose increasing the beer tax. When I looked into it I learned there hadn't been any proposals to increase the beer tax for at least five years and the distributors came to Washington every year to keep in touch with members of Congress. When I explained there was no story here, the response was that I should do a story about the fact that beer distributors were coming to Congress to lobby against a tax increase that no one was proposing. It was one of those times I just threw up my hands and did the story hoping the anchors, producers, and stations were smart enough not to use it.

Whenever things get boring in Congress, a sex scandal seems to pop up. Some are serious, most are stupid, and a few are extremely entertaining. There was a string of them involving members sending out dirty pictures of themselves on the Internet. Chris Lee, a married Republican from New York, posted pictures sans shirt on Craigslist, then followed up with e-mails using his own name on his congressional e-mail account. New York Democrat Anthony Wiener sent his pictures sans pants on Twitter, and at one point used the pseudonym "Carlos Danger."

A common theme in congressional sex scandals was Republicans who had stressed conservative family values in their campaigns getting caught with their pants down. Mark Souder, a Republican from Indiana who was a major backer of mandatory abstinence education, had to resign after an affair with a female member of his staff. In that same year, 2010, New York Republican Eric Massa resigned after he admitted groping many of his male staffers, though he insisted it was mostly just "tickling."

Louisiana Republican Vance McAllister fell victim to his own security system when a surveillance camera in his district office caught him making out with a female member of his staff.

The scandal that brought down Nevada Republican Senator John Ensign had more serious overtones, though it too began with an affair. In this case it was with the wife of a close friend at a time both she and her husband were working for Ensign. When the man discovered the affair, Ensign funneled hush money to try to keep things quiet, but it didn't work. It rarely does.

Idaho Republican Senator Larry Craig was arrested in an airport bathroom and pled guilty to soliciting sex from a male undercover officer. He tried to change his plea later and vigorously denied he was gay but his political career was over.

One senator who survived and even thrived after a sex scandal that might have brought down a lesser politician was Louisiana Senator David Vitter, whose name showed up in the address book of the famous "D.C. Madam" after her large prostitution ring was broken up. Vitter would only acknowledge that he had "sinned" and asked for forgiveness. He got it from the voters of Louisiana, who continued to re-elect him.

Telling the truth in cases like that can certainly be embarrassing, but the cover-up never works, and in some cases makes things much, much worse. In May of 2001 Chandra Levy, a 23-year old intern in Washington, disappeared, and reports soon surfaced that Gary Condit, a Democratic congressman from California who knew Levy's parents, had been having an affair with the young woman. He first tried avoiding reporters, leading to absurd scenes where we would chase him through the Capitol. Then he lied and when he stopped cooperating with the police things got serious.

There was never a shred of evidence that Condit had anything to do with Levy's disappearance, but his refusal to admit to the affair and continuing to try to cover it up led people to believe he did. By trying to hide his affair he managed to convince a big chunk of America and even some in law enforcement that he had killed a woman. Eventually Levy's killer was found and brought to justice, but by that time Condit's political career was over.

Then there was Democratic Congressman Steve Cohen, who sent messages to a young college student that weren't flirtatious but seemed to be improperly familiar, using Twitter in what he wrongly thought was a private conversation. He signed off with "I love you," and once the tweets were made public said the young woman was a close "family friend." Pushed by reporters who were now harassing the young woman too, Cohen said he learned several years before that this was the daughter of a woman he had been romantically involved with when both were single and believed she was his daughter, though never told her that. With the attention growing every day he agreed to take a paternity test, and it turned out the girl wasn't his daughter after all. A rather absurd story all around that I never thought was news and certainly felt the young college student hadn't done anything that should have earned her the notoriety.

Some of these cases showed questionable judgment, others truly bad judgment, and some involved abominable behavior. But they also reflected a change in the relationship between politicians and reporters. There simply is no zone of privacy any more.

I remember a day in college when Pete Williams and I were in the newsroom at KZSU and a story came in that a student had died in his dorm room. Obviously a hugely important story for a campus radio station, we pursued it and learned the young man had built a device to sexually stimulate himself by delivering electrical shocks to his genitals, and had been electrocuted. We had an intense discussion over whether we should report that detail and concluded there was no benefit to anyone to do so. We simply reported accurately that he had been accidentally electrocuted in his dorm room.

It is sad to note that faced with a similar situation today with a celebrity or politician we cover it is inconceivable that either NBC where Pete is now a correspondent, or CBS where I worked, or any other news organization would decide to skip over that salacious detail. And what is even more disturbing is that the question would never even be raised; the discussion would never take place. If it is titillating or shocking it is fair game. The question we struggled with as college journalists of whether the benefit to the public in reporting explicit details is sufficient to justify causing private pain and embarrassment is no longer even asked.

When the congressional elections of 2006 came along, the Republican brand was having some serious problems. The war in Iraq was becoming increasingly unpopular, the economy was not doing well, and the federal response to the devastating Hurricane Katrina in New Orleans had been horrendous.

Republicans were on the defensive and weren't helped by a particularly nasty congressional scandal involving Florida Congressman Mark Foley. Foley led the Congressional Caucus on Missing and Exploited Children, and like almost all Republicans was a consistent opponent of gay rights. When he was accused of sending sexually suggestive instant messages and e-mails to teenage boys who were serving as House pages, it became a huge story. He resigned but an ethics investigation uncovered evidence that members of the House Republican leadership and their staffs were aware of what he had been doing.

The Democrats swept those elections and returned to power in the House and Senate. Nancy Pelosi became the Speaker of the House and the highest-ranking woman in the history of the U.S. government. Pelosi had grown up in a political family in Baltimore but had raised her family in San Francisco before running for office herself. She had worked her way up fairly quickly in the Democratic House and is an extremely able politician. She is friendly and generally a pleasure to be around (plus she always has chocolates in her office) and is in many ways an old-school politician. She gained power by helping others, including as a prodigious fundraiser and built a fierce loyalty among the Democratic members in Congress. That is not to overlook her tough side. She certainly has one and repeatedly outmaneuvered competitors to move ahead. She represents one of the most liberal districts in the country and helped pass a lot of major legislation.

It was an historic day when she became speaker surrounded by her grandchildren, as Republican Leader John Boehner handed her the gavel, which she would have to return to him just four short years later.

American politics tends to be cyclical for a variety of reasons, but mostly I think because there is a very strong pull to the center. While some other democracies in Europe have swung wildly from conservative to socialist, Americans seem uneasy if their politics swings too far in one direction or another. And as the Bush administration wound to a close the country was clearly ready to shift back towards the Democrats.

PRESIDENT OBAMA SHAKES THINGS UP

President Obama came into office with enormous political capital. He had good will from a big election victory, the historic significance of being the first African American President, and most importantly, a Democratic Congress. Not only did Democrats control the House, but had a 60-vote margin in the Senate, enough to overcome any filibusters. Now of course Democrats are no more monolithic than Republicans and there were plenty of disagreements among them, but still the opportunity was enormous.

President Obama had a number of big things he wanted to accomplish, including universal health insurance, Wall Street reform, immigration, and dealing with the growing threat of climate change. He also had a financial crisis that needed immediate attention: the collapse of the real estate market and the risk of failure of a big chunk of the banking industry that was pulling the country into a deep recession.

Finances had to be the top priority and he followed the lead of many presidents before him and the advice of most economists, which was the best way to help a country out of recession is to spend money. Spend lots of it and spend it fast in order to get the country working again. During the last days of President Bush's presidency, Bush pressured Congress into taking the first critical step of preventing a meltdown of the banks. The "bailout," as it later came to be called, was a tough sell, especially for Republicans, but if the major banks had collapsed there is little doubt that a depression would have followed.

But that still left a recession that led to massive layoffs and much suffering. So President Obama's first priority in Congress was a stimulus bill to pump money into the economy. The measure included quick cuts in the FICA tax, which put cash into the hands of consumers who would spend it, along with massive government spending projects on everything from building roads, bridges, and schools to funding clean energy programs. There was also aid for states, which unlike the federal government had no ability to go into deficit to pay for what they needed. While large numbers of teachers, police, and firefighters were laid off as state budgets were squeezed, it would have been far worse if the federal government hadn't stepped in.

There was some reason to believe that President Obama might be able to get Congress to address climate change, especially since it was one of the few things he and his Republican opponent John McCain agreed on. But McCain, who had seen the real-life impact of climate change in Arizona where droughts were becoming longer and more severe, was still a relatively lone voice among Republicans in Congress, most of whom opposed any steps to address the issue. Some simply denied the science or pretended not to believe it, but most were reflecting the powerful interests of coal, oil, and other industries, which would be hurt by any steps to reduce the burning of fossil fuels and move the country more quickly to renewable energy. The recession also clearly played a role; as unemployment grew it became harder to support measures like a carbon tax or strict limits on emissions that, at least in the short run, could lead more people to lose their jobs. In the end whatever chance there might have been to tackle climate change in Congress was lost.

Wall Street reform was a different matter. It would be extremely difficult, but the public was clearly outraged that the recession they were suffering from was caused by a handful of big banks and investment companies that had created an unsustainable real estate bubble and then turned to taxpayers to bail them out when it all started collapsing. The argument was they were "too big to fail" and in fact they were. The Great Depression of the 1930s, along with more recent events in other countries, demonstrated clearly that as upsetting as it is to bail out banks, letting the banking system collapse is far worse. And so President Obama and Democrats in Congress set out to pass new rules and regulations to stop it from happening again. They were in essence not regulating Wall Street and the banks as much as re-regulating them, since the massive de-regulation during the Reagan administration had set the stage for the financial collapse of 2008. Many of the protections put in place after the Depression, including preventing banks from speculating in the stock market and making other risky investments, had been taken away, and though it took a while for the genie let out of that bottle to become full grown, it certainly happened.

The fight over that bill during 2009 was enormous. There is no small irony in the fact that the lobbyists for the same banks and investment companies that taxpayers had bailed out just a few months before were out in force, trying to stop any rules that would force them to be more responsible in the future. That is not to say that the details didn't matter or to suggest that the resulting Dodd-Frank bill that eventually was signed into law in 2010 was perfect, but those fighting it were the same interests that had abused the system and brought the country to the brink of economic collapse.

One of the biggest fights was over whether this new law should protect consumers. While the big banks eventually were resigned to the fact they would have stricter supervision and have to maintain reserves and other protections so no matter how badly they screwed up, they would never again threaten the entire economy, they fought vehemently against protections for consumers. Though every voter is also a consumer, they have never been a big lobbying force. But the final version of that law did contain unprecedented protections for consumers, including a new government agency with the power to try to stop them from being taken advantage of not only with mortgages but credit cards, debit cards, and payday lenders too. In later years Republicans would continually try to undercut the power of the Consumer Financial Protection Bureau, including blocking Senate confirmation for years of its director, making clear they didn't care who was nominated; they didn't want the job filled.

While trying to explain to listeners the ins and outs of the Wall Street reform bill was challenging, understanding the Affordable Care Act, which later became known as Obamacare, was a lot harder.

Presidents of both parties, including Teddy and Franklin Roosevelt, Harry Truman, Richard Nixon, and of course Bill Clinton, had tried to get universal health coverage for Americans. Obama knew how difficult this was going to be but if it was ever going to happen, having a Democratic House and a filibuster-proof Democratic majority in the Senate was the time. I spent the better part of two years covering the health reform debate and fear that along with the president and other politicians, we in the media failed to ensure people fully understand it, because enormous confusion remains.

A substantial chunk of the Democratic Party in Congress, including Speaker Pelosi, favored a single-payer health care system of the type in Canada and most European nations. Opponents call this "socialized medicine," but part of the confusion is that our health care system is a hybrid of government-paid, insurance-paid, and private-paid care.

On the pure "socialized medicine" front, we have the Veterans Administration health care system. Fully supported by taxes, the government owns the hospitals, pays the doctors, nurses, and other staff on salary and makes all the medical decisions. Drugs and other supplies are purchased in bulk and that savings is substantial.

Then we have Medicare for everyone over 65 and Medicaid for low income Americans of any age. These programs are basically government-provided insurance. Patients can choose their doctors and hospitals and the government pays the bills at a negotiated reduced rate; the money comes from taxes. Under pressure from drug companies, Congress doesn't allow the government to negotiate for lower drug prices under Medicare, which is one reason costs are rising so quickly.

Most Americans who work have health insurance on the job, the bulk of which is paid for by employers, subsidized by a tax system that allows full deductions for the cost. Self-employed people and others who pay for their own insurance have much steeper costs and fewer tax benefits, while the uninsured have only the access to health care they can afford along with emergency rooms, which treat them and pass the cost on to everyone else through higher charges to insurance companies.

Starting this process was not a question of whether to have a "government" health care system or a "private" one. We already had a mishmash of both that was wildly inefficient and left millions without proper health care. That was why many people believed a government-only system made the most sense since it would take the enormous amount of money spent on insurance companies out of the mix, and like most other industrialized nations simply tax everyone and give everyone health care.

But there are downsides, and politically it was untenable, even with a Democratic majority in Congress. Doctors and other medical professionals were (of course) vehemently opposed because they make far more money under the current system, drug companies would no longer be able to have prices in the U.S. that are dramatically higher than in Canada and other nations with single payer, and of course insurance companies would be put out of business. And there is a healthy and oft-times deserved skepticism about government among the American people that make them very resistant. There is also, of course, the massive confusion of what these terms mean, best exemplified by protestors over 65 whose medical care is paid for entirely with tax dollars carrying signs reading "Government: Hands off our Medicare."

And so President Obama set out to stay with our hybrid government-private health care system but change things so everyone could get health insurance. The cleanest and simplest way to do this would be to just put everyone on Medicare. That way everyone would have insurance that they could use for any doctor or hospital and taxes would be raised to pay for it. The taxes could come from employers, who were already paying the bulk of health insurance costs across the country, or through a national sales tax or some other form.

Instead, the president went with a plan that had actually been devised at the conservative Heritage Foundation and was a Republican idea offered as an alternative to single payer. The basic premise was a grand bargain with insurance companies to require them to cover everyone without regard to pre-existing conditions, and in exchange the government would require everyone to have health insurance and provide subsidies to help those who couldn't afford it. This way the insurance companies would have millions of new customers and make enough money to be able to stop discriminating against people who were sick.

The details were understandably complicated and quickly got into the political muck, but in the end Obamacare turned out to pretty much follow that outline, which had previously been used successfully in Massachusetts under Republican Governor Mitt Romney.

One issue that came up and led to later court battles had to do with setting out basic requirements for what provisions had to be in a health insurance policy. This was a critical element because it made no sense to subsidize the insurance companies and then let them sell policies that didn't take care of people's health needs. In the same way it was critical to find a way to hold premium costs down and to make sure that insurance companies could no longer cancel people's policies when they got sick, which they did with some frequency among people who bought their own insurance on the private market.

Debates arose over every detail and some stand out. There was a huge problem over abortion because most health insurance policies covered abortion, but federal law had for years prevented tax dollars from being used for abortion. So the question became: if a tax credit helped someone buy an insurance policy that covered abortion, does that mean tax dollars are going for abortion? Clearly there were ways that argument could go too far—for example, if a member of the congressional staff pays for an abortion doesn't her paycheck come from taxpayers? There were enormous amounts of time spent on trying to settle the issue, which ended up in a fig leaf solution that satisfied some but certainly not all abortion opponents. Health insurance companies would have to pay for abortion from funds not provided by the government, even if tax dollars paid for other health care for the same woman.

A key element in getting moderate Democrats in the Senate to go along was that the law couldn't increase the federal deficit. In the end it actually reduced the deficit, but that was because of new taxes on businesses providing top quality health insurance to workers, medical device makers, and upper-income individuals—those were certainly controversial.

Besides the real controversies there was a lot of time spent covering the phony ones. One of these was the nutty charge that the law would set up "death panels" to decide which older people should be allowed to die. Ignoring something that was so obviously nonsense seemed a good first choice but once it started getting attention, we had to cover it. It arose from an amendment first proposed by a small bi-partisan group in the House. Generally Medicare only paid doctors for exams and procedures, but they argued that it is important for older Americans to get good information about end-of-life issues, especially living wills, that allow them to make treatment decisions ahead of time if they become unable to do so later. The language was pretty simple; it just said Medicare could reimburse physicians for the time they spent with their patients helping them to understand and make those kinds of decisions, and most importantly answering their questions.

Already by this time a growing number of conservative Republicans had decided they would oppose the health care law no matter what was in it (in large part because President Obama was behind it) and latched on to this small provision. It was Sarah Palin who first started using the phrase "death panels" and soon conservative talk radio ginned up the fake controversy.

Sometimes the bill ran into problems from the left. That was the case with Senator Edward Kennedy's insistence that the law include some long-term care insurance for people who would need to go into a nursing home. Kennedy, who was a key author of the law and one of its most important supporters, was adamant that the provision for a voluntary government-backed program be included. The problem was that long-term care is extremely expensive and no one was willing to come up with a revenue stream that would pay for it. In the end, one of the absurd compromises that only in happen in Congress was agreed to, and a long-term insurance program was added to the law with a provision that it would only take effect if it was deemed fiscally sound and could pay for itself. After the law was passed the Obama administration quietly jettisoned it because everyone knew it couldn't pay for itself.

The debate over health reform consumed Congress for two years and much of that time was spent in efforts in the Senate to get Republican support for a proposal that had started with conservatives. But in the end no Republicans would support the Affordable Care Act. That delay had very costly results.

Senator Edward Kennedy died in August of 2009 of brain cancer. While most states allow the governor to appoint new senators to serve until the next election, Massachusetts requires a special election. In a stunning political development the following January, Republican Scott Brown won that election and suddenly the filibuster-proof margin in the Senate was gone and the health care law was in peril.

In the end, a convoluted series of parliamentary maneuvers was used to pass the law with a simple majority vote in the Senate, but that meant the House and Senate versions couldn't be properly reconciled and the normal process to fix flaws and mistakes in the law was cut off. Big laws always have problems; both Medicare and Social Security were changed numerous times by Congress as issues came up.

But the last opportunity to fix the Affordable Care Act passed because Republicans took over the House in 2010 on a campaign against the law they had come to call "Obamacare," and since they were committed only to repealing it, even the most simple fixes couldn't be made.

Republicans managed to keep Obamacare as a valuable political issue and convince many Americans it was a terrible thing. There were battles in Congress and battles in the courts, but in the end, millions of people without health insurance got it for the first time. An interesting historical parallel is Medicare. When it passed in 1965 over strong Republican objections (as a hired spokesman for the AMA, then-actor Ronald Reagan made ads calling it "socialized medicine"), it was quite unpopular. In fact, Republicans made big gains in the 1966 congressional elections, in part by running against Medicare. It took years to convince older Americans to sign up; for a while people were hired to go door to door trying to convince older Americans to get Medicare cards.

In the end, of course, Medicare became an accepted part of the social safety net and untouchable politically. It seems likely Obamacare will end up the same way.

MOROCCO 2012

I headed to Morocco for Congress's spring break, mostly, I think, because of two movies: "Casablanca," of course, and "The Road to Morocco," with Bob Hope, Bing Crosby and Dorothy Lamour; and a song: "Marrakech Express," by Crosby, Stills & Nash. Actually Morocco has long been Hollywood's go-to place for the exotic land of camels, sand dunes, mysterious souks and magic lamps with genies.

I flew Air France to Marrakech via Paris and Toulouse. I thought about a return routing that would take me on the late flight from Casablanca to Lisbon, to recreate that famous closing scene in "Casablanca," but it wouldn't have been the same without the fog.

Stepping out of the airport in Marrakech, it looks like parts of the American Southwest—flat and dry with palm trees and cactus, and all the buildings are low and adobe style. Things change fast when you enter the thousand-year-old city center. Narrow streets are jam-packed with motorcycles and donkey carts and an amazing assortment of characters.

The enormous main square has snake charmers, fortune tellers, musicians, acrobats and story tellers. Big crowds gather around the best story tellers, though a local tells me it's always the same story. (Well, I guess Broadway doesn't change its plays every night, either.)

There are stands selling delicious fresh-squeezed orange juice for 40 cents and monkeys on leashes to pose on your shoulder. They aren't little monkeys, either, but the big Barbary macaques that live in the mountains.

Around five pm, the food stands are rolled into the square, dozens of them, all pulled by hand. Ovens fire up, benches are put out, and giant tents erected. It seems everyone in Marrakech is here for dinner. I pass on the lamb's head (a specialty) and try a pastilla, fried pastry dough stuffed with chicken, and very sweet.

The women wear long, flowing traditional dresses with colorful scarves (only a few are veiled) and older men wear long, flowing robes with hoods lying flat that look like the boy wizard's uniforms at Hogwarts. But younger men are all in Western dress.

The city is a mélange of smells and sights, though the streets are surprisingly clean and the weather was pleasantly cool, with a few thunderstorms. Other than the occasional pickpocket, there is virtually no street crime. It's safe everywhere at night in the kind of dark, narrow alleys you would never venture into in any other big city.

There is a definite café culture of sitting and people-watching. The drink of choice is a tasty and very sweet mint tea. Lingering is a way of life.

People are friendly and welcoming, though they do seem to yell at each other a lot when donkeys, bicycles, motorcycles and cars get jammed up. I really don't like bargaining, but it is inescapable.

Headed to dinner at a small restaurant recommended by the French owners of the riad where I was staying. Had the national dish, tagine, which is both the food you eat and the clay dish with a pointy cover it is cooked and served in.

The riad I stayed at is similar to a B&B. Located in a converted house in the medina, the ancient walled city center, it's at the end of a tiny alley with a nondescript heavy metal door. Inside it has a lovely little courtyard and enormously high ceilings. My room has a fireplace, lots of Arabian Nights touches and a big shower. There are six rooms and it is a pleasant way to be right in the middle of the madness. The guests were mix of nationalities and a couple of kids came to breakfast in their pj's.

The owner gave me a detailed map with lots of directions, but I was lost within three minutes of leaving and spent most of my time in the tiny alleys of Marrakech having no idea where I was.

Even with a good map and iPhone GPS (which worked well but still is limited if you can't read the street names), I mostly just wandered until I decided to ask someone for directions. I generally am using French. My French is terrible but I don't know Arabic and everyone here speaks both. Shopkeepers all have enough English to sell something. The other tourists (mostly European) are concentrated in just a few areas, and lost in my alleys, I'm often the only foreigner.

I visited the Ben Youssef Madrasa from the 16th century. Since Muslims can't portray faces (especially you-know-who's) it is decorated with incredibly complex and beautiful geometric designs.

For lunch I go with an upscale Frommer's recommendation, Café Arabe. Chicken rolled in a Gruyère cheese sauce, pommes frites, and terrine of three chocolates with giant, sweet strawberries. Served in the courtyard with WiFi. Aretha Franklin playing on the stereo. Nice.

Took an hour ride around town on a horse-drawn caliche, because when you are a tourist you have to do those things.

I passed a gourmet restaurant deep in the medina that is rated number one on TripAdvisor, but fear I can never find my way back. I get a reservation anyway, and my riad arranges a taxi that can get me close and point me in the right direction.

Gastro MK has one seating a night with a fixed, five-course dinner for 55 euros, which sounds much more reasonable if you don't convert it to dollars. Canapés start on the terrace and the meal lasts for three hours.

The room was dramatic and the food fantastic. There were two amazing soups; the cumin bread was great, but the olive bread even better. I went with fish as the main course and one of the more interesting accompaniments was "mango spaghetti" with lychee nut. The warm chocolate "cigar" eaten with mascarpone cheese was a slice of heaven.

Took a full day trip to the Atlas Mountains with my Berber guide, Ali. He told me how the Berbers were here long before the Arabs conquered them and converted them to Islam. Jews lived among them here as far back as Roman times. (Though none are left in the Atlas now, a small number still live in Morocco's cities.) I later bought an intriguing little hand-shaped Berber good luck charm with a Jewish star in it, not believing for a minute the shopkeeper's insistence it was an antique.

We stopped at a weekly market out in the countryside where hundreds gathered in a muddy field selling fruits, vegetables and live animals. Unlike in Marrakech (or any other market I've ever seen) there were no women. They are allowed, but by tradition it was all men selling and all men buying their weekly groceries. They come down from the mountain villages by foot or donkey to the nearest road, then donkey or shared taxi from there.

The language in the market is Berber, not Arabic, and there is no power or running water, but there is cell service.

Climbing the mountains (which have some fresh snow on the peaks) I see vast groves of olive trees stretching all the way back to Marrakech.

Best site in a mountain Berber village is a satellite dish held in place on the roof with rocks. The dishes are not expensive and the 120 TV channels are free, a gift from Saudi Arabia, which is very generous with our oil money.

Passed on a one-hour donkey ride to a more isolated village and so stopped in the village where Ali lives, and went to his house for a cup of his special saffron tea. (The saffron is grown in his garden.)

After a long day of climbing around mud-covered mountain villages, I was ready to be scrubbed clean in a hot private hammam with the local "black soap," and then massaged for an hour. The country is Muslim where modesty is critical, but my riad is French, so it was a very nice young lady who expertly scrubbed and kneaded my body.

Dealt with the muddy shoes by saying yes to one of the ubiquitous shoeshine boys who cleaned the mud with the juice from an orange sliced in half. Effective, and my shoes smelled great!

Oddest song to hear on the radio: the old spiritual "Swing Low, Sweet Chariot."

Weirdest dessert: a kind of cold, green, slightly minty vegetable soup with chocolate shavings.

Biggest animal surprise: Marrakech is filled with storks. The giant birds have nests at the tops of the mosques and other high places.

Strangest friendly gesture: taken out of line at a tourist site waiting to buy an entrance ticket, hugged, kissed on the top of the head, and let in free.

Had to get to the train station to buy a ticket for my onward journey and after half an hour trying to find my way out of the maze to a street wide enough for a taxi to drive on, I hired a kid (and two of his friends, it turned out) who got me to a taxi. $3 well spent.

After four days in the wonderfully exotic city of Marrakech, I head to Essaouira, a much smaller and quieter city on the Atlantic coast. The French built railroads in Morocco, but never got past Marrakech; the next journey is by bus.

Amazing sight on the way were goats climbing trees. They were high up in the argan trees to eat the nuts that are made into an oil unique to Morocco, which every third person tries to sell me.

I was dipping my bread in that oil later that night at a beachfront restaurant (great sea bass) and it has a nice smoky, almost hazelnut taste. It's also good for the skin and cures almost anything, I'm told.

Essaouira is a laid-back, pretty seaside town known for its seafood and has a compact and vehicle-free walled medina. To mix things up, I'm staying here in a western-style resort hotel on the beach with a pool, spa and turndown service with a chocolate on the bed. I'm planning some substantial lounge chair time.

The picturesque port is filled with small fishing boats and was once used by the Carthaginians (didn't they win the Super Bowl one year?).

Everywhere in town is walkable; it's an extremely pleasant place, popular with ex-pats. I stopped by Orson Welles Square (really!). He is famous here because he came once to film a movie.

The beach is long and wide and stretches around a bay starting right outside the old city walls. The ocean is a bit chilly and the most popular beach activity appears to be soccer on the sand. Police occasionally patrol on horseback.

I can tell my hotel caters to upscale French tourists because the room service menu includes a selection of meals for dogs, with a choice of two different burgers, two chicken dishes with rice, and croquettes for around $15 each.

Went traditional Moroccan for lunch at a place where I sat on a couch with pillows. Started with the "sardine balls" my waiter suggested, which were actually pretty good, followed by a nice chicken, fig and almond tagine.

I was captivated by an odd scene on one street where a group of older men in white robes were in a circle carrying very old rifles. Women would go in the middle of their circle and sit on a little stool. They would chant and raise their rifles up and down, put a cloth on her head, then take it off. Then she would pay them

I learned later they come every year at this time and people come from all over to find them. They are paying for a wish to come true, and apparently if it does you are supposed to come back the next year and pay them more. My source seemed perplexed when I asked if they get a refund if their wish doesn't come true.

Find of the day is an outdoor cafe right on the main square serving terrific Italian ice cream. The cherry flavor has whole cherries in it!

I spent a full day at the beach, then walked to the "fish grills," 45 identical little stands next to the fishing boats displaying the day's catch and competing for business. You pick your shrimps, crabs and fishes, negotiate a price, then they grill it up and serve it on wooden tables. I picked stand number four. The guy had the best multilingual spiel and fixed me an assortment for $10. An experience for sure, but not my best meal.

The next night I tried the local lobster at a more traditional outdoor cafe and it was most fine.

I encounter a slight transport complication caused by what I'm told is a common habit of people working at train and bus counters saying all seats are sold out when they're not. To avoid additional hassle, I negotiate with a taxi driver to take me back to Marrakech to catch my train up to Fez. On the way I see why the guidebooks recommend staying clear of the smaller bus companies. A man signaled he wanted to get on one; the driver opened the door and slowed just enough so that at a full run the passenger could jump on.

Shaking hands is big here. Every transaction, getting a taxi, buying a soda or asking directions requires one. Locals who know each other kiss once on each cheek, French style, but men kiss men and women kiss women. I'm sure men and women are kissing each other, but not in public.

The Marrakech train station is modern and quite beautiful and even has Le McDonald's. Since I'm an American tourist well past my 30th birthday I buy a first-class ticket (which is still only around $35) for the seven-hour ride. I have two bottles of water, a bag of cookies and "Marrakech Express" on the headphones as the train pulls out of the station.

Terrain is hilly with a lot of dry scrub and eucalyptus trees. Take out the goat herders and occasional donkey cart and it could be Southern California. This gives way to flat farmland as I move north, then we climb a bit as we approach Fez.

Fez is a hilly city and quite steep in places. It dates back well over a thousand years with its center intact, pretty much as it was built in the Middle Ages.

On the drive from the train station we passed a huge royal palace and gardens, one of several I've seen. There are at least ten. It's good to be the king.

The alleys of Fez are so narrow, a man with a small hand cart took my luggage from the nearest road and it wasn't wide enough for us to walk side by side.

The riad here is wonderful. Behind a nondescript door is a soaring courtyard with a fountain, hanging brass lamps and incredible tiles. My room has a wooden door 20 feet high, with a little human-sized door cut into it. It is totally Arabian Nights, with tiles, oversized furniture, Berber carpets and some really nice, locally mixed soap and shampoo. And of course, there's WiFi.

It was already evening after a long travel day, so I had dinner in the garden under the orange trees: three salads, including pumpkin flavored with honey, tagine, and a crisp, light, fluffy sweet thing for dessert.

Interestingly, only the old Jewish section has houses with windows facing out. The ancient Arab style has only windows facing into a courtyard or walled garden.

The medina here is tighter, older and different in tone from Marrakech. It's also easier to navigate, with color-coded signs showing the way to major sites and gates. And since it's on a steep hill, heading downhill can always get you to a gate and a cheap taxi to go back up around the outside walls.

A young man latched on to me to show me the tanneries (it's how it's done) and led me into an incredibly disgusting place where the skins of sheep, cows and goats are peeled off, processed and dyed by hand. The nearby leather stores suddenly weren't so appealing.

Another square has brass workers loudly hammering giant pots while woodworkers are busy in another alley and silver is being worked nearby.

Everyplace is full of steep, narrow curved stairs and being old and decrepit now, I'm doing my best to avoid them.

Wandering the old medina I pass dozens of mosques, which are big inside, but the doorways are tucked between shops and there's no way to judge the size of the building. As an infidel I'm not allowed in, but can peek in some of the doors, including into the huge Kairouine Mosque (holds 20,000) attached to what is said to be the oldest university in the world. They won't let me in there, either.

So far I haven't seen anyone in Fez wearing a fez.

You can get some sense of the depth of the differences in culture, but a talk with the French owner of my riad showed I was just glimpsing the surface. He told me when he first bought the house he had to kill a sheep in the main courtyard to keep away evil spirits (called jinns) and the staff would run away whenever he turned on the tap for hot water. The cold water had to run first or the jinns would come out.

Tried a pastilla from a cart in Marrakech and it was okay, but at an upscale restaurant in Fez, it was delicious. A crisp pastry shell about the thickness of a deep dish pizza, with shredded, gently spiced chicken inside, dusted with cinnamon and powdered sugar on the top.

Fez also has a "new" city with wide streets and banks, grocery stores and modern apartments with no donkey carts. Easier place to navigate but not nearly as interesting.

On a full-day trip to the mountains, called the Middle Atlas here, saw waterfalls and a pretty lake with paddleboats, picnics and donkey rides for the kids.

There was a house built into a cave and I visited the elderly Berber woman who lives there.

Lunch in Ifrane, a pleasant little mountain resort town that looks like it was dropped in from the Alps, which also has a large American University at which the children of the Moroccan elite are educated in English.

It's 300 miles across the mountains to the Sahara where the sand dunes and camels are. Maybe next time.

Saw some other nice small towns and a cedar forest in a national park, where I hung out with the big Barbary macaques. Don't tell the environmentalists, but people here feed them and give them plastic water bottles to drink from, which is why these big monkeys stay out right next to the parking area and are happy to hang out with the humans.

I broke my no steep curved stairs without railings rule for five flights for a two-hour dinner at one of Fez's best restaurants, Palais de Fes, with a sweeping view of the old medina.

Multiple interesting salads (twelve actually, enough for a table full of vegetarians), followed by a wonderful pigeon pastilla with almonds (yes it tastes like chicken), beef brochettes and three plates of dessert. With some nice white wine on the house for climbing the stairs despite their offer to carry me up.

There was live traditional music and candlelight, but the best part was they sent a driver to pick me up at the end of my alley and to take me home after dinner.

Part of the medina is called Andalusian and is half a century or so younger, with an interesting history. After the inquisition in Spain 500 years ago, a large number of Muslims and Jews who were expelled came and settled in Fez, greatly expanding the city.

My fourth and last day in Fez it is pouring rain, and I decide to curl up on a couch filled with pillows in my riad's courtyard with mint tea and a book.

Headed by train on my last day in Morocco to Casablanca (which everyone here calls "Casa"), where I will stay one night before my flight home. (Interactive schedule of all Moroccan trains? There's an app for that!) Casablanca is a very big, busy city with a kind of faded-glory European architecture.

Now you have to know there is only one place I would go with an evening in Casablanca, and that's Rick's Café. I'm pretty sure it's not the original, since that existed only on a Hollywood sound stage, but an American entrepreneur recreated Humphrey Bogart's fictional café, and as they said in the movie, "In Casablanca, everybody goes to Rick's"

There is a vintage 1930s piano on which "As Time Goes By" and similar tunes are played and at the second floor bar the movie plays continuously. There was a group of German tourists who completed the picture but I'm not sure they got the joke.

It really is perfect down to the lamps and the potted palms and I half expected to see Ingrid Bergman walk in. The food was excellent: goat cheese and fig salad, filet of sole with mushrooms, walnuts and shrimp and a chocolate sundae.

It was good to look a little Moroccan on my trip, but going through U.S. immigration, not so much, so I decide to shave before flying home.

FINDING NEWS IN TONGA

I've been lucky in my career to have covered stories in virtually every state and many foreign countries. Reporters go where the news is; sometimes nice places and other times pretty miserable ones. When we do go to nice places we are often too busy to enjoy them or we are there because something terrible has happened: an earthquake, hurricane, flood, fire, or war.

Getting lucky enough to be assigned to a really nice place with time to enjoy it does occasionally happen, like my two-week assignment in Rio De Janeiro in 1992 for the first UN Earth Summit, or hanging out in Carmel, California, to cover actor Clint Eastwood's successful campaign for mayor in 1986. But more often it involved the art of the boondoggle, such as the time when Route 1 along the California coast was closed by a mudslide in Big Sur. The national reputation of that stretch of highway is well deserved; it is one of the world's truly breathtaking drives.

Still, it was a stretch to propose covering the "grand re-opening" of this highway for a national radio audience. Since the road was still closed, I had to stay near the blockage on the north side, which just happened to be where the Ventana Inn & Spa is. It is a truly wonderful little resort tucked into the forest with giant outdoor hot tubs and a great gourmet restaurant. The re-opening of the road wasn't very memorable, but my trip was.

But my best boondoggle by far was New Year's Eve, 1999.

In August of that year it was clear the arrival of the new millennium was going to be a huge media event. I was working at CBS Radio at that time and the network was already making plans for all kinds of special coverage.

At the same time everyone was worried about the overly hyped Y2K bug. When computer programmers started out, they used a shortcut to tell computers what year it was using just two digits, for instance "88" for 1988, and the habit stuck. Not until 2000 was approaching did people start thinking about what would happen when computers saw 00 and assumed the year was 1900 instead of 2000. Predictions of horror abounded, especially of bank computers wiping out everyone's savings to what the balance might have been 100 years before.

And so, on a slow August day in the CBS News Bureau in Washington, I spoke with my colleagues about the upcoming millennium. I quickly concluded that if I didn't come up with something really good to propose I would spend the only millennium New Year's Day I'd ever see freezing my ass off on some Washington street corner, waiting to see if the ATM still worked after midnight.

As we tossed ideas around, the key spots of Times Square, London, and Paris were all taken, but it got me thinking about time zones. What if I could report live from the very first time zone, from the first place on earth to bring in the New Year and the new millennium? I got out an atlas (the thing we used to use before Google Maps) and saw the first time zone was almost all ocean in the South Pacific. There were three places I spotted where people lived: some small islands off New Zealand where they raise sheep, Fiji, and Tonga.

I ruled out the sheepherders and I had already been to Fiji—plus, they cheated. They had been in the second time zone but changed as the millennium approached.

But Tonga had just the right ring to it, an exotic dateline where I was pretty sure no network correspondent had ever broadcast live before. As a bonus, it still had a king who was over 300 pounds, like South Pacific kings were supposed to be. And it had great snorkeling. As I studied the map a little more, I noticed Tonga was right next to the international date line and its closest neighbor, Samoa, was just on the other side.

So my plan was hatched. I would propose to broadcast live from Tonga as the first people entered the new millennium, then hop over to Samoa and 24 hours later report on the last place.

I wrote a memo stressing how exciting this would be for our stations and it was received in New York with bales of laughter. But this was too good a plan to give up on and I kept sending follow-up notes stressing how promotable it was and how it would set us apart from ABC Radio and our other competitors. A few weeks later Harvey Nagler, vice president of CBS News for Radio, my ultimate boss and the one the memos were all carefully targeted at, was speaking at a broadcasting convention in Las Vegas. He was telling CBS radio station executives about our millennium plans. I'm not sure if he planned it or just realized he needed something sexy to excite the crowd, but he told them we would offer live broadcasts from the world's first and last time zones.

The next day I got a call. The trip was on.

I quickly booked my business class ticket to Tonga, started contacting tourist bureaus, researching hotels, and thinking about the technical aspects of doing live broadcasts. Then I hit a snag. A big one.

It turned out there were no planes, no boats; not even an outrigger canoe that could get me from Tonga to Samoa on New Year's Day. I was in big trouble. I had sold my boss on this crazy idea, bought a $10,000 airline ticket and now couldn't do it. The man who had hired me at CBS promised live coverage from the first and last time zones and I wasn't going to be able to deliver and I certainly couldn't tell him that.

I was in full panic mode, sending out dozens of e-mails, scouring web sites, even reaching out to the congressional representative from American Samoa, which shared an island with the place I was trying to go. Finally, I found a travel agency in London offering a once in a lifetime millennium fantasy tour for golfers that would let them play the last round of golf in 1999 and the first in 2000.

That could only be done in reverse order; they would play the first round of the new millennium at the one course on Tonga, then go back in time across the international date line to play the last round in Samoa. And they were traveling on a chartered jet. I called the organizer in London and explained I needed a seat on his plane from Tonga to Samoa. I was desperate and willing to spend any amount of CBS's money to salvage the situation, but he quoted me a reasonable price and I paid it immediately.

The day after Christmas 1999 I headed out to Tonga. The pretty nation of small islands had never been colonized, the oversized king still ruled, there was little in the way of modern technology, and the people were friendly as could be.

I spent a few days broadcasting features on this charming place, planning my live New Year's Eve broadcast logistics, and snorkeling. While no European nation ever conquered Tonga, Christian missionaries did. All traces of the Tongans' original religion were gone and they were very religious Christians. Everything closed on Sundays and their tradition on New Year's Eve was to gather in their local churches and sing hymns at midnight.

It wasn't quite what I was looking for, but thankfully the king, recognizing what a special day this would be, announced people in the Capitol would gather on a giant lawn in front of the palace and he and the royal family would join them, and they'd sing hymns together. Perfect!

And so, on New Year's Eve I set up a card table at the edge of the grass, piled up spare batteries for my satellite phone, and got out my flashlight. At midnight the king and his people began to sing and I broadcast live as they led the world into the new millennium.

I filed stories well into the morning and did interviews with many of our biggest stations around the country. Every one of them asked if the ATMs still worked and I had to tell them Tonga didn't have any.

After a quick late-morning nap I headed to the airport to join up with the wacky British golfers and flew with them to Samoa. I checked into a lovely resort hotel and had them run a phone to the back of a ballroom where their New Year's Eve party had rock music instead of hymns. I celebrated my second millennium New Year's Eve with more live broadcasts, spent New Year's Day snorkeling, then flew to Hawaii for a little vacation.

Altogether a great boondoggle.

SO MANY PRESIDENTS, SO LITTLE SLEEP

I've covered eight presidents: President Nixon when I was in college, then after he left office, and Presidents Carter and Ford when they visited California or elsewhere in my western territory at UPI Radio, but Ronald Reagan was the first president I knew well and traveled with. Though he came close to grabbing the Republican presidential nomination in 1976, 1980 would be his year and mine.

I went with him to New York in November 1979 when he formally declared his candidacy and covered his campaign right up to his victory speech at the Century Plaza Hotel in Los Angeles on election night a year later.

Traveling with a presidential campaign is exhilarating and exhausting. I was 26 and we all flew on the same plane, Reagan and his wife, Nancy, and staff up front, and the press and Secret Service agents in the back. Friendships between reporters and agents were common because while our jobs were very different and we sometimes clashed, we were in many ways in the same boat. Everyone else on the campaign was there because they had a deep personal stake in the outcome, from the campaign manager to the young volunteers who carried the luggage. But the agents and reporters were there to do a job, which didn't change with the fortunes of the campaign. Win or lose, we would just go on to the next assignment.

Reagan wasn't the smartest president we ever had, but he was the nicest of the eight I have known. He struck me as a grandfatherly kind of figure who always had a joke or story to tell and was always pleasant to be around. While different in most every other way, he shared with Bill Clinton a powerful natural charm. Both had the ability to send a crowd into a frenzy and make each person they met feel they had his full attention.

Reagan was also unfailingly polite and if a reporter asked him a question, he always answered, even when he didn't know the answer or the answer was wrong or politically embarrassing. That's the reason after he became president his staff would go to extraordinary lengths to prevent him from hearing questions shouted by reporters, often by having him stand next to a helicopter or plane with the engine running. That way Reagan couldn't hear the questions, which he otherwise would feel compelled to answer.

While campaigns chartered the planes and press buses, arranged the hotels and the meals, news organizations paid for it all, and it is incredibly expensive. Just the charter airfare runs thousands of dollars a day as candidates hit five or six campaign stops.

We rarely knew the schedule of which states we would be in more than two or three days ahead. In the final days of a campaign last minute changes were common as polls showed where the candidate was most needed.

In 1980 security hadn't gotten as crazy as it is now and candidates were also less controlled and less afraid to be themselves around reporters. Those of us on that first Reagan campaign would frequently find ourselves just chatting with Reagan or being amused by his Hollywood stories. He also told ethnic jokes (a rabbi and an Irish priest walked into a bar...) that were never mean, and were common among those of his generation. When a story came out in a magazine about some of the jokes, my boss asked me why I hadn't reported on them. They struck me as pretty innocent and far less important than the fact that Reagan was repeatedly promising to cut taxes, spend more on defense, and balance the budget, which was clearly impossible. But it was a sign of things to come; politicians learned they couldn't let down their guard for a minute around journalists. Reporters in future years would have a much harder time getting to know the candidates they covered.

While Reagan was always friendly, Nancy could be a little prickly. Among other things, she didn't think women reporters should wear pants. I'm not sure she really thought they should be on the campaign plane at all, but was quite sure if they were they should be wearing a skirt or a dress. She made her view perfectly clear when she would occasionally come through the back of the plane with a box of chocolates. She would smile and offer a chocolate to each of us, but if she came to a female reporter wearing slacks would just walk right by. No chocolate for her.

While Reagan spoke often of family values his own family was kind of a mess. His two older children from his previous marriage to actress Jane Wyman were clearly out of favor and there were problems too in getting along with his younger son, Ron Junior. I remember at the 1980 convention in Detroit, Reagan's oldest son, Michael, brought his son, Cameron, who was two years old at the time. We all enjoyed this adorable little boy and were pretty shocked to learn that Reagan had not yet met his first grandchild.

That convention was the scene of a truly bizarre negotiation over the "dream ticket," the notion that Reagan would choose former President Gerald Ford as his running mate as a way to counter his lack of foreign policy experience. Intense secret negotiations went for 24 hours at the Detroit Renaissance Hotel where Reagan, his team, and his press corps were ensconced during the convention. Reagan had won the roll call vote Wednesday night, but all anyone could talk about was whether the former president would join the ticket. When Ford suggested in an interview with Walter Cronkite that it might happen, the Reagan people realized they had to move quickly.

I was in the press room at the hotel when a staffer rushed in and screamed for the pool to follow him. I was one of the reporters designated for pool duty that night, to stick with Reagan wherever he went.

We were led in a televised mad dash through the hotel lobby, knocking more than a few bystanders out of the way, and then loaded up in the motorcade and driven to the convention hall where Reagan took the podium and stunned everyone by announcing George H.W. Bush would be his running mate. Bush was a moderate Republican who ran against Reagan in the primaries and coined the phrase "voodoo economics" to describe the repeatedly debunked but still popular claim that lower taxes on the wealthy would lead to more economic growth and more revenue for the government. (In fact, under both Reagan and Bush's son it led to massive deficits, just as Bush Senior had warned.)

Back at the hotel we pieced together the story of how the negotiations with Ford had broken down over demands from Ford's team to give him so much authority, including the choice of several cabinet appointees, that he would in effect be a "co-president."

Reagan was a great storyteller, but sometimes would get hold of a story somewhere (not infrequently from "Reader's Digest") that was just plain wrong, but he liked it and used it anyway. At a rally during the fall campaign he was giving a speech railing against "environmentalist extremists," a favorite target, when he declared "trees cause more pollution than cars." It would be a line he would return to often.

I was honestly perplexed about how to deal with that. I didn't want to make fun of him, but it was such an outrageous thing to say. I remember asking the advice of Bill Plante, the CBS News correspondent on the campaign who I greatly respected. He told me you just report it straight with no hint of a snicker and let people decide whether it's good or bad, smart or stupid. Just give the facts, that's our job, and if someone wants to make fun of Reagan because of it that's their choice. It was excellent advice and served me well in covering politics in future years.

One of the first to make fun of the line was Reagan's own press secretary, Jim Brady, who understood humor was a good way to try to defuse a truly embarrassing claim by his candidate. On the flight to the next campaign event, he ran back to the press section of the plane pointed out the window and shouted "Killer Trees!"—a line that soon took on a life of its own.

One of Reagan's most powerful political tools was his optimism. Politics has become so negative these days we sometimes forget that the most successful politicians are never the ones who tell us all the things that are wrong with the country, but the ones who look ahead to something better. Reagan's optimism was a deep part of his psyche and an important reason he was so popular, even with people who by any reasonable logic had no business voting for him, like blue-collar union workers who would be severely damaged by his economic policies.

At almost every stop he would tell some version of the "Pony Story" to show the difference between a pessimist and an optimist. It always ended with a little boy happily digging with his hands through a giant pile of horse manure, exclaiming that with this much manure there had to be a pony in there somewhere.

What people loved about Reagan is that he could always make you believe that there really was a pony.

There was always tension between reporters and the campaign staff, many of whom were young volunteers who believed Reagan walked on water and were horrified that reporters didn't always agree. The printed schedule would use a shortcut for Reagan's name, "O&W," which stood for "oldest and wisest."

Many of these fights had to do with access, a theme that was repeated on every campaign I covered. The staff wanted reporters close by when the candidate had something to say or was doing something photogenic, but far away if we might overhear something we shouldn't, or ask a question that would get the candidate "off-message."

On the Clinton campaign in 1992, these young press aides decided the best way to keep reporters and photographers where they wanted us was to use ropes. Every time we left the plane they would run out with long yellow ropes and use them to try to corral us. Position is important for reporters, but critical for photojournalists taking still pictures or video, and they were not going to put up with it. So on the second day of the ropes, one of them took out a small pocketknife and cut the rope. After a few weeks of having to buy new ropes after each campaign stop, they gave up.

The Secret Service agents on the Reagan campaign were a good bunch and had a very tough job. There were a few frightening moments, one when Reagan decided to make a campaign visit in a burned-out section of the South Bronx, that was very tense. It was one of the few times I have seen agents with their heavy weapons out. They are always close but rarely visible.

Which brings me to one of my favorite Secret Service stories involving Bobo. He was a toy monkey that one of the agents had picked up at one of our stops that became a kind of mascot on the Reagan campaign plane. He had a Secret Service pin and a little earpiece and when he was wound up he would clap his hands, which had little cymbals on them.

Rules on those charter fights were pretty lax. People were often standing and talking during take-off and landing and a favorite pastime was "aisle-surfing," where someone, usually a TV cameraman, would stand on the little plastic emergency cards during take off and try to slide down the aisle from the front of the plane to the back without falling. Trying to roll an orange the entire length of the plane was another favorite pastime during take-off.

One day they had to change to a different flight crew because while we could work 16-hour days for weeks on end, there were at least some FAA rules they had to follow. So that day we boarded and had a new crew that had never done a campaign charter before.

One flight attendant was trying without much success to get people to sit down and fasten their seat belts and obey the rules that on regular flights everyone followed. She was getting upset, and by the time she got to the agent holding Bobo was really frazzled. She decided to make a stand and demanded that the agent put the large black bag by his feet in the overhead bin. He held up the little toy monkey with the cymbals and the Secret Service pin and said "Bobo says no." She was not amused, and insisted, to which he responded, "Bobo says the bag stays here." While those of us sitting nearby were roaring with laughter, the flight attendant started to take the bag to put it in the overhead bin. The agent grabbed her arm and then slowly opened the bag to show her the Uzi submachine gun. She turned pale as a sheet and walked away without saying a word and we never saw her the rest of the day. No one fools with Bobo.

As a trained actor, Reagan learned his lines and pretty much gave the same speech word for word at every stop in every city. Finding something new to report was often a challenge, but I was expected to file new radio stories after every event. This was before cell phones and so a representative of AT&T (back when it was the only phone company) traveled with the campaign and would make sure phones for all of us were installed at every stop, sometimes in an arena or hotel ballroom, and other times on a hastily built wooden camera platform at an outdoor rally.

Our days were long and after the final event of the evening, we usually had several more hours of work to do to prepare and send our stories for the morning. By the time I covered my sixth presidential campaign the exhaustion overwhelmed the excitement, but in my 20s with Reagan it was pure adrenalin.

Though the polls weren't showing it, I was convinced by October that Reagan would win. The crowds were larger and more enthusiastic each day. Though many of the campaign reporters went with Reagan to the White House I happily stayed in Los Angeles covering the western states, but that included a lot of time covering Reagan as president. He loved his ranch in the hills above Santa Barbara and spent an inordinate amount of time there, including one to two months each summer.

Reagan celebrated each New Year's in Rancho Mirage, California, near Palm Springs, at the estate of Walter Annenberg, who became fabulously wealthy as the publisher of "TV Guide." The press corps stayed at the Gene Autry hotel, which was pretty run down, but it was owned by Reagan's buddy, that famous singing cowboy. The hotel wake-up call was Autry singing his theme song, "Back in the Saddle Again."

Reagan only had a skeleton staff on those trips and I remember one year towards the end of his second term his new National Security Advisor was with him. Colin Powell, who would later become Chairman of the Joint Chiefs of Staff and Secretary of State, wasn't invited to join the exclusive party at the Annenbergs' home, and so he and his wife came by the Gene Autry and rang in the New Year with the reporters at our party.

I was never invited inside the Annenberg estate either, but I was almost arrested there in January of 1979. The Iranian Revolution was in full swing and the Shah of Iran, who the U.S helped put in power and supported to the end, fled and went into exile. There was a crazy rumor that he was heading to the California desert to hide out at the Annenberg estate and I was dispatched to check it out. After the third time I had circled the high walls a police officer pulled me over demanding to know what I was up to. I explained why I was there and he asked me if I knew when the Shah was coming. We both waited, but he never showed.

The 1984 presidential race was notable mostly for the inclusion of the first woman on a national ticket, Geraldine Ferraro, chosen just before the Democratic convention in San Francisco to be Walter Mondale's running mate. I was among a happy group of reporters covering their "get to know each other" sessions before heading to the convention.

They did this in Lake Tahoe where my main memories are joining other reporters in sailing trips on the lake.

With or without Ferraro, Mondale never had a chance to defeat Reagan for a second term and I spent the fall mostly covering other stories.

I went back on the presidential campaign trail in 1988 covering Democrat Michael Dukakis running against then-Vice President George H.W. Bush. Dukakis was smart and earnest and ran the worst campaign in modern political history. Coming out of the Democratic convention in Atlanta, Dukakis needed to define himself since he was not well known nationally. Instead we spent weeks in Massachusetts with Dukakis explaining his first job was to be governor. It was an incredibly stupid choice and traveling around the state to events at county courthouses with Dukakis we couldn't figure out what he was trying to do. It's not the job of reporters to advise campaigns, but the never-shy Sam Donaldson of ABC regularly screamed at the Dukakis people that they were blowing it. He also insisted on calling Chris Wallace, then a correspondent for NBC and son of "60 Minutes" legend Mike Wallace, "Junior," which drove Chris crazy, and there were times on that campaign we feared they'd come to blows. Donaldson loved to make trouble but was also my hero for pushing ceaselessly to get smoking banned on White House and campaign charter flights.

Since Dukakis didn't act to tell voters who he was, the Bush campaign was happy to define him. Lee Atwater, who was smart, funny, and totally ruthless, managed the campaign. He ran appallingly misleading and vicious ads using a picture of an African-American criminal named Willy Horton, suggesting the brutal murder he committed after being freed on parole in Massachusetts showed Dukakis was soft on crime. It was the worst kind of underhanded politics and was blatantly playing on racism but it was very effective.

When asked repeatedly (often by Donaldson) why he wasn't more aggressively answering the attack, Dukakis explained people cared about the issues and wouldn't be swayed by tawdry tactics and innuendo. It was noble to think the voters were smarter than that, but they aren't. If nasty and unfair attack ads didn't work, political campaigns wouldn't keep using them.

When we finally started real campaigning (on an awful old plane we nicknamed "sky pig," whose pilots would sometimes land so hard the oxygen masks would fly open), the mistakes continued. One of the worst was at a debate where Dukakis was asked whether he would continue to oppose the death penalty for a criminal who raped his wife, Kitty. It was a pretty tough question, but the Bush campaign had painted him as soft on crime and here was an opportunity to answer it in a forceful way showing some emotion, which Dukakis rarely did. Instead, he gave a detached, wonkish explanation of his opposition to the death penalty that sounded as if he wouldn't be that upset if his wife was raped. It was horrible.

The second stand-out awful moment of that campaign came at an event designed to let the country see Dukakis as a potential commander-in-chief when he visited a General Dynamics plant in Michigan and had a photo op riding an M1 tank. The number one rule of politics is never let yourself be photographed wearing a silly hat. The helmet on Dukakis looked comical, like a kid playing dress-up, and the picture was extremely damaging, playing into the unfair but effective Bush campaign message that Dukakis couldn't be trusted to keep America safe from foreign enemies or scary-looking black men.

Towards the end of the campaign Dukakis launched a desperate attempt to catch up and inadvertently started a trend that has been the bane of campaign reporters ever since. He went on a marathon round-the-clock finish ending on Election Day with no sleep, a practice expanded in later years to three and even four days of round-the-clock campaigning.

One of the events in this final, insane push was a dawn rally in New Jersey. While most of the campaign staff and reporters stayed in San

Francisco, the candidate and a small group of us flew across the country overnight in a Lear jet, then returned for a full day of campaign events on the West Coast. I slept on the floor of the plane but was still in no mood to deal with the substantial ego of NBC correspondent Andrea Mitchell. It was pouring rain at the rally site and there was limited cover for reporters and our equipment. Mitchell was going live on the "Today" show, and sent her producer over to tell me I was in the background of her shot and needed to move. Out into the rain. I declined.

The silver lining in Dukakis's Massachusetts-centric campaign strategy was I got to spend a lot of time in Boston. So many American cities have become homogenized with the same stores and chain restaurants that you can be plopped down and have no clue if you are in Atlanta, Houston, or Cincinnati. But a few places retain their own unique character and Boston is one of them. I was glad I got to spend so much time there and eat so much great seafood.

The Republicans had their 1988 convention in New Orleans and if I had my way, all political conventions would be required to be held there. Unlike the Democrats, Republicans generally have a committee write their platform in the convention city the week before the convention opens. And many of the most interesting fights at Republican conventions have been at the platform committee meetings on issues like abortion. More importantly, I had a week in New Orleans to try out all the good restaurants before the convention started.

There was no suspense at that convention in the nomination of Vice President George Bush, but a huge surprise when he introduced his running mate, Senator Dan Quayle. There has been a lot of speculation about why Bush made such a bad choice, but I think sometimes smart politicians just get frustrated and angry at being "handled" all the time, told by consultants what to say and how to say it, and hammered not to acknowledge things they know are true because it will upset some of their supporters. Bush Senior repeatedly took positions he didn't believe in, including endorsing the notion that cutting taxes on the wealthy would lead to more government revenue, something he had derided when he ran against Reagan for the 1980 nomination. I'm sure there were other reasons, but I think some of it was likely just a way to declare his independence and do something no one was telling him to do. In that way it was not dissimilar from the bizarre choice Senator John McCain made years later in picking Sarah Palin to be his running mate.

By the time the 1992 campaign came around, I was in Washington and working for Mutual and NBC Radio. I joined the rest of the political correspondents in the quadrennial trips to Iowa and New Hampshire for the first caucus and first primary. There is no rational reason to start the campaigns there; they are profoundly atypical states and are freezing in the winter. Iowa has a very liberal Democratic Party with a strong populist history and a Republican Party top heavy with religious conservatives and those who want to cut government spending on everything, except ethanol subsidies for corn farmers.

New Hampshire has a history of embracing fringe candidates of both parties and both states are as white as a loaf of Wonder Bread. But that's where it all begins and where we all go and pretend these voters are somehow representative of the rest of the country.

For one New Hampshire primary, my boss decided at the last minute I should cover the first votes cast in the hamlet of Dixville Notch, at midnight. My argument that it was silly and a really long drive fell on deaf ears, and so off I went, driving through the snow and avoiding moose as I headed north. The radio stations all were in French as I drew closer to the border region with Quebec. I pulled into the ski resort that is the entirety of Dixville Notch about 11 pm and managed to watch the handful of residents cast their ballots an hour later. It was over by 12:15. I grabbed a few hours sleep before driving back to Manchester (a quicker drive in the daytime when it's not snowing).

Iowa was flatter with no moose, but distances between campaign events are much longer. My favorite memory there is of a Des Moines restaurant recommended by Bill Plante, a gourmand and wine expert as well as a top-notch reporter. My friend and colleague Peter Maer and I decided to give it a try for lunch. We looked up "Butch's Hollywood Bistro" and gave them a call and were given directions, the final part of which was to look for the green door next to the laundromat with no sign. Reason enough to call the whole thing off, but if Bill Plante recommended it, it had to be great.

We found the green door, went in, and found ourselves in an empty restaurant decorated in a Wizard of Oz motif. Before we could retreat we were greeted by Butch—the owner, chef, and waiter. He pulled up a chair to join us at our table and began telling us his story. Born in Des Moines, he studied cooking in France and worked in New York before deciding to return home and open his own place. With no advertising or even a sign, his customers come only by word of mouth and included leading political and media figures. He told us there was no menu and asked what we'd like to eat. We left it to him and out came a penne and chicken dish that was mouthwatering, followed by the best cheesecake I've ever eaten. The bill was less than ten dollars each and the memory priceless.

The big story in New Hampshire in 1992 was Bill Clinton, whose campaign almost ended after the first of many women emerged to say he had affairs with them. His proclivities were certainly no secret to anyone who knew him (including his wife), and I'll leave it to others to try to explain how someone so brilliant in so many areas could be so dumb in that one. But he survived that and many other close calls in part because he was without doubt the most gifted politician of his generation. He could in every possible way charm the pants off people.

Early on, before he knew who I was, I remember stopping him as he walked by to ask a question. As I held my microphone up he put both hands on my shoulders and looked deep into my eyes as he gave me a totally innocuous answer. He could speak with in-depth knowledge on virtually any issue and has an incredible memory, but mostly he had that same ability Reagan did to connect to people and make them believe everything was going to be all right. I would stay with him until election night in Little Rock.

As we left the Democratic convention in New York, Clinton was trailing in the polls and facing a tough fight to defeat the incumbent president. But on that first of many bus campaign trips it was immediately clear this was something different, and Clinton was really reaching people. There were times we pulled into a small town with maybe a population of 10,000, and there would be 20,000 people waiting for him. Supporters would line country roads as the bus caravan went by and wait hours, late into the night, to see him. It was more like a rock & roll tour than a presidential campaign, and very exciting to cover.

There were complaints at the time from Republicans that Clinton was getting much friendlier press coverage than President Bush. It wasn't that we liked him better, but the story was better, and he was getting phenomenal crowds unheard of in the early weeks of a campaign.

Many of the bus trips also included running mate Al Gore and both families. Clinton always ran late. By the end of a long day (and they were all long), he was hours behind schedule and 9 pm events routinely slipped past midnight, but the crowds always stayed.

A big reason they were always late was the handshaking. If the schedule called for 15 minutes to shake hands after a speech it could easily stretch to three hours because Clinton wanted to shake every hand. No matter what his staff did, Clinton wouldn't leave until all the hands were shaken. At one point, some of the buses were repositioned after a rally to hide a big part of the crowd, the idea being if Clinton couldn't see them he couldn't shake their hands. He could get so carried away he couldn't be stopped. One night we got to our hotel after 2 am and there was a small crowd just outside. As Clinton and Gore shook their hands, the Secret Service blocked the elevator, leaving a handful of reporters trying to get to our rooms stranded in the small lobby. As Clinton finally got inside he started shaking our hands. As Gore chuckled we told Clinton it was nice he wanted to shake our hands, but it was time to go to bed.

The Republican convention in Houston that year was the most unpleasant political story I covered. The atmosphere was poisonous and the animosity towards journalists was palpable. We were routinely harassed and harangued even walking down the street outside the convention hall.

Believing wrongly that firing up the social conservatives was the key to his victory, Bush gave a prime speaking position to Pat Buchanan, who had done well in a few primaries with a virulent anti-immigrant, anti-liberal, and pretty much anti-everyone platform. Buchanan had built a nice career for himself campaigning for president every four years and then cashing in on his fame with TV gigs and books. He would fire up crowds with angry rhetoric and then try to pretend he wasn't really responsible for his followers. I'm not sure he was as anti-Semitic and racist as it often appeared, but there is no doubt many of his supporters were, and he egged them on.

His speech at the convention declaring America was in the midst of a "culture war" probably did more to hurt the Republican party that year than anything the Democrats did, driving women especially away in large numbers.

Still, defeating a sitting president isn't easy, and George H.W. Bush hadn't done anything bad. But the country was in a recession and Americans tend to reward presidents when the economy is good and punish them when the economy is bad, despite the fact that presidents have very little control over economic conditions.

Bush was hurt by the impression, fair or otherwise, that he didn't really care about average Americans and their problems and his somewhat patrician air didn't help. Clinton was the perfect candidate to take advantage of this weakness, since he came across as someone who cared deeply about absolutely everyone. Towards the end of the campaign when polls were showing Clinton pulling ahead, Bush turned to a tried and true Republican strategy of blaming the media, arguing we were biased against him.

The irony is that reporters who knew them both generally liked Bush better as a person. He was always kind and genuine and seemed to actually like reporters more than Clinton did. Though talking to Clinton was always fun, he had an amazing range of interests and knowledge and was always charming, he never let his guard down and was always deeply suspicious of us.

There is a kind of love-hate relationship between journalists and politicians. We pester them with questions they don't want to answer and reveal secrets they want to keep. Especially when at the level of a president or presidential candidacy, politicians are surrounded by people who are respectful and flatter them constantly, and we journalists most assuredly do not. But they need us desperately because no one is going to vote for someone they never heard of. The worst thing I can do to a politician is not to reveal some deep, dark secret; it's to ignore him. Reporters do that and they disappear.

My favorite example of this love-hate relationship was when I was covering President Bush (the elder) on vacation at his summer home in Kennebunkport, Maine.

I was with the "press pool," a small group of journalists that always stays near the president just in case something happens. President George H.W. Bush liked fast boats and liked to golf fast, but we still had to hang out at the clubhouse for a few hours waiting for him. The practice was we would watch him on the first hole, the ninth, the 18th, and then ride back in the motorcade to his home.

So we go to the first hole, and while the president is standing around waiting to tee off, one of my fellow reporters shouts out a question. We are reporters after all; it's what we do. Bush got angry and scolded us and explained that we could never ask him another question when he was on the golf course. So when we got back to the clubhouse we decided it was stupid to waste our time and would just wait until it was time to ride his motorcade back to the house.

But when he got to the ninth hole and didn't see any reporters he got furious and told his aide he'd better get those reporters back. So they quickly rounded us up. It may have been bad for reporters to ask him questions when he was golfing, but it was far worse for reporters not to be there to watch him golf. Being questioned is annoying for a president; being ignored is intolerable.

The other wrinkle in the 1992 campaign was Ross Perot, a Texas billionaire who decided to enter the race as an independent. A folksy, energetic speaker, Perot was gaining a lot of support over the summer before a bizarre episode in which he dropped out, claiming Republican operatives were plotting to disrupt his daughter's wedding. Then he came back into the race at the beginning of October. He took part in the debates that fall, and despite his flakiness got 19% of the popular vote, the best showing for an independent since Teddy Roosevelt tried to win a third term in 1912. Perot ran again in 1996 and created the Reform Party, which for a while gave us some fun, wacky conventions to cover. But his real contribution came by raising an issue that both Democrats and Republicans would have rather ignored, the growing deficit spending by the government. I have no doubt the focus during the Clinton Presidency on trying to balance the budget would never have happened without Perot.

Clinton won handily in 1992 and after several weeks in Little Rock, Arkansas, covering his transition, I returned to covering Congress, though I continued to cover Clinton on and off over his years in the White House. He presided over a period of enormous economic growth, got some major important legislation passed in Congress, and balanced the federal budget, even leaving office with a surplus. But he did have his quirks.

His eye for the women, which would get him in such trouble in his second term, was obvious to any of us who spent time around him. I remember being at a summer picnic for journalists and their families on the White House lawn. There was a "girl band" to play oldies on the stage as Hillary Clinton gave a speech welcoming us all to the picnic. As she was talking in front of a crowd of hundreds of reporters, her husband slipped behind her to chat up the girls in the band.

Another time I remember being in a small press pool that was going along while the president went jogging. We were waiting at the point where the jog would end and would watch Clinton get into his limousine to return to the White House. A small group of people had gathered behind some barricades to see him and I spotted a young woman in the front row who I recognized immediately as being Clinton's type.

The press aide told us to get back in the cars because the president would leave immediately after he finished jogging. I said I didn't think that would happen and would wait outside the press van, despite several threats that I would be left behind. Sure enough, Clinton arrived and his staff started moving him to his limo—and then he saw the woman in the front row. He immediately went over and chatted with her for a few minutes and posed for a picture.

There wasn't much doubt about the outcome of the 1996 presidential election, and while I very much liked Republican Bob Dole and enjoyed covering his campaign, we all knew he couldn't beat Clinton and I think he knew it too. The president was popular and the economy was booming.

The unfortunate part of the campaign was what Dole tried to do to cater to the increasingly more conservative base of the Republican

Party. Make no mistake, Dole was always a conservative and could be a very tough politician. But Dole had spent his entire career in the Senate battling for fiscal responsibility and seeking a balanced budget, so when he went on the campaign trail in 1996 calling for tax cuts that he knew would reverse everything President Clinton and Republicans in Congress had achieved in reducing the deficit, it was obvious to all of us he didn't believe it. He could give a good speech, but generally didn't inspire the kind of enthusiasm in a crowd that Reagan or Clinton could and had the very odd habit of constantly referring to himself in the third person, as in, "Bob Dole is very happy to be here today."

Having been severely wounded in World War II and still without function in his right arm, Dole also had been a key player in passing the Americans with Disabilities Act. Despite the general mood in the Republican Party against social programs, Dole always believed the government had an obligation to help those who needed it. After traveling for months on his campaign, I received a nice note from Dole about my ability to deal with the rough and tumble of a campaign on crutches, which coming from him meant a lot.

Towards the end of the campaign when polls were showing how badly Dole would do and with fear rising that Republican voters wouldn't bother to show up, Dole began to attack the polls and tell his crowds that the "liberal media" was just lying and shouldn't be believed. There were more than a few times after this became a regular line in his speeches that the crowds got riled up and began shouting, and in some cases physically assaulting those of us who were traveling with him. We always had good relations with his Secret Service detail but their job was to protect him, not us.

On several occasions Dole came back on the plane after a particularly raucous rally to apologize and remind us what we already knew, that he didn't really mean any of it. Things did get bad enough, though, that we had to confront him about it. He started toning it down and would say the liberal media was lying, but pointing to his traveling press corps to say we were all right.

The best part of the Dole campaign was the tanning stops. They weren't officially called that, but Dole loved to sit in the sun. After all, he was 73, and so there were lots of rest breaks. We never went longer than a few weeks without stopping for several days in a sunny place, usually Miami Beach, where Dole had a condominium, or San Diego if we were on the West Coast. They were called "debate prep" or some such thing, but they were basically tanning and resting breaks, and when Dole took a few days off to sit by the beach, so could we.

Several times during the 1996 campaign I got calls from my boss asking why the bills from the Dole campaign were so much higher than the bills from President Clinton's re-election campaign. I gave the honest but incomplete answer that I had nothing to do with the bills and the campaign made all the decisions of where we stayed and what we ate. But I knew full well why the bills were so much higher.

While berating reporters from the stump for our alleged bias, Dole and his campaign advance team were taking very good care of us. Every time we stopped anywhere, the press room set up for us to work in had a full buffet, more often than not an open bar, and occasionally musical entertainment. When we had our longer breaks in Miami there were always elaborate parties with amazing food and drink, and one time a "cigar roller," who came in to hand-make cigars.

While our bosses complained regularly to the Dole campaign about the high costs of having reporters travel with him, we were all quite happy with the arrangement.

When presidential campaigns visit a city or especially a small town, it is an exciting event for the people there and an opportunity for the civic boosters to seek some promotion for tourism. This was often the only time a town would ever see the national press corps, and so they tried to put their best foot forward, often providing us with t-shirts and other little trinkets in hopes we would say nice things about their town, or at least not forget its name.

On a bus trip through Michigan, the Dole campaign pulled into Frankenmuth, a cute little town that relied on its German heritage to appeal to tourists. It was kind of a German "theme" town, with bakeries and restaurants and kids dancing in lederhosen. When we returned to our buses after the rally, there was a box on every seat and inside a cornucopia of tasty snacks including salami and ham, sausage and cheese, mustard, and a big fresh loaf of German bread. And in each box was a foot-long and very sharp Frankenmuth souvenir bread knife. We sliced the bread and cut the sausage and had a wonderful feast as we drove to the next event.

But the next morning when we lined up all our bags in the lobby of our motel for the Secret Service to check them before putting them on the buses, the first bag that was opened had a great big knife right on the top. The agent called over the owner of the bag, who explained that the previous day in Frankenmuth every one of us had been given a big knife. The show must go on, and so the bag was zipped up and the campaign moved on to the next stop with a well-armed press corps.

Dole had resigned his Senate seat to run for president. That was too bad. The Senate has had a series of leaders, both Democratic and Republican, who never measured up to his standard. During my last years covering Congress, Democratic Leader Harry Reid and Republican Mitch McConnell spent most of their time spewing invective at each other on the Senate floor, and the "world's greatest deliberative body" basically just ground to a halt.

A very sad commentary on how much the Senate and his party changed after his departure came in December of 2012 when Dole, in failing health and a wheelchair, came to the Senate floor on the day of a critical vote to urge ratification of a U.N. Treaty on the rights of the disabled. It was a treaty negotiated under President George H.W. Bush, and already ratified by 126 countries, that simply said all nations should stop discriminating against people with disabilities. Its language came straight from the Americans with Disabilities Act and would have no effect on the U.S. at all, since that is already the law here. Under any circumstances no U.N. treaty can supersede federal or state law, but that didn't stop most Republicans from opposing it.

After many Republican senators came up and shook Dole's hand and honored their former leader who had come to urge a "yes" vote, they voted once again to block the treaty. Some gave the totally fabricated excuse that it would allow the U.N. to interfere with American laws and home schooling of disabled children, but the real reason was that a substantial minority of the Republican base so hated the United Nations, senators feared they would be punished at the polls if they voted to ratify any U.N. Treaty.

As President Clinton's second term was drawing to a close in 2000, the economy was still booming, the federal budget was balanced, and we had gone eight years without a war. The odds certainly favored Vice President Al Gore going into that campaign against George W. Bush, the governor of Texas and son of the former president. Bush had run a brilliant campaign for the nomination, in essence locking up all the money before the first primary was held, and clearly establishing himself as the heir apparent leaving little room for challengers.

But while he scared off most traditional Republicans, Bush hadn't counted on Arizona Senator John McCain. McCain is one of the most interesting characters in the Senate. He is a fascinating and complex man who I always enjoyed being with, but who also has a nasty temper and has gone through some dramatic changes over the years.

McCain identified himself as an independent thinker and a reformer and in those days he certainly was. He was a strong proponent of campaign finance reform, believing that there was too much money in politics and too much influence by the wealthy and the powerful, certainly not a popular message among the Republican establishment. He worked for years with liberal Democratic Senator Russ Feingold to pass a major campaign reform law limiting political contributions and wanted to go further. Sadly, that law would later be totally gutted when conservatives on the Supreme Court decided the first amendment allows unlimited political spending by individuals and corporations. McCain was also a war hero, having survived years of torture as a prisoner of war in Vietnam, and that provided him with a certain clout and a stiff spine.

When McCain entered the race, Bush had locked up the Republican establishment and so McCain skipped the Iowa caucuses, where the GOP is dominated by religious conservatives, and instead went to New Hampshire, where voters are fiercely independent and can vote in whichever primary they want. When McCain won the New Hampshire primary, the Bush campaign was stunned. They were counting on the argument of inevitability to sweep to the nomination and suddenly things weren't looking so inevitable. If Republicans felt they had a real choice, it could be trouble for Bush.

McCain's brief campaign for the 2000 nomination was one of the most extraordinary in recent history; from a reporter's point of view, it was pure heaven. McCain always liked reporters. He turned what had become the traditional campaign of tightly controlled access and talking points on its head, basically letting reporters talk to him all day long and ask whatever we wanted.

Unable to raise much money since Bush had pretty much locked up major contributors, McCain traveled by bus, nicknamed the "Straight Talk Express," and invited reporters to be on the bus with him. He would open himself for questions all day and into the night as we rolled along. He answered every question, showing not only reporters but the public that there was another way to seek the White House besides hiding behind focus-group-tested pablum.

He took positions on everything we asked him about, and while that sometimes meant he said things that would alienate some people (especially the religious right), it was a breath of fresh air not only for reporters, but for millions of voters who wanted real answers to important questions, and were tired of politicians telling them only what they thought they wanted to hear. It was an amazing experience for those of us used to fighting constant battles to just be able to ask a single question on the campaign trail. With McCain, there were literally times on that bus when reporters would just run out of questions and we would talk about sports or just take a nap.

I'm not sure if McCain could have won the nomination, but I do know he was stopped in the most vicious and nasty campaign I ever had the misfortune to cover. It happened in South Carolina, where the Bush campaign decided it had to stop McCain any way they could. They did it with a below-the-radar smear campaign that was truly disgraceful. It included fliers claiming McCain had fathered an African-American child, and had pictures of McCain's dark-skinned daughter Bridget, who he and wife Cindy had adopted from an orphanage in Bangladesh. There were despicable rumors spread through something called "push polls." In a push poll a voter is called and someone pretending to be a pollster asks questions, and if the voter said they supported McCain would follow up with questions like, "Would you still vote for John McCain if you knew he had fathered a black child out of wedlock?" or "Would you still support him if you knew he was a homosexual?"

Bush won the primary in South Carolina and though McCain did go on to win in his native Arizona and in Michigan, the race was basically over. He formally dropped out in early March after Super Tuesday and those of us covering him gathered in Sedona, Arizona, near McCain's ranch for the announcement.

I traveled with the Gore campaign in the fall of 2000, and while he didn't challenge Dukakis for the worst campaign ever, he did manage to blow the election. One of the main reasons was his decision to distance himself from Clinton and not let the former president campaign for him.

Now there was no question Clinton's personal reputation had been severely tarnished by the Lewinsky scandal that had led the Republican House of Representatives to impeach him. Gore seemed to be personally offended by Clinton's behavior, a contrast to his own squeaky clean image (at least until his divorce many years later) and it seemed to me there was also a fair amount of ego involved in that truly terrible decision. Despite all his problems Clinton was still the best and most effective politician out there, and if he had been able to turn just one small state, and there is little doubt he could have, Gore would have won.

That being said, of course, Gore actually did win the popular vote.

As the U.S. encourages new democracies around the world, we would never dream of suggesting they create anything like the Electoral College, an anachronism that goes back to concerns at our country's founding that the larger states would dominate the smaller ones. And so instead of directly electing our presidents, they are chosen in a roundabout fashion in which each state has its own winner-take-all election and the candidate with the most electoral votes becomes president.

In a modern nation this makes no sense at all and leads candidates to only bother campaigning in fewer than half the states. The reason for this is that winning by fifty thousand votes in a state like California gives you the same benefit in the electoral college as winning by two million votes. So if a candidate is confident he will win a state, or lose one, there is no reason to go there.

The strategy of simply ignoring most states reached its zenith in the Clinton campaign of 1992 led by James Carville, a great character who always said things he shouldn't but was a brilliant political strategist. He devised a strategy that took full advantage of the quirks of the Electoral College by focusing in on a literal handful of states that would decide the election, the swing states that could go either way. That excluded places like New York, California, and Texas and local politicians there were not happy about it, but the fact is that Democrats were not going to lose New York or California or win Texas, and so there was no reason to spend a dime campaigning there and Carville didn't.

So in 2000 Gore and Bush focused on the handful of states they knew would decide the election and those of us covering the campaign spent an enormous amount of time in Florida and Ohio. There were some smaller states that should have gotten more attention and if Gore had managed to turn West Virginia, Arkansas, or his native Tennessee he would have won.

Instead we ended up with a crazy election night that left the nation without a clear winner until the Supreme Court justices decided they should pick the next president.

I was with Gore in Nashville when the results started coming in. Though there were very close races in several states including New Mexico and Oregon that took days to resolve, it was clear that the election would turn on Florida. Based on exit polls and early returns, the TV networks and the usually more careful Associated Press all reported that Gore would win Florida and since I was working for CBS News at the time, I reported it too.

But then the numbers started changing and some of the official results that had been reported were wrong. The networks withdrew the calls for Gore about two hours later and as the night dragged on we all started calling the election for Bush. Fox was the first and the others all quickly followed. It was humiliating for those of us on the air that night. Competitive pressure was certainly part of the problem as no one wanted to be the last one to make a call. Even if it was wrong.

At about 2:30 am, Gore called Bush to concede and then headed out to give a speech to his supporters, who had been anxiously waiting all night. But then the Florida numbers started getting flaky again and it wasn't clear at all that Bush had won and we withdrew our second wrong call of the night. Gore was actually starting to head towards the stage to talk to his supporters when his staff called him back. He returned to the hotel where he saw the latest results and called Bush and "un-conceded."

The experts at all the networks had blown it twice at this point, and as dawn came we had no idea who had won the election. I remember going live on radio stations all over the country trying to explain what was happening and not having any good answers to the questions I was being asked.

The vote in Florida was by any statistical measure a tie. It was within the margin of error and there were lots of errors in voting, counting, and reporting. In New Mexico they have a law that when local elections end in a tie, the tie is broken with a single hand of five-card stud poker. It might have been a better way to handle things.

Gore had gotten half a million more votes than Bush across the country, but the extra votes in places like California and New York didn't count. All that counted at that point was Florida and Florida was a crazy mess. Most of the attention soon focused on Palm Beach County, where the old-fashioned paper punch ballots were confusing, and it was clear a large number of elderly Democrats who had meant to vote for Gore had in fact punched the hole in their voting card for conservative Pat Buchanan, who was on the ballot as the candidate of what was left of Ross Perot's old Reform Party.

As both sides started sending lawyers into Florida, I covered court hearings, then settled into Palm Beach watching the recount, with protestors outside and election officials inside looking at "hanging chads" on the punch cards, trying to figure out who the voter had meant to choose and whether their ballot should count.

It was while in Palm Beach reporting on our unresolved presidential election that I received word that my father, who had been seriously ill and in a nursing home, was close to death. I left the recount in the capable hands of my colleague Peter King and headed out to California, where I was able to say a final goodbye the night before my father died at the age of 77.

The fact that I had known for well over a year that this day was coming and suffering the sadness with each visit with my dad of knowing it might be the last didn't make things any easier. Being prepared for the death of a parent is of no help at all. It is still shattering.

When I returned to Washington two weeks later, the election saga was exactly where I had left it. It still wasn't clear who had won Florida and the court battles over what votes needed to be recounted continued. Bush and Gore were both acting as if they would be president but time was running out and there were some serious nightmare scenarios. If the governor of Florida, who happened to the brother of Republican candidate George Bush went ahead and certified electors for Bush, the validity of those electors could be challenged and things could ultimately be decided in Congress. If that were to happen the House, with its Republican majority, would choose the president, but the newly elected Senate would choose the vice president. The Senate was evenly divided 50-50 at that point, creating the possibility that the House would make Bush president and the Senate, with Al Gore himself casting the tie-breaking vote, could make Gore's running mate Joe Lieberman the vice president.

The Florida State Supreme Court ordered a new recount of contested votes and when the Bush campaign lawyers asked the United States Supreme Court to intervene and stop it, the justices surprised many by taking the case. There was no precedent for the nine Supreme Court justices to step in and decide who should be president in a contested election. The Constitution clearly gives Congress that power, which it used three times in the 1800s.

But the Supreme Court did step in. An argument could be made that the country was heading into a serious constitutional crisis as the calendar ticked towards January and they were the only ones who could stop it. But having unelected judges decide who the president should be certainly carried its own risk.

The high court ruled late on December 12th. I remember being part of the team at CBS Radio in a very hairy live broadcast that night. Those who have covered the Supreme Court understand that its rulings are often complicated and confusing and don't lend themselves to immediate live broadcasts from the courthouse steps by breathless reporters. Indeed, most of the early reports that night were wrong. Happily our reporter on the scene, Barry Bagnato, is one of the best in the business and we fought back the intense pressure to rush to judgment and remained cautious until we were certain. The decision was not only convoluted, it was downright strange, the justices saying they were deciding this election only and were not creating a precedent that could be used in any future cases. While they technically sent the recall issue back to the Florida Supreme Court, leading to the early false reports, they allowed no time for any recount to proceed and cleared the way for the very partisan Republican secretary of state in Florida, Katherine Harris, to certify the results. Many consider the reasoning in the case to be questionable at best. But someone had to end this and the justices did that. In their five to four ruling, the conservative majority made George W. Bush the next president, and Al Gore conceded the following day.

I find two important takeaways from the chaos that followed the 2000 election. The first is that everyone accepted the results. It demonstrates the extraordinary resilience of our American democracy, not to mention respect for a Supreme Court that may or may not have had the right to do what it did. It has taken far less in other nations to bring riots to the streets or the military taking over a government. A bitterly fought election in which the candidate who got more votes was denied the presidency ended with a peaceful and calm transition and that is pretty impressive.

But I was surprised by the lack of any serious movement to get rid of the Electoral College. The 2000 election proved beyond any shadow of a doubt that this throwback needed to be changed. There were some rumblings in Congress and some academic conferences but no real effort to amend the Constitution to avoid this kind of thing from happening again.

In 2004 I spent a lot time covering the campaign of Democratic Senator John Kerry in his unsuccessful effort to defeat President George W. Bush. Kerry is a smart and accomplished man, who later served as Secretary of State, but was hurt by his patrician air, and despite growing doubts about the war in Iraq and the economy was never able to truly take on Bush. The Bush campaign focused on Kerry's perceived "wishy-washiness," and the underlying message of his ads was that it was better to have someone who was strong, even if his decisions were wrong. Like Dukakis, Kerry took too long to respond to some nasty underhanded attacks concerning his experiences in Vietnam and let the opposition define him. He never posed in a tank, but inviting us all to come watch him wind surf off the coast of Nantucket was nearly as bad.

2004 was the last presidential campaign I covered as one of the "boys on the bus" traveling non-stop for months. Those were exhilarating and totally exhausting times and I was ready to step away.

I did cover parts of the 2008 Democratic primary race, which was extraordinary and historic. Barack Obama had been in the Senate less than one term but had caught fire politically, was a great speaker, and was on his way to becoming the nation's first African-American president. Hillary Clinton, who had made a smooth transition from former first lady to New York senator, was trying to become the first female president. One of the problems Obama and Clinton had was they really didn't disagree on very much. They tried to create differences between themselves on issues like health care, but they weren't real. In fact, the Affordable Care Act, Obama's biggest accomplishment as president, ended up close to what Clinton had been proposing during the primaries.

And so the campaign became personal and at times nasty as the two candidates tried to figure out ways to make themselves look better by making their opponent look worse. They were evenly matched in many ways and the campaign stretched into early summer before Obama finally won. One reason he did was a critical strategic decision made early on that was helped by his unprecedented campaign war chest.

While it makes sense in a general campaign to only focus on the swing states, in a primary fight every delegate in every state counts. While the Clinton strategists felt they would be able to win with big states, Obama's people understood this could go down to the wire and they were playing a very different game. And so Obama was working in little states, especially Republican states, and as Clinton was winning critical big primaries, including California, New York, and New Jersey that split their delegates among the top finishers, Obama was picking up delegates in places like Alaska and North Dakota and those numbers added up.

While in some ways the campaign illustrated how far equal rights had come in this country, it also frankly provided evidence that racism and sexism were alive and well, and not only in the manufactured charges Clinton and Obama threw at each other. I remember talking to voters when covering the West Virginia primary and hearing a lot of pretty horrible things being said about Obama because of his race. Then, talking to male African-American voters in Mississippi, I was struck by how many told me they would never vote for a woman for president.

John McCain has undergone quite a few transformations over his career and the one in 2008 was rather sad to watch. The former fierce independent and reformer allowed himself to be handled and took positions on issues like taxes opposite to those he had previously held. His choice of Sarah Palin was stunning in so many ways and led many to question his judgment. If there was a constant in McCain's public life, it was dedication to America's defense and the importance of a steady hand in the commander-in-chief. The notion that he would seriously want Palin in that role is just not believable.

After he lost and returned to the Senate, McCain in many ways was transformed again, this time into someone who struck me, and many others, as bitter and sometimes just plain cranky. He attacked Obama constantly and backed away from things he clearly believed in. Those who were concerned about global warming were encouraged in the 2008 campaign because it was the first time that there were two candidates who strongly believed in the risks of climate change and wanted to do something about it. But that dedication vanished after Obama was elected. McCain joined other Republicans in attacking the president at every turn. However, his cantankerous nature was not limited to fighting Obama and Democrats. He attacked the increasingly isolationist positions of Republicans, pushed for U.S. military action in hot spots all around the world and when Tea Party Republicans started to get too extreme for him, coined one of the choicest lines ever uttered about them, describing them as "wacko birds."

THEY RAN TOO

Several shorter presidential campaigns were memorable too, including that of Gary Hart, a senator from Colorado who came within a hair's breadth of winning the Democratic nomination in 1984 before losing to Walter Mondale, and then decided to try again in 1988. Mondale had been crushed in 1984 by Reagan, and Hart was considered the front runner for 1988.

He was a self-described "new Democrat" who would move the party in a more centrist and pragmatic direction, away from the liberal label (interestingly the same tack taken by the next Democrat to win the White House, Bill Clinton). He was a smart and attractive candidate, but those of us who covered him always thought there was something just a little off. There were little things, like an unexplained change of his name and lying about his age, for no discernible reason.

That is part of the reason rumors of an extramarital affair were pursued with maybe a little more vigor than was common at the time. When he was asked he angrily denied it and challenged reporters to "follow me around," one of the dumbest things any politician has ever said. We did, and thus emerged the infamous picture of him with a young woman named Donna Rice on a yacht named "Monkey Business." He dropped out of the race soon after.

There was a lot of criticism of the media afterwards. Many see that event as a key turning point from the days when reporters ignored presidents' affairs as private matters to the awful obsession journalists now have for politicians' sex lives. But at the time, the way I saw it was that those of us who covered Gary Hart were already uneasy about his character and honesty, and the episode brought it out in a way everyone could understand.

Colorado Congresswoman Pat Schroeder was one of Hart's national campaign co-chairs and after he dropped out began exploring her own bid for the Democratic nomination. Well respected, smart, and accomplished, she had a real chance to be the first serious female candidate to seek the presidency. She was running third in the polls and as someone with more reason than ambition, struggled with the decision to run. She had no interest in being a symbolic candidate for women's equality, but focused on whether there was the time and money to mount a winning campaign and what it would mean for her family. She made a decision and scheduled an event in Denver to announce it. Nothing had leaked and those of us gathered for that outdoor event waiting for the announcement had no idea which way Schroeder was going to go. As the crowd began to chant, "run, Pat, run," she got through one line saying that she would not be running and then began to cry.

It was excruciating to watch as she tried several times to regain her composure, and then began sobbing again. Nothing else from that speech made the news but her tears were seen around the world. Some jumped on it as evidence women weren't tough enough and were too emotional to be president. Schroeder liked to remind reporters in later years how many male presidential candidates and presidents cried in public and had a large collection of examples. But even today, with John Boehner, the Republican speaker of the House crying at the drop of a hat, the double standard is still there and women seeking high office try to never show any tears.

Jerry Brown, who as a young man was governor of California and won that office again in his 70s, was fun for reporters to cover because he was unpredictable. Very few politicians surprise those of us covering them. By the end of the Reagan campaign, most of us who traveled could recite his speech along with him from memory, but you never knew what was going to come out of Jerry Brown's mouth. He could be giving a well-reasoned speech on clean energy, a subject on which he was well ahead of his time, and then launch into a riff on why we need to set up colonies on Mars. He ran for president three times. In 1976 he entered the race after most of the primaries were over and rode a wave of "anyone but Carter" sentiment as many liberals started having second thoughts about the Georgia governor who had come out of nowhere to lead the pack. Brown won a few late primaries but couldn't catch up to Carter. But approaching 1980 he was considered a strong contender, and I was among a large contingent of national political reporters who followed him when he formally declared and headed to the all-important first primary state of New Hampshire. When he pulled his large motorcade over to get ice cream it was cute, but then his offbeat side got the better of him.

We were spending the night in Boston when Jacques Barzaghi, his longtime friend and constant companion on the road, told him one of his favorite swamis was in town at a swami convention. Before any of his more grounded political advisors could stop him, Brown and Barzaghi headed off to see the swami with a small group of reporters and photographers in tow. Needless to say, by the next morning the story shifted from Jerry Brown the leading Democratic challenger to Jerry Brown the flake. It wasn't the first time Barzaghi led him off the straight and narrow political path, but the timing was perfect to sink him. Within days the national press corps was gone and we moved on to Ted Kennedy, who decided to challenge President Carter for the nomination, and came close to beating him.

Ted Kennedy was a great senator who fought hard for liberal causes but also reached across party lines and created coalitions and got important legislation passed into law. One of his close friends was Utah Republican Senator Orrin Hatch, as far away politically as it was possible to get, but they found common ground. On opposite sides on abortion, for instance, they knew they couldn't bridge that gap, but could come together on providing health care for poor pregnant women and young mothers and their infants and making adoption easier.

But traveling with Kennedy as he sought the presidential nomination, it was clear his heart wasn't really in it. That came through in dramatic fashion in an interview with Roger Mudd on CBS, broadcast on November 4, 1979, as Kennedy was traveling around the country in the run-up to his formal announcement. Mudd asked what should have been a softball question, "Why do you want to be president?" and Kennedy seemed stumped. He paused way too long, looked like a deer stuck in the headlights and gave a rambling non-answer. It led many to believe the real answer was, "I don't," or perhaps, "Because it's my turn," that he was running out of a sense of obligation to his family and his two assassinated brothers. Once his campaign was over and he lost to Carter it was as if a weight had been lifted from his shoulders. At the Democratic convention in New York he gave an inspiring speech, far better than any he gave while halfheartedly seeking the nomination.

There were smaller election battles that stand out too. The first I covered was in 1978 with the passage of Proposition 13 in California, a state with a long history of ballot initiatives where citizens get together and change the state constitution. Some in the 1960s were pretty wacky, including one to allow racial discrimination in housing and another to ban cable television, which was still in its infancy. Both of those were eventually thrown out by the courts, but not Proposition 13, which was the brainchild of Howard Jarvis, a wonderfully quotable cranky old fellow and his more straight-laced partner, Paul Gann.

They launched what came to be known as the "taxpayers' revolution" and played no small role in setting the groundwork for Ronald Reagan's presidential campaign two years later. The initiative was fairly simple. It rolled back property taxes in California, stopped them from being increased, and made it extremely difficult for the state legislature to raise any other taxes. California had high property taxes and the initiative passed overwhelmingly.

It can certainly be seen as the start of a powerful anti-tax movement that continues to this day. Some of its effects, including a dramatic cut in funding for California's public schools, which at the time were some of the best in the country, are still felt.

Another important election I covered in California was the 1982 governor's race, not so much for who won but who lost. Republican George Deukmejian won the race, beating Los Angeles Mayor Tom Bradley. Bradley, a former police officer, had been a popular mayor for 20 years, and his candidacy was significant because he was African American and would have made history. (It would be eight years later that Doug Wilder in Virginia became the first African American to be elected governor.)

It was an extremely close race and I was covering the story on election night at the hotel where Bradley supporters were gathered. Several of the television networks projected that Bradley would win based on exit polls. Exit polls were considered very reliable and were based on interviews done by hundreds of people hired by a consortium of news organizations at a scientifically chosen sampling of precincts. I was working for UPI Radio and we had much stricter rules about not calling any race until we were sure based on actual counted ballots. But Bradley went to sleep that night a few floors up from the hotel ballroom where his supporters were celebrating convinced he had been elected governor.

He woke up in the morning to learn that he had lost in a squeaker.

It was obviously a tough day for Bradley (who tried again four years later and lost by a much larger margin) but it also caused a lot of handwringing in the media and years of research into how our exit polls could have been so far off. The answer was as simple as it was frightening for those of us who count on polls in our political reporting: people lied. Not just a few people, but large numbers of people just flat-out lied to the exit pollsters.

One theory was that it had to do with race and people who voted for Deukmejian thought it made them look better to tell the pollster that they had voted for Bradley. Not that they voted against Bradley for reasons of racism (though there certainly was some of that) but because saying they voted against him might suggest they were racist. Pollsters even started using the term the "Bradley effect" to suggest that there were times voters lied to tell pollsters they voted for a minority candidate when in fact they didn't.

Twenty-six years later when Barack Obama was running for president his pollsters were very aware of the Bradley effect, and those of us in the media looking at polls that year were concerned that we not get misled the way we were in the Bradley race. But in 2008 the pre-election polls and the exit polls turned out to be pretty accurate.

Another interesting local race I covered was the governor's contest in Louisiana in 1991. Louisiana has a long, colorful history of corrupt politicians and one of them was Edwin Edwards, a Democrat known for living large, who had already been elected several times as governor and was trying for a comeback. He had not yet been convicted of any felonies (that would come later and he would eventually go to prison), but his reputation was well established and no one thought he could win another election. That was until the state's Republicans nominated David Duke, a renowned white supremacist and Holocaust denier, who was the former Grand Wizard of the Ku Klux Klan.

When polls a few weeks out showed that Duke was leading in the race there was panic in Louisiana and panic in newsrooms, which is why reporters like me suddenly were rushing to cover this off-off year governor's race. Business leaders in the state saw a future in which there would be boycotts of New Orleans tourism and they started pouring money into the Edwards campaign. Even Republican President George H.W. Bush came out to publicly endorse the corrupt Democrat over the Klan Republican. Edwards won in the end and it produced what I believe to this day is the best political bumper sticker of all time. It read: "Vote for the crook. It's important."

Over the decades I developed a kind of subspecialty covering presidential vacations and some were better than others. Reagan was of course the best, spending a month or longer at a time several times a year at his ranch in the hills above Santa Barbara. He would spend his days "chopping wood and clearing brush," or so we were told. I think if he did that as much as was reported there wouldn't be a tree left standing. The ranch was a great place for horse riding and just relaxing. His ranch house was small and rustic, decorated in cowboy movie style and he desired nothing bigger or fancier. The best thing was when he went there he never came down the mountain, leaving those covering him to enjoy the beautiful beach town with its great restaurants and perfect weather. The network TV correspondents each rented big beach houses and held occasional parties. And other than a few times when Reagan held a party for reporters or came down to go to church on Easter we never saw him. Major news would happen, including some international crises, when we covered Reagan at the ranch but nothing ever brought him down. It wasn't always clear his staff had even told him about developments in the world.

Still, he was the president and you just never know, so we stayed and took our beepers to the beach and restaurants. Every few days we would gather in a hotel ballroom for the press secretary to tell us the president was still chopping wood and clearing brush.

The first President Bush couldn't have been more different in style. His vacations were hyperactive and frequently interrupted by news he would want to comment on. He vacationed at his family home in Kennebunkport, Maine, and was always out playing golf or riding his speedboat. But it still wasn't exactly hardship duty. We stayed at an aging hotel on the water, ate lots of lobster, and sometimes headed out sailing. That first Bush Administration was also very family-friendly. The very expensive charter plane our news organizations had to pay for always had lots of empty seats and the White House allowed family members to fill them for minimal or no cost. So the press corps in Kennebunkport always included lots of reporters' kids, who President Bush sometimes invited out for rides on his speedboat.

There were lots of news stories on those trips and we would head out to the Bush compound for him to make a statement out on the lawn. One of those times was when he nominated Clarence Thomas to the Supreme Court to replace Thurgood Marshall, the great liberal and first African American on the high court. After making the announcement and stating with a straight face that Thomas was the "most qualified person he could find for the job," a reporter questioned him but he stuck to it. Clearly telling the truth, that he was the most conservative black nominee he could find and Democratic senators wouldn't dare block him, wouldn't have been prudent.

I was happy to join President Clinton on some excellent vacations, more varied because he had no vacation home in Arkansas or anywhere else. His wife Hillary had always been the breadwinner in the family and while the Clintons became extremely wealthy after leaving the White House, they weren't that way coming in. One nice trip was to Jackson Hole, Wyoming, one of the nation's most beautiful mountain resorts. I rode the chairlift to the top of the mountain for great views and hiked around nearby Jenny Lake.

Clinton generally spent his New Year's holidays in St. Thomas in the U.S. Virgin Islands, which also was a nice place to work. He stayed at a private villa and so we stayed at a resort and barely saw him. Days were generally spent at the beach with rum drinks and happily very little news was made.

I was with Clinton on a trip to Florida in 1997 when he learned a lesson I had long known about Air Force One. It is a very nice plane, comfortable and with all the latest gadgets, but it doesn't use the jetways that commercial planes do. Instead, to board Air Force One you have to climb a long flight of stairs outside and another narrow set of stairs on the inside to get to the passenger cabins (separate ones for the president, his staff, Secret Service, and press).

I was never really happy about the hassle of having to climb two flights of stairs with luggage to get on the president's airplane, but on this Florida trip the President learned about it first hand. He was visiting golfer Greg Norman and they stayed up late talking before a planned golf game the next day. Walking down some wooden steps at 1:30 in the morning, Clinton missed the last one and fell, damaging his knee. Doctors determined he needed surgery and the decision was made to fly him back to Washington to have the operation at Bethesda Naval Hospital.

They then discovered what I could have told them: there was no way he was going to be able to climb those two flights of stairs to get into his plane.

They ended up putting Clinton in a wheelchair on the open platform of a catering truck that could lift him up to the door used to put food on the plane and he got in that way. It all ended up for the best because he got crutches to use during his recovery that were made to order by a small company in Pennsylvania. They were great titanium crutches that were strong and super light, completely quiet, and jet black. I saw them up close at a small reception I attended with the president, one of those black-tie Washington events where reporters mingle with the politicians we cover. We posed for a picture with our crutches that is on this book's cover and I got the name of the company that made his crutches. They've made mine ever since.

VIETNAM AND CAMBODIA 2011

It's a long way.

First stop, Hanoi, is uber-bustling and overflowing with life. People are friendly, streets are filled with vendors selling everything imaginable, and you can pretty much find a massage or karaoke on every block.

There appear to be no traffic laws at all and crossing the street takes nerves of steel and a lot of luck. You pick your time and just walk in a steady pace exuding confidence that the motorbikes will swerve around you because they won't stop. Walking along the street isn't much better. There are sidewalks but that's where the motorbikes park, and tables and chairs are set up for eating (which the Vietnamese do constantly), and so the only place to walk is in the street with the traffic.

I lucked out with a great little hotel right in the center of everything. It has an extremely helpful staff and a spacious room that comes with breakfast, flower petals on the bed, and its own laptop computer and is in the upper tier for Hanoi at $60 a night.

It is modestly named "Hotel Elegance Diamond" to distinguish it from its sister hotels, including the Hotel Elegance Ruby, Emerald, and Sapphire.

The hotel breakfast was a fine and eclectic buffet with fresh baguettes and fruits both familiar and exotic, and everything from eggs and pancakes to the national soup dish, pho; steamed dumplings and fried rice.

I took a free full-day city tour with an organization that pairs up college students with foreign devils. It was a fun tour with a young woman in her senior year studying economics. We had some good conversations in which she explained how capitalism is doomed and communism will prevail in the world. I tried to gently point out her nation is a whirlwind of capitalist fervor, and she explained you needed some capitalism as long as the government was in control. She wanted to know if American students study Marx and Lenin and was shocked to learn we have no government-run media and are not allowed to eat our dogs.

Our first stop, as required by tourist law, was the tomb of Ho Chi Minh (who everyone here calls "Uncle Ho") who fought against the imperialists (French, Japanese, and us). He doesn't look bad for a guy who's been dead almost 40 years. He even still has his beard.

Hanoi in summer is somewhat hotter than hot and far wetter than wet and if Guinness has a record for the most sweat produced on a single day I may have broken it. The old city center is a warren of small, crowded streets, each with its own specialty. One sells only clothes, another shoes, toys, or bamboo baskets. A favorite is a street selling fake Vietnamese and American currency to burn as offerings.

Though they were imperialists, the French influence is everywhere from the food (baguettes and fries) to the architecture. I ate at the upscale Green Tangerine in a classic French colonial house that could have easily been in New Orleans.

The city is crowded, smelly, and noisy and trash is thrown in the street, then occasionally swept into small piles and burned. But Hanoi is also exhilarating and fascinating.

During the frequent downpours (it is monsoon season), everyone takes cover under storefront awnings. During one of them, a young man offered me a chair and asked if he could practice his English with me. He said he follows many famous Americans on Twitter (you know who you are!).

In another rainstorm I ducked into a bar and was served wonton nachos with chile sauce.

A giant gothic cathedral in the center of Hanoi seems quite out of place, though no more than Mediterraneo, a truly fine Italian restaurant just up the street from it (ravioli with sausage, walnuts, and mushrooms in cream sauce and chocolate mousse!).

Religion here is a fusion of Buddhism, Confucianism and Taoism, ancient gods of the sea and the fields, with a little Uncle Ho worship thrown in. Confucius was big on learning and his shrines fill up with students praying at exam time. Offerings at the altars run the gamut from rice and incense to cash and whiskey, though my favorite was at a small Buddhist shrine where the offering was several bottles of orange soda with the tops off and straws placed inside.

In Argentina you go see tango; in China you must go to the circus; in Hanoi, it is the "world famous" water puppets. It is an elaborate tourist show with an orchestra of classic Vietnamese instruments. The 1000-year-old art form is impressive and the puppeteers skilled, but it's also a tad silly as giant wooden puppets of people, buffalo, and dragons splash around in a big pool of water.

After collapsing early, I woke up at 5:30 am and headed to the nearby Magical Tortoise Lake, the heart of the old city. The streets were filled with the smell of pho cooking for breakfast on the sidewalks and at least a thousand people were out exercising at the lake: walking or jogging around it, doing tai chi, playing badminton with and without nets; one group was taking lessons in ballroom dancing.

I visited the museum at what's left of Hoa Lo prison, better known as the Hanoi Hilton. Sad and interesting, it focused on the earlier use of the prison built by the French for Vietnamese who resisted their occupation.

Still it was very unnerving to see John McCain's parachute and flight suit on display. The history of war is generally written by the winner and it's jarring to see it from that perspective when it isn't us.

Lunch was at Quan An Ngon, a wildly popular spot with communal tables under a giant tent with lots of fans and scores of Vietnamese dishes, all being prepared in open kitchens encircling the dining area. Delicious food and absurdly cheap prices.

Walked around the "French Quarter" with wide streets, beautiful buildings, and swank stores, though I'm not sure what Ho Chi Minh would have thought about a Gucci store in his capital.

Splurged on dinner at Club de L'Oriental, arguably Hanoi's most elegant restaurant. Started with spring rolls stuffed with big chunks of crab in a wrapper so light it just melted in my mouth. The tiger prawns were outrageously good in a garlic sauce. The steamed rice was filled with goodies including more crab, mushrooms, lotus and other bits I fear may have been vegetables.

The Vietnamese serve fresh mint with everything and it was put to excellent use in my mojito. The bill topped a million dong! About $50.

It was only about a ten-minute walk back to the hotel but I was walked out and opted for a 79-cent cab ride.

The next day, in a van heading to my ship to visit Halong Bay, the representative of the cruise company asked if anyone had any special dietary needs. One French couple spoke up and said, "We don't eat dog." The guide looked confused so they repeated it and she dutifully wrote it down.

Upon arrival we boarded Prince 2, a lovely Chinese-style junk for three days on Halong Bay. It's a truly unique and amazing landscape with an ethereal beauty as we sailed among 2000 islands, most of which are sheer limestone cliffs towering straight up. Some are just rock towers, others rounded at the top with trees and plants and the occasional sea eagle flying overhead. Parts of the bay are mobbed with hundreds of tour boats, but I picked this trip because it goes far afield and we rarely saw another boat.

We kayaked through a dark low cave under one island to a magical little lagoon on the other side and later jumped off the side of our boat for a swim in the warm salt water. The legend is that there are baby dragons here and it looks like they belong.

Best rule posted in my room: "Don't smock in the cabin."

Anh is our young guide and cruise director and kept us engaged and entertained. He explained in the safety talk that we have an alarm and life jackets. Asked where the lifeboat was, he said there wasn't one, but we shouldn't worry because if the boat sinks a fast rescue boat would come right away.

We had perfect weather and didn't sink.

We did visit a friendly floating fishing village and were offered a terrifying homemade moonshine made with honeycombs, with several bees visible in the plastic jug.

As we kayaked into pitch-black caves with no flashlights, Anh lied with a smile as he told us it wasn't dangerous. But it was tons of fun. A highlight was after a morning of kayaking and swimming we were served lunch on a small sand beach with table, chairs, umbrellas, linens, two waiters and a bottle of champagne.

This is a very good life.

Back in Hanoi I went for a change in cuisine and tried the city's top French restaurant La Badiane, a tiny place just off a narrow alley with Western prices. The mojito had mango, the crab appetizer was tasty, and the duck excellent, served over cooked apples on a crisp pastry shell.

I'm down to my last million dong, so it's time to hit the ATM, which was next to Fanny's Ice Cream, where I passed on "young rice" flavor but enjoyed chocolate and passion fruit.

Overnight trains are one of those things that always sound better in theory.

The hotel sent a bellman with me to the station who got me through the chaos on to the right train heading to Hue and didn't leave until I was safely in my compartment. Signals at Hanoi station were provided by people standing next to the tracks holding different colored lanterns.

This being the off-season for tourists, the fancier sleeping compartment cars (with sit-down toilets!) weren't full and I had a four-bed compartment to myself. That is, until the train attendant came in to have his dinner followed by two railroad security guards. They slept in the three empty berths and never left until our arrival in Hue.

Hue is a calm and pretty city along the Perfume River. The former imperial capital, it is the site of some of the worst fighting during what people here call the "American War."

I spent several hours wandering through the Citadel, the walled "forbidden city" of Vietnam's last emperors surrounded by a very cool zigzag moat filled with floating lotus flowers. It wasn't a very old empire. The complex of palaces, temples, and residences for hundreds of concubines and the eunuchs who watched over them was built in 1805 (when Thomas Jefferson was president) and the empire officially was ended by Uncle Ho in 1945, but lost its power long before then to the French.

It is annoying to have to bargain over everything. I asked a cyclo driver for a short ride in his bike-powered cart and he quoted me 500,000 dong ($25), probably enough to buy his cyclo. He eventually came down to 50,000, but it is an exhausting process.

On the other hand, miracles do happen.

As I was getting out of a taxi at a lovely little restaurant that served French and Vietnamese food, a motorbike driven by a tourist smashed into the back of my cab, badly cracking the bumper. No one was hurt. But about 30 minutes later, after the spring rolls and before the duck, I realized that in the confusion of the accident my camera had slipped out of my pocket getting out of the cab. The waitresses saw how upset I was and spent 20 minutes on the phone tracking down the taxi. When they did, the driver found my camera and brought it back to the restaurant.

Best things about small Vietnam hotels: extraordinary service and helpfulness and ridiculously cheap minibar and laundry prices.

Worst things: The air conditioning goes off when you leave so you always return to a hot room and the soaps are half the size of what would be needed by an average Munchkin.

Took a tour out of town to see the tombs of the emperors, big complexes of tombs, temples and man-made lakes. At the ticket booth were the rules. My favorite is number three: "Not to bring in the dynamite, poisons and weapons."

The most beautiful tomb by far, with elaborate mosaics made with Chinese and Japanese porcelain, belonged to Khai Dinh. Odd, because he was a very unpopular emperor installed by the French as a puppet. He gambled, smoked opium and, most unforgivably, raised taxes.

Hue is known for its "cakes," but clearly the bakers here have no idea what a cake should taste like.

After some very half-hearted bargaining on my part I was happy to pay $16 to rent a 10-passenger dragon boat to cruise the Perfume River for two hours to visit the Thien Mu Pagoda.

I had lunch at a large luxury hotel just to refresh my credentials as a rich American (and to use their well-equipped bathroom).

I am old.

I find I can go about half a day of walking, touring, fighting off vendors, climbing steps at temples, and sweating enough that my clothes are dripping. Even after a leisurely lunch, by 3 in the afternoon I'm in bed at the hotel, napping with the air conditioner all the way up. Pretty pathetic.

After three days in Hue I hired a car and driver for the five-hour trip south to Hoi An with several stops, including a scenic beach along the way. It's a pretty drive through lush green countryside with the occasional water buffalo, and crosses several mountain passes. The beach had another great set of rules, including "Drunkards cannot swim."

Hoi An is a touristy historic town of well preserved old buildings, a pretty riverfront, and lots of color. I am ensconced at a sweet little resort in a small villa opening on to the pool. Good place for napping.

But first, I headed to the Mermaid Cafe for a late lunch. Hoi An is known for its food and I had a local specialty, "white rose," a light-as-air steamed rice paper dumpling with a shrimp inside, topped with crispy toasted onions. I'll need more of those.

I am an aficionado of the spring roll and believe I now have eaten the world's most exquisite spring roll at Mango Rooms, a small, very upscale eatery. I'm beginning to fear three days won't give me enough meals in this town.

The only cooking class I ever took was in high school. We needed two "practical arts" classes—home economics for girls and shop for boys. I, and an equally rebellious friend, decided spending an hour a day cooking and eating with the girls would be much more fun than auto shop. We were right.

So I figured it was about time to try another cooking class and headed to the Red Bridge Cooking School.

First, our group, which hailed from half a dozen countries, was guided through the outdoor market, learning about all the fruits, vegetables, spices, chickens, seafood and fish. I learned how to test if a squid is fresh and trust me: you don't want to know.

Then we traveled 30 minutes by boat deep into the countryside, up a small river to this modern facility in the jungle, where for several hours we made delicious food and ate it. My crisp shrimp-stuffed pancake wrapped in rice paper was a masterpiece. My tomato that was supposed to be carved into the shape of a rose? A total disaster.

Tonight's massage included tiger balm, which burned a bit as she rubbed it into my neck and scalp but is supposed to cure everything. I'll let you know.

I'm running into a fair number of Australians, Brits, French, Spanish, and Japanese tourists, but very few other Americans. That's why I was surprised at Miss Ly's, a longtime fixture of the Hoi An dining scene, to be greeted at the door by a New Yorker. Turns out he married Miss Ly last year. Had another fantastic local specialty, cao lau, a kind of salad made from cold thick noodles, shredded lettuce and cilantro, pork slices and deep-fried spiced wonton croutons.

After leaving Hoi An I flew to Ho Chi Minh City, which everyone except the government still calls Saigon. It is a huge, frenetic noisy city but with a very different feel from Hanoi or Hue. There are tons of motorbikes but also lots of private cars. It has skyscrapers, traffic lights, and a more modern feel. Walking down the street no one is shouting, "Hello! Where are you from?" trying to sell me something. I quickly run across a French bakery run by a real Frenchman and pop in for a chocolate pastry.

Saw the sights, many of which relate to the victory over the American imperialists. The city has some beautiful buildings left over from the French, but isn't as scenic or exotic as Hanoi. The American influence is overwhelming on every street.

They are seriously into hair and body care here. I got a haircut and was massaged many times. That included a $3 one-hour body massage at the Institute of the Blind, where blind men and women massage in a style that involves a lot of slapping and some head thumping.

I had dinner at Xu, a super-hip restaurant with waiters all in black and techno music that would fit right in on the west side of Manhattan, if the prices were tripled. I passed on the tasting menu (which included pork and snail spring rolls and curried goat) and went with a yummy crab appetizer and sea bass that was heavenly.

Passing government buildings, it strikes me this is one of the last places on the planet you see the hammer and sickle flag still flying, usually right next to Vietnam's single star flag,

I fly next to Siem Reap, Cambodia, to see Angkor Wat and head to

The One Hotel. I first heard of it on the Travel Channel, which listed the ten most exclusive hotels in the world and it topped the list. It has only one room and the front desk and the chef and the bellman and the rest of the staff are all working just for one (or two) guests. It was the first reservation I made for this trip, paying about half what the Marriott in Manhattan charges.

Things got off to a good start as my personal concierge met me with a driver at the airport and gave me a local cell phone with him on speed dial so I can call when I need him. The hotel owner, a transplanted American from Indiana, has his number in there too.

The room has a giant bed on a wooden platform, the bathtub is sunken stone, there is a big shower and a second outdoor shower on the roof deck next to the private Jacuzzi and oversize bed for lounging or massage. The room comes with a stereo system with speakers in every room and at the Jacuzzi and a loaded iPod, DVD player with DVDs, complimentary stocked mini-bar that will be refilled daily and an iPad. Breakfast is served in your room or on the roof deck.

Siem Reap has a small, walkable tourist center filled with charm and unlike in Hanoi or Saigon, I can safely cross the street. There are tons of kids who latch on to you trying to sell postcards or some little trinkets. It's tough because people here really are very poor. I don't need postcards but once or twice did buy a kid a meal at one of the food stands located every few feet. The people are friendly and low key and the town is filled with restaurants, bars, massage parlors, and tanks with fish that eat the dead skin off your feet.

I'm anxious to get started seeing the temples of Angkor Wat and hire a driver with a tuk-tuk, a motorcycle pulling a little cart with padded seats and a roof, rather like a surrey without a fringe on top. His English is good and he charges $15 for a full day. (I paid him more.)

Angkor Wat really does take your breath away, as does climbing the incredibly steep steps. The scale is amazing. It's said to be the largest religious structure ever built by man (or visiting space aliens). The inside walls that go forever are completely covered with intricate carvings telling stories, including when the monkey god went to war against the demons (and thankfully won).

Angkor Wat is the granddaddy of the temples, but many of the others are equally or even more fantastic. The walled ancient city of Angkor Thom has the Elephant Terrace, the wall of a thousand Buddhas (I took their word for it) and half a dozen temples, including Bayon. For almost a mile its walls have intricate, carved illustrations of stories on three vertical levels and at the top of an absurdly steep stairway terraces with hundreds of huge faces look down on you. Each has a rather cryptic smile and there is always one seeming to watch you.

My tuk-tuk driver Chen was terrific and I rode to different temples with him over four days. He knew them well and was helpful, friendly and reliable, always waiting with a bottle of ice-cold water as I emerged from the temples.

There were tons of tourists, but these temples are so vast you can easily turn down some small passage and find yourself alone to quietly contemplate the place. After one such turn I found a monk who tied a red string around my wrist for luck. Then he asked for a dollar. Another turn brought me to a young artist and I bought one of his small paintings.

Chen is a singer but says now that he has two young children he needs the income a tuk-tuk driver can earn. He says the largest number of tourists come from Korea and Japan, but always travel in big groups. He says they are told at home if they hire a Cambodian driver he might kill them. (They are probably told the same thing about New York.)

Some of the temples are older, Hindu instead of Buddhist and brick instead of stone. The most spectacular and my favorite is Ta Prohm. It is in the jungle amid the trees and branches and roots are wrapped around archways and the ancient stones. It is a marvel.

One of the smallest temples is also one of the most scenic. Banteay Srei is made of a pinkish limestone and built, not by a king, but by a wealthy member of the king's court, and is dedicated to Hindu gods. The carvings are incredibly well preserved, as are large, sculpted monkeys lining each courtyard.

It's about 20 miles away, which is a fair distance in a bouncy tuk-tuk, but I think it was a much better experience than going in a car would have been. You see so much more and the people you pass can see you. It was a fascinating slice of rural life with farmers in knee-deep water tending their rice with plows pulled by water buffalo, women cooking palm syrup in giant vats on clay ovens heated with wood fires, and children swimming in the nearly endless supply of ponds and rivers that appear in the rainy season. A handful of wells producing clean drinking water each had a sign of which Western charity donated it. There were no gas stations but roadside stands selling gasoline in small glass bottles. (No pesky government safety regulations here.)

When downpours came the tuk-tuk had surprisingly effective rain flaps.

Some of the less famous and less well-preserved temples were monumental in their own right and nice because the tour buses skip them. It's quite an experience to walk through one alone. One distant temple was next to a Buddhist monastery and my driver was perplexed that I didn't want a photo but wanted instead to go inside to visit. I spent 20 minutes or so chatting with the monks. They were mostly boys who come when they are quite young, get an education, and can leave whenever they want to return to a secular life and most do. They get up at 4 am and pray, and around 6 walk to the nearby village, where people with barely enough for themselves always come out to bring them rice and other food.

I went upscale to dinner at Visoth, a lovely garden setting with waterfalls, candles, and the all-important fan. I asked be moved closer. Tried fresh passion fruit soda. The seeds stay in it and the sugar syrup comes separately, so you can decide how sweet you want it. The spring rolls were crisp and delicious and I thoroughly enjoyed the special fish amok. (Fish is always just "fish." What more would anyone need to know?)

It came in a bowl submerged in a rich broth with coconut milk and lemongrass. Had ice cream for dessert, so the bill was a princely $15.

The Cambodians, by the way, like the Thais, generally eat with a fork, not chopsticks. The comma is important because they don't LIKE the Thais and there are occasional firefights along their disputed border, which is a fine spot if you want to go looking for land mines.

A wild nighttime tuk-tuk ride out of town on pitch-black, partially flooded dirt roads brought me to Touich, reputed to be Siem Reap's best restaurant. It's a tiny dining room under a thatched roof with a nice assortment of sculptures, far enough in the sticks they put mosquito coils at each table and the sound of the frogs competed with the soft music. (An aside: though I brought enough DEET to launch a major jungle expedition, I've barely seen a mosquito anywhere and only got one bite, though it could have been from a sandfly or small crocodile.)

Back to dinner. The mojito came with a flower in it and a touch of ginger.

The beef salad was nice with more beef than salad and the red snapper ("fish") was served whole at tableside and was perfectly cooked.

It has one serious flaw though, no desserts. None. Shocking.

I made up for it the next day with a rather amazing find. As a kid in Los Angeles, Swensen's Old-Fashioned Ice Cream Parlor was my favorite. They are only in a few states besides California so I hadn't seen one of their stores in many years. I was stunned to find one in Siem Reap, Cambodia. Same old-fashioned lighting fixtures, same company—and they still make a mean chocolate sundae.

There was a nice spa down the street, so I popped in for a traditional Cambodian massage (2 hours, $32, plus generous tip). First she washed my feet, and then asked if I wanted the massage medium or hard. I said medium, but should have said "newborn baby soft." Still, in the end, after the post-massage lemongrass tea, I felt good and managed to stumble in a half-stupor back to my hotel, where the fridge was stocked with cold drinks and my glass was chilled.

I've lost all track of time and feel like I've been here forever. If it wasn't for my iPhone, repository of all knowledge, I don't think I'd even know what month it is.

My journey next led me on a five-hour drive in a shared minivan to Cambodia's capital of Phnom Penh. Even when the two-lane bumpy "highway" to Phnom Penh passed through good-sized towns, none of the other streets were paved, and for most of the way trucks were outnumbered by carts drawn by horse, cow, or water buffalo. Coming here from Vietnam really is like traveling back in time.

Phnom Penh is a big, busy, polluted city but has an interesting character and the area along the Mekong River is lined with parks and wide boardwalks. Worried I needed to ease back slowly from a life of pampered luxury at The One Hotel, I picked a lovely little hotel with lush tropical gardens right behind the Royal Palace. I got a room with a private swimming pool in its own walled garden ($90 a night). I'd never had a hotel room with its own swimming pool before. It's nice.

The restaurants here have some interesting names. One by the river is called "Titanic" and my favorite is "Mother-in-law House Two," which raises the question of what happened to Mother-in-law House One.

There are a lot of weapons left over from wars in Cambodia with no one to shoot them at, and so tourists can head to shooting ranges to try out AK-47s, machine guns and even grenade launchers. I'll pass.

I also pass on two of the top tourist destinations, the killing fields and the torture museum. The people of this country suffered horribly at the hands of the Pol Pot regime but I don't need to go see it. While Siem Reap is an extremely safe city, Phnom Penh has a street crime problem, so I'll be a bit more careful at night and keep a grenade launcher close.

I head first to the Royal Palace. Even in a very poor country it's good to be the king. The throne room is an entire building, but the highlight is the Silver Pagoda. Its floor is covered in silver tiles. Not silver plate, but solid silver tiles, each weighing about two pounds. It is filled with hundreds of Buddha statues of marble, jade and silver, and a life-size gold Buddha studded with more than 2000 diamonds. But while there is plenty of opulence, including one display of hundreds of carved elephants in silver, gold and marble, the main feeling walking around the palace grounds, with its low pavilions, pagodas, gardens and the occasional monkey, is serenity. It is a very peaceful place.

Hit a "good deed" restaurant for lunch. It's run by an Australian charity that helps hundreds of street children, some who served my shrimp spring rolls and stir fried chicken along with a very tasty watermelon-passion fruit slushy. It's a little more expensive than other places, but you get to feel like you are being generous when you order dessert (crepes with chocolate sauce and vanilla ice cream).

Cambodia feels much more like Thailand than Vietnam (though its Khmer empire included much of both) and you see it especially at the Buddhist temples. I climbed the city's only hill (a very small one) to the impressive Phnom Pagoda, with many fine Buddhas and surrounded by a popular park. A sign indicated foreigners (that's me) have to pay a dollar to get in.

Across the street is the American Embassy. Sadly, like so many of our embassies around the world, it is built like a fortress, sending the architectural message to "stay away."

Everything you could need here is on the sidewalks: from food, drinks and clothes to haircuts, manicures and motorcycle repair. It is very hot and in the afternoon I head back to my hotel for a siesta. The main pool has little couches with individual fans, but I decide to swim in my personal pool and then lounge under my banana tree.

Decided on my last night in the old French Indochina to go to Van's for French food in a very elegant dining room (two flights up, no escaping the stairs in this country). Though very expensive for Cambodia, it was also only the second place on this trip that served purified water without having to buy it in bottles. I started with some scrumptious scallops in a mushroom and cheese sauce, then tried the Mekong lobster. Not as big or sweet as we grow them in Maine and served with a spicy brown sauce instead of drawn butter, but tasty nonetheless.

I NEED A BREAK

Words are the stock and trade of journalists and we not only use them, but have an obligation to defend them against a constant effort to twist and abuse them, from the Orwellian naming of the MX ICBM missile as the "Peacekeeper" during the Reagan Administration, to the everyday actions of political spinners.

In 2001 as part of a broader effort to reduce taxes, President Bush and Republicans in Congress launched a strong move to repeal the estate tax. This tax on large inheritances was first imposed in 1916 and like all taxes was designed to bring in revenue, but had a broader purpose too, to try to break up the wealth of a few powerful families that had an outsized influence over American business and politics.

The idea that began in the progressive era with Republican Teddy Roosevelt was that it wasn't good for a democracy to have extremely wealthy families stay extremely wealthy forever, and it did have an impact. The tax was only imposed when wealth was passed down from one generation to the next (spouses were always exempted) and only applied to large inheritances. It was only the very wealthiest of Americans who ever paid the tax, a far smaller group than what we later called the "one percent."

But some of those Americans were big donors to the Republican Party, including families of privately owned companies like Mars Candy, whose main political goal was to get rid of the inheritance tax. They tried first to convince people that this was hurting family farms, and when that wasn't doing the trick some bright political consultant came up with a great idea: instead of calling it the estate tax, they would start calling it the "death tax."

They would make the argument that people shouldn't be taxed after they died, that this was un-American and unfair and must be stopped. If successful, voters would think this was a matter of fairness instead of an effort by a handful of wealthy families to hand down their fortunes without paying any taxes. They also counted on a quirk of human nature that also explains why people buy lottery tickets, the belief that no matter how unlikely it was, there was still some chance they themselves would one day inherit a large fortune.

I and other reporters covering Congress at the time saw right through this, of course, and referred to the tax by its proper name when covering the debate. The tenor of the time prevented Democrats from defending the tax as a way to prevent the excessive build-up of wealth in families over generations. I remember pressing defenders of the tax to talk about what its creators and early backers had in mind to break up family wealth and whether that was still important, but they were fearful of doing that.

So the argument ended up being over whether the government could afford the loss in revenue and whether this was indeed a "fair" tax. But the opponents won the battle over words, and with incredible discipline no Republican ever referred to it as anything other than the "death tax." Many reporters started using that wording too, and in the end the tax cut bill of 2001 included a repeal of the estate tax. However, it didn't quite work out the way supporters wanted it to because of something called the "Byrd rule" named for Senator Robert Byrd of West Virginia, a great orator who knew the Senate rules backwards and forwards and used them to limit all the provisions of the tax law to only ten years, since that was as far as budget projections would go.

Backers of repeal believed once the tax was gone it would never come back but they too had to deal with the realities of the ballooning federal deficit. And so instead of being repealed all at once the estate tax was phased out over ten years and in 2010 it disappeared entirely. But by that time the deficit was concern number one and a Democrat was in the White House. The law was going to run its course and one year after the estate tax disappeared entirely it was going to kick back in at its old high level. A compromise lowered the rate a bit and increased the exemption (it still only affected those with the very largest inheritances), but created a bizarre situation in that final year in which if a wealthy person died by December 31, 2010, his children could inherit millions or even billions tax-free. But if he held on until January 1, they'd pay millions in inheritance tax.

Basically Congress created an incentive to hasten the death of wealthy relatives. Though I have no reason to think anyone killed their rich uncle that December because of the tax law, it was insane public policy.

When my good friend Mike Freedman left CBS News Radio in 2000, he was replaced as general manager by someone who didn't like stories about politics or Congress, and starting in 2001 there was a sudden end to my travel to out-of-town stories that started me over the next few years thinking about leaving. As I began to seriously start looking for an exit, I realized I was also growing disenchanted with journalism, which was being dominated by cable networks, which were dramatically lowering the bar and the standards. I quietly explored teaching and some other options, but what I really wanted to do was win the lottery and just travel for a year.

Over the July 4th holiday in 2003 I was with friends at Lake Louise in the Canadian Rockies, one of the world's most scenic spots. My two friends decided to go play golf and I chose to walk around the lake, which would take me most of the day. As I walked in solitude I began to think seriously about what I needed to do and concluded that because I had been diligently saving money, I actually could afford to take a year off from work and travel and do it without winning the lottery. I decided that's what I would do. I would quit my job and just travel for a year, and then come back and be in a fresh frame of mind to find another job. I had saved enough for the travel as long as I stuck to a pretty strict budget and then be able to support myself for another few months while looking for work. If I timed it right and left in August, I would be able to keep my union health insurance for that entire period. I returned to the hotel feeling as if a huge weight had been lifted from my shoulders. I told my friends and family, and as soon as I got home began immediately planning for my trip.

I arranged a house sitter who would live in my home and take care of my dog. It was an arrangement with no money changing hands, in which he and his young daughter would live rent-free in a nice house and I would not have to pay for someone to care for Chewy. I began serious planning for my journey, laying out a two-month driving trip across the country, using miles to book a flight from the West Coast to Australia, and then leaving the rest open.

Two weeks before I was ready to go I sat down to write my resignation letter to CBS News vice president Harvey Nagler, whom I liked and admired. As I was drafting it, it struck me that I had nothing to lose by asking for a leave of absence instead of resigning. I certainly didn't expect to get it and made clear I would be leaving in any case. Harvey wanted to give me a leave, clearly hoping I would return, but the longest he could offer was six months. I felt it was very unlikely I would come back, but there was absolutely nothing to lose by taking a six-month unpaid leave and that's what I did.

ON THE ROAD 2003-2004

The feeling of freedom is overwhelming as I drive off August 31, 2003, to begin six months of traveling, with no intention of returning to my job, but my leave of absence like an insurance policy in my back pocket.

I am a vagabond with a gold card as I hit the road heading west.

I take Highway 68, the National Freeway, to head over the Appalachians and cross the Eastern Continental Divide. I pass a sign that Noah's Ark is being rebuilt here, but am not quite ready for that. I keep going past the birthplace of Clark Gable in Southeastern Ohio.

My first overnight stop was the Malamar Farm Hostel, where I was the only one in a room with five beds and it cost $15, less than the gas to drive there. I will stay at a number of hostels, which vary greatly in quality and atmosphere. This one has a cozy living room, shared kitchen and a dining room. Other guests include Sue, a woman in her 60s spending a quiet weekend with her grandkids, and a German woman with a one-year-old baby.

My next stop was Columbus where I stayed with my college friend Randy, his wife Allison and son Alex. We had stayed in touch but it had still been years since we'd actually seen each other. But some friendships can just pick up and it was like we had just been together at Stanford the week before. I had spent a lot of time in Ohio on Presidential campaigns and never liked it much, but never had the chance to slow down and really see it, either, and enjoyed my time in Columbus.

I drove off in a rainstorm that lasted all the way through Indiana to Chicago, where I would spend several days with my longtime friend Bob Berger.

A massage takes out the kinks from driving, a visit to the zoo reminds me of Congress as the gorillas pound their chests and try to be the top ape, and I take a fun gangster tour of all the Al Capone-related spots. I end up staying a few days longer than planned before heading on towards Wisconsin.

Madison is a pretty state capitol and even from the rest stop you can tell this is a liberal place. There isn't just one recycle bin but separate ones for green glass, brown glass, clear glass, tin foil, aluminum and plastic.

Next stop is Taliesen, where I tour the architecture school out in the middle of farmland built by Frank Lloyd Wright, a crazy egomaniac, but a brilliant architect.

Heading west on Route 60, a two-lane road along the Wisconsin River to Prairie du Chen, I turn north on a scenic byway along the Mississippi River. Years before I had interviewed the author of the book "Blue Highways," and those smaller roads were the ones I kept heading to. I camped along the river with some deer and a blue heron, and then on day eight crossed the mighty Mississippi at La Crosse, which puts me officially out of the East.

One thought as I head through the Heartland is that our country may have a lot of problems, but we will never run out of corn.

I take Highway 16, another "blue highway" through the hilly farm country of Southern Minnesota and stop at the post office in Grand Meadows, where I saw a woman leave her car not only unlocked but running when she popped inside. It's a very different America out here in the small towns of the Midwest, where many of the people tend to look the same. We are an ethnically diverse nation, but it is not an even diversity. It still surprises me to find places where pretty much everyone is of German or Swedish descent, but there are still lots of those places.

I stop at the Spam Museum in Austin, Minnesota, dedicated to the infamous canned meat. Because how could I not?

I spend a night in Mitchell, South Dakota, home of the "World Famous Corn Palace," decorated inside and out with different colors of corn. I'm not quite sure why.

I stopped at an overlook of the Missouri River where Lewis and Clark camped in September of 1804 to take a rest, so I took a rest too. I never planned to seek out Lewis and Clark historic spots but my route was similar to theirs, and I ended up at quite a few of them.

The badlands of South Dakota, stunning pinnacle formations with horizontal bands of red, rise up like some kind of enchanted castle out of the seemingly endless grasslands. I stopped at one overlook and just stared in wonder at a thunderstorm over the prairie that must have been fifty miles away, with a rainbow rising from one end and bands of rain and lightening visible beneath the dark clouds.

Since Minnesota I have seen billboards advertising "Wall Drug Store," the biggest thing in South Dakota after the Corn Palace. It is a great big store where no store has any business being, but they make a great ice cream soda. I spend the night in Rapid City enjoying a $50 a night room facing a small lake.

The Black Hills aren't really hills at all, but a mountain range with peaks over 6000 feet. I hate to say this, but at my first view of Mount Rushmore I started laughing. It struck me not as monumental but as a rather silly thing to do to a mountain. After watching the video narrated by Tom Brokaw, I have more respect for the tenacity and skill it took to carve such realistic sculptures with dynamite, but still think the mountain would look better without it.

I much preferred the nearby drive on Iron Mountain Road, an amazing route filled with hairpin turns, old wooden bridges and single lane stone tunnels. It is one of several wonderful driving roads through

Custer State Park, which is filled with buffalo, antelope and donkeys that like to stick their heads in the car windows looking for handouts. I got a flat tire, which a very nice couple from Kentucky helped me change. My next stop was Frenchman's Creek Feed, where you can buy food for your horse, shells for your shotgun, and get your tire fixed.

I spend two nights in Hot Springs, South Dakota, in a little cabin on a creek. The mom and pop motels are uneven but so much more interesting than chains, which I've avoided on this trip. I drop off some clothes at the laundromat and have a soak and massage.

My next stop is Deadwood, where Wild Bill Hickok was shot in the back in the saloon while playing poker and holding two pair—aces and eights—which later became known as the dead man's hand. The restored western town is filled with casinos with penny slots and $2 blackjack tables.

I had been to 49 states, most for work but some just for pleasure, and now I need to get to the 50th, so I head north on Route 85, to cut into a little corner of North Dakota. I stay long enough to take a picture of the "Welcome to North Dakota" billboard, then go back to Buffalo, South Dakota, to pick up lunch at the grocery store and cafe. As I chat with the owner and tell her what I'm doing she tells me I need to go to Yellowstone. I explain I've been there several times before and was planning to drive north of there, but she said it is fall and the elk are bugling and I simply have to go.

So I check the map over lunch and head west on Route 12 to hear the elk.

After a night in Red Lodge, Montana, I decide to take the dramatic Beartooth Pass Highway into Yellowstone. I start in sunshine and shirtsleeves, but at about 9000 feet it starts to snow. By the time I reach the Wyoming border, snow covers the road and I'm in a full-fledged blizzard. A truck in front of me has stopped and starts backing up; it turns out to belong to a road crew who tell me the pass is closed at 11,000 feet and this is the last place to turn around. It was a slow and difficult process, inches at a time to make sure I'm not heading off a cliff. I head down the mountain as the snowstorm continues to worsen and then take a 200-mile detour to the next entrance to Yellowstone. After all, the elk were bugling.

The weather starts to clear as I enter the park and the elk are out in force. A big buck with impressive antlers is surrounded by six cows and is bugling. It is a kind of plaintive screech, incredibly loud, and clearly can be translated as "these females are mine and I want them now!" An unconcerned coyote is walking down the side of the road.

I camp that night at Grant Village near the southern entrance. The low was 19 degrees and my sleeping bag keeps me warm, but just reaching my arm outside is like putting it into the freezer. The campground has showers, but in this weather I immediately rule that out.

After another day at Yellowstone enjoying a lot more elk, gurgling hot pools and mud volcanoes, I head out of the park north back into Montana on another small road, 287, following another river. I like roads that follow rivers, which is why I keep finding myself in the same places Lewis and Clark went.

Had a wonderful fried chicken lunch at Grandma's Old Fashioned Buffet and Casino in Butte, probably the best meal I've had for $5.75 (and no sales tax!). I spend the night at Lolo Hot Springs, where I soak and swim for a few hours and go to sleep in a teepee. I love the high ceiling, but kind of miss having a floor.

Heading north to Glacier National Park, I hear there is a hurricane threatening Virginia and hope my house sitter is able to take care of everything. It's been over two weeks since I've read a paper, watched the news or worn a watch and don't miss it. I do need a haircut.

At Glacier National Park I start with waffles with chocolate chips and whipped cream at the Lake McDonald Lodge before heading up the Going-to-the-Sun Road. The leaves are turning and it is a magnificent drive, with clouds hanging like a Shangri-La mist over the highest peaks.

Perhaps the most beautiful mountain road in the world, it barely hugs the cliff with a low stone wall with lots of gaps and no guard rails. A favorite t-shirt in the local stores says, "Real Men Don't Need Guardrails." The view of the scenery and the road disappear close to the pass at the top where I drive into a cloud, and it snows all the way down the other side as I head towards the Canadian border, where the park continues and is named Waterton.

It is still snowing when I get to the hostel at the park headquarters, where there is a pool and a hot tub and I'm assigned to share a room with two young women from Japan. You have to love Canada.

When the snow lets up the next day (it is still September!) I take a pretty hike to a waterfall, surrounded by mule deer with their floppy ears. As they take each bite from low-hanging tree branches, they get covered with falling snow and shake it off and eat some more. I visit a shop and buy some chocolate from a woman who is partially blind and asks me to read the price tag.

I hike alone in a beautiful canyon of red rocks as snow starts falling again in grizzly bear country. Not prudent, but sublime, and when the sun comes out a few other people show up.

I decided to continue driving west in Canada and headed out on Highway 6, then Highway 3, which hugs the U.S. Canadian border through prairies under snow-covered peaks. I crossed into British Columbia and the Pacific Time Zone and stopped at Sparwood to see the world's biggest truck. Who knew?

Finally got my much-needed haircut in Creston, a cute town that was having a quilt festival along its one and only main street. The drive west from here is one of the prettiest of the trip, with high mountain passes, rolling hills and more lakes than I can count. There were also wonderful little towns, all of them selling cherries from the local orchards.

The jacket that came out in Montana goes back in the suitcase as the temperature is in the 70s just in time to visit Harrison Hot Springs, which, besides wonderful soaking waters, was having a world championship sand castle building contest. Charlie's Lakeside Restaurant serves a mean potato chip-crusted trout.

Day 22 of my car trip and I cross back into the U.S. and head to visit my good friends Brian and Wendy in Bellingham, Washington. We go sailing out to the San Juan Islands and after dinner at a fine Thai restaurant I realize this is a small town I could live in.

I visit more friends and relatives and play tourist for a while in Seattle, going up the space needle, wandering through the Pike Street market, and visiting the wonderful rock and roll museum there, where you can perform as a rock star with spotlights and screaming fans accompanying you.

I follow the Columbia River west from Portland with the rather awful smell of pulp mills until I reach the Pacific Ocean at Astoria, where Lewis and Clark did. I visited the re-creation of Fort Clatsop, where they wintered after reaching their goal.

Driving the Oregon coast is wonderful, especially with lots of time. Sand castles on the beach and great little towns with salt water taffy. The coast gets more dramatic as you go south, with giant rocks and caves with pounding surf, and tree-covered slopes that go right down to the sand.

I camped at Nehalem Bay State Park just over the dunes from a wonderful beach. I set up my tent, then sat on a dune watching the sun set over the crashing waves as two people rode by on horseback. It doesn't get more perfect.

I had a wonderful dinner at the Blue Sky Café: salad with hazelnuts and warm rock shrimp and chicken in a coconut curry. No credit cards, but out-of-town checks are fine.

I stopped at Tillamook on a pretty bay known for its famous cheddar cheese. At the cheese factory I had a grilled cheese sandwich and Tillamook ice cream. They send their cheese all over the country but the ice cream you can only buy within a hundred miles or so.

The Three Capes Scenic Drive off Route 101 got me to the "octopus tree," an ancient Sitka spruce whose immense trunk has grown to resemble candelabra.

The next day brought me to a pretty bridge, a haunted lighthouse and the Oregon Coast Aquarium, where I saw sea dragons, which are like sea horses but look just like little dragons with "wings" that appear glued on. That put me in the mood for Yachats crab and chowder house and some Dungeness crab.

I took a wild ride on a dune buggy in an area of giant sand dunes, holding on for dear life. Lots of fun and it took an hour to get all the sand off before sleeping that night in a wooden yurt, complete with power and a skylight.

The coast now has giant boulders and tons of driftwood. I stop at an odd little zoo where I can pet a baby black bear, a cougar and a young white Bengal tiger that tries to grab my crutch.

South into California I drive though the redwoods, which is like being in a giant outdoor cathedral. Those trees are amazing.

I had dinner at the Samoa Cookhouse near Eureka, the last surviving cookhouse from the era of company logging towns, where the food is served family style on long tables with red-checked table cloths.

After several more hours in the incredible redwood forest I turned west over a deserted mountain road to head to Route 1 along the Mendocino coast.

Back in familiar territory now, I cut inland to Harbin Hot Springs, where you can't use cell phones, talk above a whisper or eat meat. But you can soak nude in wonderful hot pools and meditate. It's kind of like a naked co-ed monastery.

After driving south through the wine country I was glad to be back in San Francisco. I got to visit my nephews Ilan and Ari and niece Rina and checked into the San Francisco Hilton, where I was upgraded to a bay view. It actually felt strange after almost two months of vagabond travel, but it was also kind of nice.

The smell of eucalyptus trees at Stanford transported me back 30 years as I visited the campus and wallowed in nostalgia, visiting more old friends and even stopped by the campus radio station KZSU, which looked exactly the same.

Moving on, I took Highway 17 to Santa Cruz back on the Pacific coast. The boardwalk was deserted on an October morning, but I spent the day at Kiva, a lovely spot with hot tubs and a giant sauna. Monterey is always wonderful, especially for eating. I had nut-crusted sole and great scallops, and stayed in a hostel a few blocks from Steinbeck's famous Cannery Row.

Taking the 17 Mile Drive I saw a number of houses I would like if I end up with an extra few million dollars, and then went to Big Sur, which never loses its ability to awe. I had lunch at Nepenthe, where they serve hamburgers on what is arguably the most spectacular outdoor deck in the world.

The Esalen compound, known for its workshops like "Healing A Broken Heart" and "Zen Hiking," transports people back to the 60s where they can feel like hippies, though they have to be pretty well-off hippies. I spent the night for $140, including a tolerable organic meal, and slept in a room where I had to make my own bed.

But oh, was it worth it.

They have soaking tubs perched right over the crashing waves of Big Sur and offer extraordinary massages in a room open to the sea breeze where you can hear the waves crashing below. After dark I soaked under the stars until the moon rose and lit the waves.

I stopped at Morro Bay and kayaked with the seals, then camped north of Santa Barbara with an ocean view. My morning walk was joined by hundreds of monarch butterflies and accompanied by a dolphin swimming up and down the beach. I got a bagel and gave my car an oil change. It had earned it.

I stopped for a few days in Santa Monica and visited my Great-Aunt Dorothy and several more cousins and friends. I was back in my old stomping grounds now. I drove past the house where I grew up in Woodland Hills, then headed out to the desert to visit my mother and then to San Diego to hang with my sister Lorri and her family.

It had been two months since I left Washington and it was time to give the car a rest and fly to Australia.

I ended up spending six weeks in Australia, including a wonderful week on Heron Island, which is out on the Barrier Reef, where I snorkeled with turtles, giant rays and the occasional shark.

Australia is a party continent and I enjoyed my time there, though I was surprised by the persistent and almost casual racism towards the native aboriginal people.

The southern coast was fantastic, Sydney is a wonderful city, and the outback was fun. I loved the kangaroos, wallabies, koala bears and penguins but hated the flies, and was not happy about salt-water crocodiles, which can attack you on some of the more isolated beaches in the north.

After returning to the U.S., I spent the holidays with family, including my sister Lorri, who has always been a bedrock in my life, then spent a month driving back across the U.S. It was January now and so I took the southern route.

I was in Taos, New Mexico, at the end of a day of skiing when I got word that my cousin Howard had died suddenly of a massive heart attack suffered at work. I had just been visiting Howard in Tacoma, Washington, on the earlier part of my journey and it was quite a shock. He was exactly my age. I left the car in Albuquerque and flew to Seattle for the funeral, then later returned and resumed my journey, more sure than ever about the importance of enjoying life every day.

After returning to the East Coast, following fun stops in New Orleans and Charleston, I headed to Costa Rica for a two-week tour of that lovely country and then took a sea-kayaking trip through the San Blas Islands of Panama, occupied by the Kuna Indians. Our small group would paddle from one island to the next, visiting with the local people and buying fish and fresh seafood from them as we went. On some of the tiny islands where we camped there was only a single Kuna family with us.

BACK IN THE SADDLE

The six months was coming to an end and I hadn't made plans for further travel, leaving my options open. I had loved the non-stop travel, but also felt that I didn't need to keep going and decided to head home. I wasn't enthusiastic about going back to work, but serendipity hit again, which led me back to CBS News to cover Congress for another ten years. Harvey Nagler, CBS's vice president, asked to meet with me and said he would take me back full-time as he had promised but if I preferred, I could work part-time covering Congress when it was in session, which is generally about eight months a year. It would solve so many of the problems that had led me to leave: I wouldn't miss traveling for work since I'd have four months a year to travel wherever I wanted, and I would only be covering Congress and wouldn't have to continually fight over the occasionally stupid stories I was asked to do when they weren't in session.

After some negotiations that left me with a reduced but still more than adequate salary and all of my previous benefits, I signed a new contract and returned to work at CBS News on my 50th birthday.

SWIMMING WITHOUT SHARKS

I looked at gyms when I moved to Falls Church but quickly concluded that the nicest and most convenient facilities were also the most reasonably priced, and those were the Fairfax County Recreation Centers, including one just minutes from my house. I would work out sometimes and for a while joined a regular group that played Wallyball, a combination of racquetball and volleyball. I had played tennis and racquetball and could have fun as long as I was playing with people who weren't overly competitive.

I soon learned of the county's adapted aquatics program, which provided one-on-one swimming instruction to disabled children, and decided to volunteer. I had never done any volunteer work before, in part because my schedule was always so crazy. I could get called out of town on just a few minutes notice. But covering Congress was more predictable and other than presidential campaign years, I could anticipate my schedule pretty well.

The Saturday morning lessons soon became my favorite time of the week. I would teach three one-hour classes in a row, working with just one student in each class for eight-week sessions that went year round. I remember one boy in a wheelchair whose father offered him $100 if he could swim all the way across the pool without stopping. Boy, was he motivated, and we worked on it until he could do it.

But children with physical disabilities didn't stay in the classes very long. If a child couldn't kick his legs or was missing an arm or was blind, it didn't take a whole lot of special instruction to get him swimming. He could then join a regular class or just swim with his friends.

And so most of those we taught and the only ones who came back year after year had developmental disabilities, the most common being autism. One of the things we were taught in our training was that children with autism don't like to be touched. While generally true, that rule certainly doesn't hold when they are in the water. Kids who wouldn't be able to even meet my glance outside the pool would wrap their arms tightly around my neck and hold on until they developed the confidence to swim. Since most of these kids were never able to move to a regular class, I taught some of them for years, starting them out when they were four or five and teaching them until they were teenagers. It was incredibly rewarding, and while it did sometimes take months or even years to get one of these special children to put their face under the water, I never had one who didn't eventually learn to swim.

Every child was different; techniques that would work for one wouldn't for another. Each new student required trial and error and creativity. There was one little boy who would never go into the deep water, but was fascinated with geography. He wouldn't carry on a conversation, but name a place, and he could give you detailed directions how to get there. We got some little plastic cards with names and pictures of different cities on them and stuck them to the side of the pool all along the wall leading from the shallow end to the deeper water. He would happily swim from one card to the next, naming the location and completely forgetting that he was afraid to go to the deep end.

Then there was the teenager who had suffered severe brain damage in an accident and didn't communicate and didn't cooperate. Two of us were working with him, trying, usually without success, to get him to swim laps, which he was quite capable of doing. One day another child swam close to him and he splashed him and was suddenly happy and smiling. We couldn't let him splash the other kids, but we had found the key, and so another volunteer and I would take turns going backwards in front of him and letting him splash us in the face and he would happily swim his laps.

Patience is a funny thing. I found as I got older I had very little for the politicians I covered; less and less for red tape or officious security people; and none at all for bad drivers, who are overly represented in the Washington, D.C. area. But I seemed to have endless patience with the kids I taught to swim.

THE WORST CONGRESS EVER

The change in Congress after the 2010 election was dramatic and led to what is arguably the worst in American history. There had of course been bitter partisanship and gridlock before, but nothing like this.

When Republicans took over the House in 2011, they elected John Boehner as speaker. Boehner is an affable guy, and though he grew up in hard times and is a self-made man, he is in many ways the archetype of a country club Republican. He favors lower taxes for the wealthy, a smaller government, and whatever is best for business. He smokes like a chimney, enjoys a good Merlot, likes to joke around with reporters, takes his orange-tinted tan very seriously, and is prone to tears whenever he talks about anything emotional. He likes nice restaurants and golfing with lobbyists.

Boehner first came to my attention early in his career when he got in trouble for passing out campaign contributions from the tobacco industry—on the House floor. He was also a real legislator who had worked closely with Democratic Senator Ted Kennedy to pass a major education bill and built coalitions to try to accomplish what he wanted. But he was put into power by a new breed of Republican spawned by the Tea Party movement, which considered compromise a dirty word. They not only wouldn't work with Democrats, they wouldn't even talk to them, and they made it clear from the start they wouldn't let Boehner do any compromising either.

One of their big issues that first year was earmarks, which are special spending projects put into bills to help a particular district. There had been some outrageous abuses of earmarks, most notably the "Bridge to Nowhere," a hugely expensive bridge for a minuscule Alaskan town. And so against the advice of more seasoned members of Congress and their own best judgment, the leadership went along and got rid of earmarks (or at least the more obvious ones).

Those few who publicly defended earmarks made the point that members of Congress are responsible directly to voters in their districts and so are in a better position to decide which bridge or road project deserves federal money. Taxpayers don't save any money by getting rid of earmarks. A $100 billion multiyear transportation bill with earmarks specifies lots of individual roads and bridges to get the money. One without earmarks is exactly the same size, but leaves the decisions on where the dollars are spent to the executive branch and state transportation departments. You can make good arguments on both sides as to which leads to better decision making for taxpayers.

But earmarks had another critically important role in the legislative process: they were used to buy votes and enforce party discipline. These are not noble goals, but the fact is, once earmarks were gone, Boehner lost a critical tool to control his caucus. He couldn't go to a recalcitrant member whose vote he needed and offer him something good for his district: a bridge or a school project or a museum. The only other power he had to try to enforce discipline and get members to vote for things they might resist was control over the perks of power within Congress, such as committee assignments. But many of those committee assignments only were desirable because they allowed members to put in earmarks. When Boehner at one point stripped some of the more troublesome Tea Party members of their committee jobs because they kept voting against the leadership, it just emboldened them.

The fact is they didn't care what committee they sat on because they had no interest in governing. Their goal was to tear down all government programs they didn't like. When Democratic Senate leader Harry Reid called them "anarchists" he wasn't far off the mark.

This led to crazy budget negotiations, where Boehner would strike a deal with President Obama that would have given Republicans far more than they could have gotten any other way, and then the deal would be shot down by other House Republicans because they didn't get everything they wanted. Eventually Boehner simply stopped trying to negotiate with the president because nothing he agreed to could pass his own House.

And so the House spent its time passing bills that would never become law. More than 50 times they voted to repeal the Affordable Care Act, which they called "Obamacare," and repeatedly passed what they liked to call "jobs bills" to roll back clean air and water rules and worker and consumer protections, knowing full well those measures could never pass the Senate or be signed by the President.

Besides setting records for the fewest number of bills passed into law, they also kept leaving town. The "do nothing Congress" of 1948 that Harry Truman campaigned against were hard workers compared to this crew. They would generally be in session from Tuesday to noon on Thursday and would be away on "district work periods" one to two weeks every month. The House and Senate refused to coordinate their vacations, so frequently one was in while the other was away, making it even harder to accomplish anything.

An extraordinary example of their incompetence was the renewal of the Violence Against Women Act. Already having a problem with women voters, it was insane for Republicans in the House to hold up renewal of a law that provided help to battered women and assisted local police agencies. But they did so for over a year after it lapsed because social conservatives objected to language in a bipartisan Senate bill that would have helped same-sex spouses who were being beaten and provide more authority to Indian tribes to deal with offenders. Finally, with self-imposed political damage mounting, Boehner brought it up for a vote anyway and it passed with mostly Democratic votes with the majority of Boehner's own Republicans voting against it.

There was a similar situation with aid to states devastated by Hurricane Sandy in 2012. The second most damaging hurricane in U.S. history caused billions of dollars in damage across two dozen states, but the worst was in New York and New Jersey. Those are states most House Republicans just plain didn't like and, incredibly, continued to resist providing the federal assistance that had been routinely provided to their own states after hurricanes, tornadoes, and other natural disasters.

After a deal to vote on the aid in the House fell through when leaders bowed to pressure from opponents, there was a firestorm with New York Republican Peter King threatening to ask wealthy Republican contributors on Wall Street to stop supporting the party. Speaker Boehner quickly turned things around and in January 2013, managed to pass the aid, but once again had to do it over the objections of the Tea Party and with help from Democrats.

Boehner wouldn't risk his job to pass immigration reform, which he and his business supporters badly wanted, or deal with the federal budget in a meaningful way, but he did do that to rely on Democratic votes to prevent the government from defaulting. The debt limit is one of the most misunderstood issues that comes before Congress and is also an incredibly stupid way to handle government debt.

Congress has to approve every dollar the government spends and authorizes the taxes to be collected to pay the bills. Since they routinely, under both Democratic and Republican leadership, vote to spend more money than they vote to raise with taxes, the government runs a deficit. The Treasury Department then sells government bonds to borrow the money to pay the bills and pays those investors back over time with interest.

The Treasury borrows the money to pay the bills that Congress has run up but Congress also has to authorize the amount of money they can borrow. That is the debt ceiling. It clearly makes no sense because the amount of money borrowed is determined entirely by the amount of money that Congress votes to spend. If they spend more without raising taxes, then more has to be borrowed, whether they want to vote to raise the debt ceiling or not.

When the borrowing approaches the debt ceiling, Congress has to vote to increase the limit. Members of Congress don't like to vote to do this because it reminds people how big the debt is and how irresponsible Congress has been in managing the federal budget. Of course Congress could avoid this entirely by spending less or taxing more, but it is easier to yell and scream about the debt ceiling than make those kinds of hard decisions.

And so over the years the party in power would bite the bullet and provide the votes to raise the debt ceiling, doing the responsible thing, while allowing those in the other party to vote against it and complain about the rising debt. Both Democrats and Republicans played this same game until the Tea Party changed the rules.

The House Republicans under Boehner decided that the debt ceiling would be their big stick to use against President Obama. They would threaten not to raise it in order to get concessions on things they wanted, which in that first go-round were lower taxes and less spending on social programs.

The problem with this strategy was that the risks of actually carrying it out were enormous. The reason the U.S. can always borrow as much money as it needs at rock bottom interest rates is because this is the safest place in the world for money. Wealthy people from other countries want their money in U.S. government bonds because nothing is safer. The U.S. had never defaulted and never would default. This confidence has helped our economy and our currency stay stable under even the most trying circumstances. Unless of course Congress screwed it up.

And so House Republicans took the faith and credit of the United States government, the bedrock foundation of our economic prosperity, and held it hostage. But they forgot the first rule of hostage taking, which is: if you want a ransom, you don't kill the hostage.

Many of the Tea Party Republicans, including Senator Rand Paul and Representative Michele Bachmann, not only were willing to kill the hostage they seemed anxious to do it, arguing it would actually help the country to refuse to raise the debt ceiling because that would force budgetary discipline. Since they and others in Congress were the only ones who decided how much to spend and tax and the deficit was entirely under their control, it was rather like that scene in the Mel Brooks movie "Blazing Saddles," where the new black sheriff is facing a crowd ready to shoot him and holds a gun to his own head and threatens to shoot himself unless they let him go.

With economists warning of disaster and business leaders, whose campaign contributions had helped put these Republicans in power beginning to panic, a deal was reached two days before the August 2nd deadline in 2011. They would raise the debt ceiling in exchange for future automatic and mindless across-the-board spending cuts and a wacky arrangement to have a special committee come up with legislation to reduce the deficit, which of course it was never able to do. Senate Republican Leader Mitch McConnell was a key player in ending the crisis, a role he often plays despite his overheated public rhetoric.

Boehner backed the deal but most of his House Republicans still voted against it. It was only with Democratic votes that the debt ceiling was raised.

But even coming that close meant confidence was shaken and damage had been done. Standard & Poor's lowered the credit rating of the U.S. government for the first time ever, and stock markets around the world tumbled, with a one-day drop in the Dow Jones Industrial Average of over 600 points. Independent estimates suggest that little political temper tantrum cost American taxpayers $18 billion in higher interest payments that had to be paid on Treasury bills and notes because investors' confidence in the stability of the U.S. government had been diminished. I escaped personal damage by temporarily moving all my retirement savings out of stocks a few weeks before the deadline, fearing these guys really were crazy enough to do this.

In 2013 they did it again. This time they also shut down the government by refusing to pass the required funding bills, hurting people around the country and wasting millions of dollars as they took the debt ceiling right to the deadline. Their demand this time was to repeal the Affordable Care Act, which everyone knew was not going to happen. And so as Speaker Boehner was mollifying his fellow House Republicans, insisting in daily news conferences that they would never compromise, he was privately assuring Wall Street that they would never allow a default and in the end, with business leaders fuming, he once again used Democratic votes to pass a compromise that his own Republicans wouldn't accept.

After that the business community finally had enough and realized the party they supported to keep their taxes low was out of control and posing a serious threat to the economy and their profits. And so in 2014 the U.S. Chamber of Commerce and other groups started pouring money into Republican primary races, directly taking on the Tea Party and trying to restore the power of the Republican establishment that was teetering.

While Republican voters out in the country were badly divided by the Tea Party, the fact is that in the House of Representatives the main tactic of Republican leaders was to try to co-opt them and move sharply to the right in hopes of mollifying them. They abandoned any effort to reach agreement on immigration reform or come up with a Republican alternative on health care, and even let a farm bill lapse to avoid angering their most extreme members.

The problem, of course, is when you invite an angry lion into your house and feed it and tell it how sweet it is, it might turn around one day and eat you.

Which is exactly what the Tea Party did in June of 2014, when it devoured one of its biggest champions, Eric Cantor, the Majority Leader in the House of Representatives. Cantor was a Tea Party favorite and repeatedly pushed House Speaker John Boehner to the right, torpedoing efforts to find compromise on spending and tax issues. The threat that he would try to unseat Boehner was ever-present. Cantor raised money and campaigned for Tea Party Republicans all around the country and built up a substantial power base in Congress. He also happened to be the only Jewish Republican in the House and was on track to become Speaker.

But he had a fatal flaw for a Tea Party favorite, and that was he wanted Republicans at some point to actually be able to govern again. Seeing his party's brand sink and being smart enough to understand if it kept alienating young people, single women, and Hispanics its long term survival would be in doubt, after the shutdown fiasco Cantor tried to find ways to actually accomplish something. He wouldn't try to get a House vote on the Senate-passed immigration bill, though his business supporters were screaming for it, but tried to push some small measures, such as a version of what is called the "Dream Act" to provide legal status and a path to citizenship for undocumented immigrants brought by their parents to the U.S. as young children.

That, and his votes not to let the nation default on its debts was enough to turn the monster he helped create against him. In a stunning development Cantor was defeated in the primary in his Virginia district by an unknown Tea Party contender, Dave Brat.

Never before had a leader in Congress been ousted in his own party's primary. While Cantor's loss stunned the political world, there was more than a little ironic justice in his defeat at the hands of the movement he had so enthusiastically embraced. He left a Republican House leadership in disarray and no closer to being able to or even interested in trying to help govern the nation, a situation unlikely to change even after the November 2014 elections gave Republicans control of the Senate.

This total failure of Congress to do its job is certainly the fault of Republicans but there is blame, too, for Democrats and the Supreme Court allowing growth in the already overwhelming role of big money in politics. Gerrymandering by state legislatures also plays a huge role. Democrats and Republicans both have an interest in protecting incumbents in Congress and having crazy district lines in order to create safe Democratic or Republican seats. That helps the parties but has been terrible for the country.

If a Republican is in a safe district he or she never has to worry about any opposition from the left and so is pushed farther and farther to the right since their only contest is a primary against other Republicans. The same is true for Democrats and so there is no incentive in any of these safe districts to move to the center.

An experiment in a few states, including California, may help this. An open primary has everyone run in the same primary with the same voters; the top two finishers face each other in the general election. In some cases it will be two Democrats or two Republicans running against each other. But the big difference is that everyone in both parties is voting in that primary and so in theory candidates would have to reach out to people who are not on the extreme end of their party.

Voters are not innocent victims in all this. The reason primaries are so dominated by the extremes is that most Americans, whose political views lie somewhere in the middle, don't bother to vote, especially in primaries. And when they do vote they seem to draw a bizarre distinction between Congress and their own representative or senator, somehow believing they are separate. How else to explain that somewhere close to 90 percent of Americans believe Congress is doing a bad job and yet more than 90 percent of incumbents are re-elected every two years.

TIME TO LEAVE

The frustration of dealing with an increasingly useless Congress was certainly a factor in deciding to retire when I turned 60, but it wasn't the only reason. I had a wonderful career covering news all around the country and the world and had a great time doing it, but it seemed to me that 40 years was enough. I still enjoyed my work and got satisfaction from going on the radio to tell people what was happening in Washington, but it wasn't as much fun as it used to be and I was ready to leave.

The state of journalism has gone up and down in cycles over those decades but has been in a dip for quite a while now. As I looked ahead there wasn't anything I really wanted to do in broadcasting that I hadn't already done.

Working in one of the few industries left with strong unions and pension plans, I drew up a financial plan and decided to retire in May of 2014 and while I would continue to write and certainly to travel, my days on the radio were over. Though I have a lot of good friends at C-SPAN, I had to tell them I would no longer be tuning in to watch Congress.

HONDURAS 2014

Within a few weeks of retiring, I headed to Honduras to snorkel on the world's second biggest tropical reef.

Avoiding any Honduran cities, where people seem to kill each other at alarming rates, I flew directly into the small airport on the tourist-laden island of Roatán, and was met by a representative of the CoCo View resort where I'd spend my week with the fish and the dolphins and maybe a few sharks.

A fun moment filling out my immigration form when I got to write "retired" for my occupation.

A short drive and shorter boat ride and we were at the resort, a laid-back spot on its own little island dedicated to scuba divers (and the occasional snorkeler like me). A chalkboard showed I'd already been assigned to a boat for my twice-daily trips to good spots on the reef, plus unlimited day and night diving and snorkeling right off the beach.

I have a spacious cabana built on stilts over the ocean, accessible by a little wooden walkway with a private deck and a hammock. No TV or phone, but WiFi, of course. Only 29 rooms altogether and everybody books Saturday to Saturday so we'll all get to know each other. All the guests are American, and most are repeat visitors.

There is a dining room and the meals are all very good, a bar that serves the biggest piña colada I've ever seen, a little store, lots of places to sit and relax, a few kayaks, three pet dogs, a loud scarlet macaw who sometimes bites, and some crazy lizards who run upright on their hind legs. There are also lots of nasty little sand flies and I brought insect repellent, but while others reported problems, happily they weren't biting me.

It's cloudy and a bit rainy the afternoon of my arrival, but I pop into the water because that's why I came. I didn't go very far but there were some big, colorful fish.

At the suggestion of the resort I had packed crayons, pencils and children's vitamins, which they collect for the local school.

On my first full day I went out on a boat with the scuba divers, as another thunderstorm was moving through. It cleared just before I jumped in about 15 feet of water, but there was still a very strong current to fight. The coral was pretty and I saw a lot of fish, but it was pretty choppy. I was right above a wall; it is dramatic to snorkel to the edge and look down and see nothing but blue. But just trying to grab hold of the boat ladder, much less climbing it, against a strong current with waves crashing was a challenge, and I think I'll skip the boat next time and just swim out from the beach to the reef.

The afternoon solo snorkel from the shore was much better. (Note to kids: never snorkel in the open ocean alone.) It was like being in a giant canyon of vibrant coral with big schools of fish swimming by. My favorites were jet black with a luminescent blue stripe all along their outside edge (blue durgon, I later learned).

I saw three lobsters and a bride and groom.

The wedding reception was set for that night at the resort and the wedding party was heading out for their underwater ceremony. I floated over them as the bride, with a short veil waving behind and a bouquet of flowers, scuba'd hand in hand with her groom about 20 feet down, as the photographer hung in the water in front of them.

The resort has an easy to spot buoy as well as underwater markers to find your way back safely through a cut in the reef so I didn't get lost.

Late in the afternoon I watched from my overwater deck as another, much bigger thunderstorm rolled in. It was still raining the next morning in clear violation of vacation weather rules.

When the weather cleared a little I headed back out to the reef and spent an hour with big fish and little ones, then it was time to settle on my deck to read and segue into my mid-morning nap, which isn't that dissimilar from my mid-afternoon nap. Something about the ocean always makes me sleepy.

Took an excursion by boat, van and boat again to go snorkeling with dolphins. First we visited and posed with friendly dolphins, who occasionally listened to their trainers, then snorkeled and played with them in deep water. It is a research center and the dolphins were born in captivity and live in a huge enclosure. It was great fun. At one point I felt something on my feet; three young dolphins pushed me forward, then passed me from behind, all close enough to reach out and pet, then came around and did it again. Others swam close or bumped me playfully.

On my next day's snorkel there were many fine fish and a mermaid with a bright yellow tail.

I would think scuba diving in a custom-made mermaid outfit (not to mention trying to get in and out of the water in one) would not be something a rational person would do. But apparently when the underwater videos are taken at the right angle by her companion, the air tank doesn't show and they get lots of hits on YouTube. It takes all kinds.

Sunshine! More snorkeling. One fish, two fish, red fish, blue fish, along with a cool stingray and a four-foot barracuda waiting for something more tasty than me.

Found the island weather station. It's a small rock hanging by a string from a tree with a sign explaining, "If the weather rock is wet, it's raining. If the rock is hot, it's sunny. If it's swinging back and forth, it's windy. If it's jumping up and down, it's an earthquake and if the rock is gone, it's a hurricane."

Hovered in the water next to a pair of lion fish. They shouldn't be here. They somehow came over from Asia and are causing huge problems all over the Caribbean, where they have no natural predators and are eating all the local fish. They are bad, but they are quite spectacular looking.

The wind blew hard on Thursday and the waves tossed me like Eric Cantor on primary night. But visibility was still good, and lots of brightly colored fish came out to play.

Friday, my last full day, is sunny and windy. Good morning to snorkel, but the strong current tires me out, and my mid-morning lying on my deck time is extended appropriately. The resort is usually empty mornings and afternoons when the scuba boats are out, but people are leaving Saturday and you can't dive 24 hours before you fly (that sport has a lot of rules), so lots more people are lounging about.

Took a final afternoon snorkel and ran into the biggest fish I saw all week. It was huge. For future reference we'll just call it "the grouper that ate New York."

Seeing lots of lobsters in the ocean was fun but seeing them on the buffet table was even better. After a fine meal of many lobster tails, there was an end of the week party with a live band and free rum punch, which everyone knows tastes better than regular rum punch.

In the morning they printed out all our boarding passes, took our luggage, then brought us to the airport by boat and van, where I paid Honduras $40 to leave their country, and headed home to continue my new life of leisure.

ACKNOWLEDGMENTS

I want to thank my fine editor Deborah Davidson for all her help and credit Pixelstudio for the cover design.

Thanks too to those who read early drafts and provided advice and encouragement including Peter Maer, Mike Freedman, Sam Litzinger, Laura King and Pete Williams.

Lorri, John and Jeff Hilbert and Jenna Anderson provided excellent suggestions and of course my mother Carrie Fuss provided encouragement and remembered things I had forgotten.

A special thanks also to Nell Minow for her guidance.

CPSIA information can be obtained at www.ICGtesting.com
Printed in the USA
BVOW11s1806290715

411011BV00012B/93/P